"A man who does not exist"

"A man who does not exist"

The Irish Peasant in the Work of W. B. Yeats and J. M. Synge

Deborah Fleming

Ann Arbor

THE UNIVERSITY OF MICHIGAN PRESS

Copyright © by the University of Michigan 1995
All rights reserved
Published in the United States of America by
The University of Michigan Press
Manufactured in the United States of America
⊕ Printed on acid-free paper

1998   1997   1996   1995   4   3   2   1

A CIP catalog record for this book is available from the British Library.

Library of Congress Cataloging-in-Publication Data

Fleming, Deborah.
    A man who does not exist : the Irish peasant in the work of W. B.
Yeats and J. M. Synge / Deborah Fleming.
        p.   cm.
    Includes bibliographical references and index.
    ISBN 0-472-10581-7
        1. English literature—Irish authors—History and criticism.
    2. English literature—19th century—History and criticism.
    3. English literature—20th century—History and criticism.
    4. Yeats. W. B. (William Butler), 1865–1939—Political and social
    views. 5. Synge, J. M. (John Millington), 1871–1909—Political and
    social views. 6. Peasantry in literature. 7. Ireland—In
    literature. 8. Literature and society—Ireland—History—20th
    century. 9. Literature and society—Ireland—History—19th century.
    I. Title.
PR8752.F57   1995
820.9'920624'09034—dc20   95-4346
                                                                CIP

For Clarke

Acknowledgments

I would like to thank Mary Helen Thuente, Declan Kiberd, and Edward Lense for their considerable help in preparing this manuscript.

Grateful acknowledgment is made to the following authors and publishers for permission to reprint excerpts and selections from copyrighted material:

Columbia University Press for excerpts from Yeats's *Uncollected Prose*, volumes 1 and 2, edited by John P. Frayne.

Cork University Press for permission to quote from *Synge and Anglo-Irish Literature: A Study* by Daniel Corkery.

Curtis Brown Ltd. and Rogers, Coleridge & White Ltd. for permission to quote "The grouse in Cruachan Cuin," "Tonight the grouse is not asleep," and "A little bird / Has let a piping" from *The Irish* by Seán Ó Faoláin.

Irish Academic Press for "Uná Bhán," "Father Leeam," and "Breedyeen Vesy" from *Songs Ascribed to Raftery*.

Macmillan Publishing Company for permission to quote the poem "Crazy Jane and Jack the Journeyman" and excerpts from "Crazy Jane on the Day of Judgement," "Tom the Lunatic," "The Fisherman," "The Tower," "Shepherd and Goatherd," "At Galway Races," "Song of the Wandering Aengus," "The Everlasting Voices," "The Madness of King Goll," "The Happy Townland," "Into the Twilight," "Crazy Jane and the Bishop," "The Municipal Gallery Re-visited," "The Three Beggars," "An Hour Before Dawn," and "Coole Park, 1929" from *The Poems of W. B. Yeats: A New Edition* edited by Richard J. Finneran; for excerpts from "What is Popular Poetry?" "Magic," "The Galway Plains," "The Celtic Element in Literature," and "The Well of the Saints" from *Essays and Introductions*; for excerpts from *Explorations*; for excerpts from the *Autobiography* of W. B. Yeats; for excerpts from *Memoirs* of W. B. Yeats edited by Denis Donoghue; for excerpts from "By the Roadside, " "Dust Hath Closed Helen's Eye," and "The Twisting of the Rope" from *Mythologies;* for excerpts from *The Hour-Glass* from the *Collected Plays of W. B. Yeats;* for excerpts from *The Countess Cathleen, Land of Heart's Desire, The Pot of Broth, The Unicorn from the Stars, Purgatory,* and "Love Song: From the Gaelic" from *The Variorum Edition of the Plays of W. B. Yeats,* edited by Russell K. Alspach.

Mercier Press for excerpts from two songs in *Songs of the Irish* by Donal O'Sullivan.

Routledge and International Thomson Publishing Services Ltd. for "The eagle of brown Glen Rye" and "All the sweetness of nature was buried" from *A Celtic Miscellany* to Kenneth Hurlsone Jackson.

Anne and Michael Yeats for permission to reproduce cover illustration, "An Island Man" by Jack B. Yeats.

Every effort has been made to trace the ownership of all copyrighted material in this book and to obtain permission for its use.

Contents

Introduction

An understanding of the Irish Revival of the late nineteenth and early twentieth centuries necessitates a study of the literature written about Irish peasants, for one central idea of the Renaissance was the revivification of Irish culture. The literary treatment of the peasant played a crucial and controversial role in the emerging sense of Irish national consciousness in the early twentieth century. In their very different ways, W. B. Yeats and J. M. Synge, the two most important figures of the Irish Literary Revival, which can be seen as part of the larger Irish Renaissance, were engaged in this revivification. Because of their literary importance, I have chosen to look exclusively at their works rather than undertake a more comprehensive study of other noted writers of the Revival who also wrote about peasants—among them Padraic Colum, Lady Gregory, and Douglas Hyde.

Yeats's and Synge's different but complementary ways of looking at Irish peasants helped to establish a new sense of cultural and linguistic identity in Ireland by transforming Irish folklore into art and by capturing the rhythms of the Anglo-Irish dialect. Synge was concerned with the peasants of his time, especially those he met in Wicklow, Kerry, and Connemara and on the Aran Islands. Yeats saw the peasants as inheritors of "Celtic" tradition, whose folklore and legends were essential for the development of a national literature. Yeats as well as Synge celebrated what he saw as the robustness and spirit of the country people, and both realized the literary potential of the peasant as archetype or poetic mask. Yeats and Synge remind us that if the peasants' culture represented a mystical and virtuous tradition, that culture too had suffered from nineteenth-century imperialism and from the degradation of modern times; yet, even though their way of life was threatened by the outside world, the country people displayed courage and the ability to endure.

In this study I have included poems from all periods in Yeats's canon and five plays with important peasant characters (*The Countess Cathleen, The Land of Heart's Desire, Cathleen Ni Houlihan, The Unicorn from the Stars,* and *Purgatory*), and have looked at passages from his many essays about Irish folklore and the necessity of the artist to be familiar with the folk culture and ancient literature of his own country.

Mary Helen Thuente examines Yeats's use of Irish folklore in her thorough and excellent book *W. B. Yeats and Irish Folklore* and emphasizes the fact that Yeats was far more interested in the 1880s and 1890s in folklore than he was in mythology, although in the twentieth century he turns to mythology as his major Irish subject matter.[1] Irish folklore, Thuente writes, was the central impulse behind one of the most distinctive literary movements of the century, the Irish Literary Renaissance (Thuente 1). Birgit Bramsbäck further analyzes Yeats's use of folklore material in three plays, *The Countess Cathleen, The Land of Heart's Desire,* and *The Shadowy Waters.*[2] She looks at the traditional tales underlying the three plays, the function of popular belief, and the impact of folk poetry and music on the songs in the plays, and shows how Yeats's revisions of his own work demonstrate the changes in his interest in folklore. Declan Kiberd shows in *Synge and the Irish Language* that Synge's plays are evidence that he knew very well the Irish language and the folklore and traditions of native Irish speakers.[3]

My purpose is to look more closely at the depiction of the Irish peasants themselves by Yeats and Synge. Chapter 1 provides background on the social, political, and economic situation of Irish peasants in the nineteenth and early twentieth centuries; a definition of the term *peasant;* a discussion of Yeats's and Synge's ideas about bringing "native" Irish culture and folklore to the attention of the urban middle classes, who, being descendants of peasants, wanted a more romanticized depiction than Synge gave them; and a consideration of Yeats and Synge as "postcolonial" writers. The second chapter discusses C. G. Jung's theory of the Collective Unconscious and Yeats's belief that peasant culture was a repository of ancient wisdom, and Yeats's and Synge's use of the literary convention of the "Noble Savage." The following four chapters discuss Yeats's and Synge's poetic treatment of the peasants—their relationship to nature, which may mean freedom, peace, and virtue, or confinement, loneliness, and destruction; the peasant and love, and the influence on Irish literature of the songs of the blind peasant poet Raftery; the peasant as vagrant and exile, as prophet, seer, or hermit, as poetic device to convey the poet's philosophy as contrasted with the convention of the peasant who possesses quaint and homely wisdom; and finally, the peasant as artist and hero, and as a suitable subject of and audience for poetry. The appendix contains additional information on the history of agrarian Ireland.

Chapter 1

"To write for my own race": Irishness and Anglo-Irishness

In his 1919 collection *The Wild Swans at Coole*, W. B. Yeats included "The Fisherman" (1914), a poem of deliberate ambiguities and timeless symbols which Yeats would echo in many other poems: the conjunction of coldness and passion ("The Wild Swans at Coole"), the confusion of dream with reality and the poet's having to look "all day" at an image ("Men improve with the Years"), the solitary man climbing up to a stream in order to fish ("The Tower"), the dawn ("Towards Break of Day"), hillside streams and gray, stony landscapes ("The Tower," "In Memory of Major Robert Gregory," "Towards Break of Day," "The Hour Before Dawn" "Ego Dominus Tuus"). Yeats discovers in this poem his ideal artist and audience—his mask or anti-self. The fisherman goes "To a grey place on a hill / In grey Connemara clothes"[1] at dawn, the time, according to Gaelic legend, at which miracles are most likely to happen. He pursues no trivial occupation but one of the oldest activities of mankind. The key word here is *dream:* this man so utterly unlike himself, being wise and simple, lives only in his imagination. The poet associates the mental image—created by his desire to embrace a more natural life—with the image in the world, the fisherman he saw as a youth in Sligo:

> It's long since I began
> To call up to the eyes
> This wise and simple man.

The fisherman has become for him a symbol of his hope that he would write for his "own race," since he sees around him only the images of an unworthy civilization:

The witty man and his joke
Aimed at the commonest ear,
The clever man who cries
The catch-cries of the clown,
The beating down of the wise
And great Art beaten down.

Here we have the crucial theme: "great Art beaten down." Yeats's greatest concern was art; seeing it rejected by the modern audience was "the reality" he faced. Scorning the trivial modern audience that prefers clever jokes, Yeats imagines his ideal of the man in "grey Connemara cloth" who climbs to a place "Where stone is dark under froth," who is wise in his simple, natural way, and who does not need to express himself in witty locutions. He is an acceptable audience because he is not, like the middle-class mob, craven or insolent, nor does he desire attention from common people. The poet now has an image with which to summon his opposite, who does not exist in the empirical world, for he is an image ("A man who does not exist, / A man who is but a dream") which enables the poet to write for him one "Poem maybe as cold / And passionate as the dawn." His ideal man is drawn from the romantic pastoral image of the noble countryman who embodies virtue, whose life under the changing skies of western Ireland is itself a work of art—so well integrated is he with his surroundings.

Because this man represents a lost nobility, Yeats chooses him as his heir:

It is time that I wrote my will;
I choose upstanding men
That climb the streams until
The fountain leap, and at dawn
Drop their cast at the side
Of dripping stone;

("The Tower," *Poems* 198)

Against the background of the west—the grey dawn, the stone dampened by froth—the fisherman is one with the landscape and its history. Yet the image is contrasted with the modern reality, the urban world full of shallow people who prefer popular comedy to great art, who

enjoy tasteless jokes. The man of the western countryside stands out
like a hero, engaged in timeless activity. Modern, urban people do
what is fashionable at the moment, beating down what is traditional
and universal; they are a mob that flocks to hear the comedian because
they would rather be amused than inspired, while the fisherman is an
individual. Finding this modern reality when he had hoped to write
for his own people, the poet resolves to write for his romantic ideal;
however, his resolution is clouded by the irony that this man does not
exist in the contemporary world apart from the poet's mind. Further-
more, he lacks identity because he lacks personality and emotions.
Both ideal and archetype, he is but an image, not a human being. The
dream of a peasant audience is likewise impossible, and so again the
man does not exist.

Readers may be uncertain as to whether the poem actually speaks of
a landless peasant or an Anglo-Irish gentleman; this intentional ambi-
guity in the poem emphasizes the similarity of the predicaments of
peasant and aristocracy: neither exists except as an image. The ideal
of a peasant audience is a feature of modernism, as is, for example, T.
S. Eliot's desire to write for an "untutored savage": it represents unap-
proachable simplicity in a complex age. The ambiguity, however, may
lead us to deeper understanding of Yeats's symbols. John Unterecker
maintains that "the fisherman" is Yeats's image of himself,[2] and cer-
tainly Yeats fished as a boy in Sligo. Unterecker identifies as a source
for the poem the incident in *The Stirring of the Bones* when Yeats had
tried to have a suit made of Connemara cloth and found to his chagrin
that it in fact came from Scotland.[3] Still, in this section of the *Autobiog-
raphy*, Yeats also discusses his notion of Unity of Being, "where all the
nature murmurs in response if but a single note be touched," found
"by the rejection of all experience not of the right quality" (235). Im-
possible without "Unity of Culture" (236), this Unity of Being Yeats
otherwise describes as a "[d]ream of the noble and beggar-man":
dream, that is, of aristocrat and peasant. Edward Hirsch sees the fish-
erman as a type of Yeats's ideal, imagined peasant,[4] while Seamus
Heaney regards him as the pattern of the aristocrat who turned away
from the Dublin audiences which had rejected great Art, the aristocrat
whose qualities included "solitude, the will towards excellence, the
courage, the self-conscious turning away from that in which he no
longer believes."[5] Edward Said compares this poem with Neruda's

"El Pueblo": "in both poems the central figure is an anonymous man of the people, who in his strength and loneliness is a mute expression *of* the people, a quality that inspires the poet in his work."[6] Declan Kiberd reads the figure as an Anglo-Irish gentleman, perhaps even J. M. Synge, who is mentioned in the first stanza as "The dead man that I loved" and whose plays *The Playboy of the Western World* and *The Shadow of the Glen* were reviled by Dublin audiences. That the peasants fished with nets from the shore, not with rod and fly, as did country gentlemen, buttresses this reading. Furthermore, the poem "In Memory of Major Robert Gregory," included in the same collection, describes Synge in terms similar to those in "The Fisherman": he goes to "a most desolate stony place" to find people "Passionate and simple like his heart" (*Poems* 133).

It is time to ask why Yeats needed to create an ideal audience that he himself acknowledged did not exist, why he chose for his model this archetype of the fisherman, and why in his mind the experiences of aristocracy and peasant were so closely aligned.

Revivalists and Peasants

One of the artistic aims of the writers of the Irish Revival, including W. B. Yeats and J. M. Synge, was to reacquaint the Irish people with their lost culture, to restore to Ireland its sense of national unity through literature; that is, through themes borrowed from Irish folklore and the ancient heroic stories. Interest in the customs and stories of Irish country people had been increasing throughout the nineteenth century, especially after the Great Potato Famine (Hirsch 1116). The Revivalists sought to use the folkloristic and mythic heritage in order to influence the development of a new national culture, what Yeats called sealing "with the right image the soft wax before it began to harden."[7]

Nationalism is a powerful ideal—in Ireland particularly so, due to its long history as a colonized nation. Indeed, it is the only Western European country to have experienced both early and late colonization.[8] Maurice Goldring describes nationalism in Ireland as a "flame" that attracts anyone "possessed by the idea of belonging" (9)—an obsession particularly marked among intellectuals (10). Yeats himself described nationality at the time as being like a religion in which "meditation had but one theme—the perfect nation and its perfect service" (*Autobiography* 240). In this new religion the writers envisioned themselves as prophets—"flaming torches of the spirit" (Goldring 11). They would guide the people in the creation of this national culture through the medium of their own work, by turning the people into audiences for themselves. Thus the relationship between autobiography and history in Ireland became inextricably interwoven (8); and a good many Irish writers not only wrote their lives as history but endeavored to create history as well.

Among their necessary fictions, the Revivalists before Kavanagh believed in the purity and innocence of a peasant nation malleable to the work of artists (16). The poets, moreover, "took the road to the country" because they were fascinated by "the living presence of legends, stories and poems in these communities" (65). To the peasants, the visible and invisible worlds were not distinguished from each other; in fact, the supernatural affected all forms of human endeavor. They believed in fairies and ghosts as a part of their society (65). In the Irish countryside, the writers of the Revival "could see their ideal alive, the image of Ireland they wanted to fashion, a rural society directed by a new aristocracy—the aristocracy of the mind" (66). One of their enduring creations was an image of the Irish peasant, characterized according to their own values, which established the terms of an elaborate cultural discourse with which subsequent Irish writers have been forced to deal (Hirsch 1116, 1117).

The Revivalists' image of the Irish peasant stemmed in part from ideas about cultural unity and identity. Like Carl Gustav Jung, W. B. Yeats believed that the human spirit was part of a Collective Unconscious—which Yeats called *Spiritus Mundi*—in which the soul was no longer individual, but one with the world. Yeats also believed in the existence of a "racial" collective unconscious, images from which could be used by poets to inform and enrich the national culture. He wrote:

Have not all races had their first unity from a mythology, that marries them to rock and hill? We had in Ireland imaginative stories, which the uneducated classes knew and even sang, and might we not make those stories current among the educated classes, rediscovering for the work's sake what I have called "the applied arts of literature," the association of literature, that is, with music, speech, and dance; and at last, it might be, so deepen the political passion of the nation that all, artist and poet, craftsman and day-labourer would accept a common design?[9]

Unlike Douglas Hyde who envisioned Ireland as a nation of Gaelic-speaking peasants, Æ,George W. Russell, who wanted to transform it into a visionary utopia, and James Connolly who worked for a socialist republic, Yeats believed that Ireland could become a land directed by pastoral mythmakers, inspired by images of past nobility and greatness. Their purpose would be to create a new sense of nationhood in Ireland by drawing from older conventions and creating a new, national art inspired by tradition. He wrote in 1904: "We must grope our way towards a new yet ancient perfection."[10]

Yeats and John Millington Synge disliked the urban, industrial world, although they spent most of their adult lives in the artistic centers of Dublin and London. Both had spent much of their youth in the country, which they learned to love (Yeats in Sligo, and Synge in Wicklow); both had been amateur naturalists as children. Thus, having learned to identify their nationality with the countryside, they turned to folklore to find images and themes for literature and found in the Irish peasantry a displaced aristocracy whose culture could help to restore Ireland's imaginative and spiritual life. Yeats's occult interests led him to study the folktales of people for whom the supernatural was still present. He wrote that the peasants were the inheritors of Ireland's cultural memory, and that their rich folklore—ballads and legends, the true beginnings of literature and the arts—could provide symbols for poetry: modern poets should recover through art the ancient, heroic consciousness of the world. Yeats's enchantment with folk literature was inspired by its passion and vitality; he described an idea for a poem that was to have been a dialogue between a "portentous professor" and a tinker, "a melodious lying Irishman," and that would have conveyed the superiority of the latter through his lively imagination and speech (Wade, *Letters* 307). Synge, on the other hand, valued what he saw as the peasants' lack of self-consciousness and freedom from urban social convention. To him, they were the people who could tell his Dublin audience about its own country. Both writers used peasant speakers to create a sense of primitive—to them, universal—emotion, and celebrated what they perceived to be the peasants' liveliness, individuality, relationship to nature, imagination, and dialect. Synge wrote in *The Aran Islands* that "these men of Inishmaan seemed to be moved by strange archaic sympathies with the world. Their mood accorded itself with wonderful fineness to the suggestions of the day, and their ancient Gaelic seemed so full of divine simplicity that I would have liked to turn the prow to the west and row with them forever."[11]

In fact, he was less sanguine about the Irish peasants than he is often accused of having been. Believing that the painful isolation of peasant communities might be assuaged by contact with the urban world, and knowing that city-dwellers needed to be in touch with the remote places of their origins and with nature, he conceived of a vast system of railways which would allow people access to both. His philosophy, like that of the present-day Green Party in Europe, included the integration of urban and rural ways of life.[12]

For both Yeats and Synge, the countryman or peasant possessed secret wisdom, consciousness of his own cultural identity, and knowledge of nature. In Synge's poetry and drama, the peasants were the tenant farmers of Wicklow, the Aran Islands, or the Congested Districts (Nora and Dan Burke and Patch Darcy of *The Shadow of the Glen*, Christy, Old Mahon, and the Widow Quinn of *The Playboy of the Western World*); farmer-fishermen of the Aran Islands (all the characters of *Riders to the Sea*); poor self-employed working people (Pegeen and Michael James Flaherty of *The Playboy*, Timmy the Smith of *The Well of the Saints*); or wandering beggars or tinkers (the Tramp in *The Shadow of the Glen*, Martin and Mary Doul of *The Well of the Saints*, and the family in *The Tinker's Wedding*). Yeats further developed the myth: beggars, hermits, wanderers, madmen, and madwomen—usually country people—became spokesmen for poetic ideas. Red Hanrahan, important in Yeats's fiction as well as in his poetry, was a peasant "hedge schoolmaster" and wandering poet; Crazy Jane, patterned on a peasant woman of Sligo and a character from a traditional ballad, represented the peasant's practical morality and lusty personality. "'The Old Pensioner'," Yeats wrote, was "an almost verbatim record of words used by an old Irishman,"[13] and he identified the revision of that poem, "The Lamentation of the Old Pensioner," as "little more than a translation into verse of the very words of an old Wicklow peasant."[14] Many of his other poems had been suggested to him by popular ballads and songs of the country people.[15]

In her 1979 forward to Yeats's anthology of fiction, *Representative Irish Tales* (1891), Mary Helen Thuente writes that after completing *The*

Wanderings of Oisin in 1888, Yeats wanted to simplify his work, and so turned to the folklore, life, and character of the Irish peasant.[16] His first literary treatment of the Irish peasantry and their folklore had been modeled upon William Allingham's and Samuel Ferguson's ballads, but Yeats had soon become dissatisfied with their work as too "literary." He began to learn about the peasants themselves through folklore-collecting. When selecting materials for *Fairy and Folktales of the Irish Peasantry* (1888), he was most concerned with the literary and occult use of fairy lore, but he realized that the character and imagination of the peasants provided better subject matter (7).

W. B. Yeats attempted to replace both Irish and anti-Irish propaganda with social history, passion, and drama in the stories he selected for *Stories from Carleton* and *Representative Irish Tales*. Thuente makes clear that Irish country people on the one hand had been portrayed as sufferers under extreme oppression and on the other as barbarians trying to bring down "rational" English colonial government (11). Recognizing that there had been inequalities, Yeats nevertheless tried to present the social lives of individuals rather than studies in caricature, their joy rather than stage-Irish humor, their tragedy rather than the melodrama that characterized much fiction in nineteenth-century Ireland (17).

Yeats also used peasant characters and idiom to help inspire a sense of Irish national tradition. He wrote in 1888:

> You can no more have the greater poetry without a nation than religion without symbols. One can only reach out to the universe with a gloved hand—that glove is one's nation, the only thing one knows even a little of . . .

and in 1890:

> There is no great literature without nationality, no great nationality without literature. . . . The first thing needful if an Irish literature more elaborate and intense than our fine but primitive ballads and novels is to come into being is that readers and writers alike should really know the imaginative periods of Irish history. It is not needful that they should understand them with scholars' accuracy, but they should know them with the heart.[17]

Much later in his career he reiterated this desire he had felt to express universal emotion through national literature. In 1937 he wrote in "A General Introduction for My Work" that he wanted to "cry as all men cried, to laugh as all men laughed," and that the Young Ireland poets, when they were not writing "mere politics," had had the same desire. Although he did not admire their poetry, Yeats respected them because they were not "separated individual men" but "spoke or tried to speak out of a people to a people; behind them stretched the generations."[18] When describing his revision of *The Shadowy Waters* in 1905, he wrote that "It is full of homely phrases and of the idiom of daily speech. I have made the sailors rough, as sailors should be. . . . I believe more strongly every day that the element of strength in poetic language is common idiom, just as the element of strength in poetic construction is common passion" (Wade, *Letters* 462).

Yeats was convinced that in order to create a national literature, Irish writers must be familiar with Irish folklore and legend. To Æ he wrote that if they (the poets) would express Ireland they must know the nation's heart: the unleisured class had its ballads and legends, upon which the writers must draw, for they were the beginning of literature and art. He wrote that Irish writers must be national (as opposed to nationalistic) and should write seriously of Irish life, that Ireland was ripe for a national literature and theater. While folklore-collecting among Irish peasants, he discovered stories about the "wild old man in flannel" who could produce from a pack of cards a hare and hounds and about Mary Hynes, the peasant girl made famous by blind Raftery's song.[19] To Yeats, nationalism was the servant of art, not the other way round: "Creative work has always a fatherland" (*New Island* 74). The treasury of Irish folklore and legend should be collected, translated, and published in order that a new national and artistic consciousness could come into being. According to his own account, Yeats persuaded Synge to believe the same, and to go to the Aran Islands: "I had just come from Aran, and my imagination was full of those grey islands where men must reap with knives because of the stones" (CW 3: 63–64).

Synge's and Yeats's attitude here may be related to the Russian nobles' embracing their peasant culture in the late nineteenth century. As Nicholas Grene shows in *Synge: A Critical Study of the Plays*, Ivan Turgenev's *Huntsman's Sketches* (1847–51) is a landmark in Russian literature because it was the first work in which the peasants were the main subject of interest. The narrator, a young nobleman, acquaints his urban, upper-class readers with the life of the people by describing incidents and recording chance encounters with peasants. He tries to be unobtrusive because he is aware that he is an outsider; furthermore, he is a dilettante, selecting from his experiences with the peasants what *he* values. In "The Singers," for example, he hears a moving folk ballad but leaves immediately afterward because he does not want to spoil the impression by witnessing the drinking-bout that he knows will follow. For Turgenev, landscape is the focus of attention, while for Tolstoy in *Anna Karenina*, the land and peasants are central to the sense of national identity. While working with the peasants, Levin comes closest to understanding and identifying with the people. Although he is divided from the peasants by immovable social barriers, he shares a bond with them when he works on the land. Grene writes that Synge more closely resembles Turgenev than Tolstoy and quotes Synge's comment in his essay "In West Kerry": "Yet I know even while I was there I was an interloper only, a refugee in a garden between four seas" (*CW* 2: 258). Still, Synge can also be called a Tolstoyan in that he recognized the peasants and their culture as a part of Ireland that could not be neglected if the Irish were to realize their cultural identity.[20]

Synge lived on the Aran Islands, shared the islanders' precarious way of life, and learned their language, and Yeats knew the Irish folk poets and nationalist poets very well, and yet, like Turgenev's huntsman, they had difficulty communicating with the people and being accepted by them. They themselves were sometimes ambivalent toward their own subjects: Yeats wrote that the peasants had great courtesy, and yet he also referred to them as "serious, reserved, and suspicious" (*New Island* 91). Synge described his own sense of isolation from the people of Aran:

> In some ways these men and women seem strangely far away from me. They have the same emotions that I have, and the animals have, yet I cannot talk to them when there is much to say, more than to the dog that whines beside me in a mountain fog.
>
> There is hardly an hour I am with them that I do not feel the shock of some inconceivable idea, and then again the shock of some vague emotion that is familiar to them and to me. On some

days I feel this island as a perfect home and resting place; on other days I feel that I am a waif among the people. (*The Aran Islands* II, *CW* 2: 113)

These sentiments stemmed from a wide gulf created by differences in background, education, language, religion, and expectations—in short, by differences in culture—that separated W. B. Yeats and J. M. Synge from the peasants they chose to write about. They were Anglo-Irish—people of remote English descent in Ireland, an Ascendancy, not an aristocracy, which included people of very different social standing, united by minority interests (Grene 1).

Grene maintains that the peculiar position of the Anglo-Irish involves complexities that make generalization almost always inaccurate. The same can be said of the Irish in general. Conor Cruise O'Brien describes the "root-relation" between Protestant and Catholic in Ireland as one of settler and native. Yet, he says, "the vegetation sprung from these roots is complex and intertwined."[21] He distinguishes six groups who were affected by the *Playboy* riots: (1) the actual peasants of the west whose life Synge depicts in heroic pastoral comedy, who are essentially precolonial; (2) country people of other areas who were profoundly affected by modernization and Anglicization; (3) the children of the second group who had become urbanized, middle- and lower-middle class; (4) alienated descendants of Protestant settlers, who refused to share in Unionist feelings; (5) descendants of settlers who were pro-Unionist; (6) the English. This outline elucidates some of the complexities among the Irish people themselves. The third group, he explains, from among whom the Abbey Theater audiences were drawn, resented the *Playboy* because, heavily Anglicized themselves, they believed comedy about country people to be a calumny against themselves in the face of English opinion. The fourth group included the writers of the Literary Revival; the people they idealized were those who, they thought, had remained distinctively "native," but the qualities the writers praised did not appeal to the Catholic middle class. They felt themselves to be the victims of colonization:

Yeats often writes (as in part of the "Tibetan monk" passage) in the persona of a man of Gaelic ancestry, and Synge cursed the English language "that a man can't swear in without being vulgar." From this point of view they resented the Catholic *colonises* as being a vulgar caricature of that part of themselves that they wished to reject: The Catholics, in this perspective, were not merely imitation Englishmen, but imitation *lower middle-class* Englishmen.

Furthermore, even the Catholic attempt to reject this imitation could be seen as a vulgar caricature of the Protestant and upper-class mode of rejection: the crude demands of the political demagogue, in substitution for a genuinely distinctive cultural growth (73–74).

G. J. Watson explains, in *Irish Identity and the Literary Revival: Synge, Yeats, Joyce, and O'Casey*, that the tension between Anglo-Irish writers and their audiences was created by insurmountable differences in culture, that as Protestants they were suspect in the eyes of the people.[22] Birth did not guarantee "Irishness," writes Frank O'Connor: one qualified on the basis of descent, religion, politics, or a combination of these. However unfair this prejudice was to people whose families had lived in Ireland for four generations or to those Protestants who, like Thomas Davis and Charles Stewart Parnell, had abandoned Unionism, the native Irish were (and are) instinctively resentful of those whose ancestors had prospered from repeated conquests of Ireland and exploitation of its native people. This was how the Catholic natives felt, and how many of them still feel, O'Connor wrote in 1967. One of the reasons Anglo-Irish writers turned to landscape as a subject was that history was full of painful allegations against their ancestors. Furthermore, any attempt by the educated to try to interpret to the people, so lately come from the country, the life of the nation through the lives of country-dwellers was received with some animosity and resentment. In *A Short History of Irish Literature: A Backward Look*, O'Connor writes that the Irish in the early part of the twentieth century were becoming a nation of town dwellers by choice, not because of industrialism or high wages; the countryside ("beyond the lamps," it was called) to them represented poverty and ignorance. Dublin, according to O'Connor, is the only city in Europe where the town dweller does not pine for a little plot of land where he can garden and keep hens.[23] While the newly urbanized did not want to live like peasants, however, they wanted to believe that country people led lives of pious devotion and virtue. Middle-class Catholics had invented their own version of the noble peasant.[24]

Another native Irishman who criticized the Anglo-Irish writers, Patrick Kavanagh, wrote that one phrase of Joyce was worth all the writing of Synge because Joyce conveyed the real life of the people while Synge romanticized, and thus idealized, a way of life that was devoid of romanticism and idealism. Kavanagh accused Synge of falsifying the story of the peasants' lives by making their suffering seem beautiful: he said that a true peasant woman would never have the imagination to desire the hero, as Pegeen Mike does in *The Playboy of the Western World*. Kavanagh scorned the romantic notions of the peasantry that were held by writers of the Literary Revival: "Although the literal idea of the peasant is of a farm working person," he wrote, "in fact a peasant is all that mass of mankind which lives below a certain level of consciousness. They live in the dark cave of the unconsciousness and they scream when they see the light."[25] The entire Irish Renaissance, wrote Kavanagh, was "a thoroughgoing English-bred lie." St. John Ervine, furthermore, called Synge a "faker of peasant speech."[26]

Flann O'Brien, a contemporary and friend of Kavanagh's, makes the same comment on a phrase of Joyce being worth the lot of Synge. He refers to Synge as a "comic ghoul" who should finally be destroyed, a "virus isolated and recognisable." "Here is stuff," writes O'Brien, "that anybody who knows the Ireland referred to simply will not have." Yet with the double-edged sword of his wit, he tells us either that life imitates art or that the Irish read Synge too credulously: "We, who knew the whole insideouts of it, preferred to accept the ignorant valuations of outsiders on things Irish. And now the curse has come upon us, because I have personally met in the streets of Ireland persons who are clearly out of Synge's plays."[27]

Daniel Corkery's analysis of Synge's writing is more positive but still distrustful. Corkery, one of the first critics to assess Synge's contribution to Anglo-Irish literature, described a national literature as one written primarily for its own people: " ... every new book in it—no matter what its theme, foreign or native—is referable to their life, and its literary traits to the traits already established in the literature" (*Synge* 2). Where the writer lived was less important than who his chosen audience was; although many Irish writers lived abroad, among them Padraic Colum, John Eglinton, Austin Clarke, James Joyce, James Stephens, Sean O'Casey, George Moore, and Liam O'Flaherty, the typical Irish expatriate continued to find his subject matter in Irish life, and although his audience undeniably included many non-Irish people, his task was to express Ireland to itself. (Corkery excluded Yeats from his list of expatriates because, he wrote, it was Yeats's practice never to spend the whole of any year abroad.) The Colonial writers, on the other hand, wrote for their kinsfolk in England; their subject was usually the "quaintness" and inferiority of the native Irish people, described to a public that thought of itself as sophisticated and "normal." All over the world, writers who had exiled themselves spiritually from the colonizing nation adopted this "quaintness" as their major theme. According to Corkery, these writers had no chance to express the people of Ireland to themselves because they had no share in the Irish native memory. Thus, the Irish during Colonial rule were without self-expression in literary form, except for the little-known writers in Irish, because any true Anglo-Irish literature would have been written for the Irish people who could not accept the "insolence" of Ascendancy writers.

Corkery maintains that the work of the Irish Literary Theater (established by W. B. Yeats, Augusta Gregory, and Edward Martyn) from its beginning to 1922, whether good or bad in itself, was done for Ireland because it made an effort to express Ireland to its own people. J. M. Synge also stood apart from other Ascendancy writers because he lived with the people and because his writings interpreted their lives; nevertheless, Corkery writes, his inability to understand their religious consciousness, and his Anglo-Irish background, separated him from the Irish people.

Corkery describes what he calls the "three great forces" that have made the Irish nation different from the English, set it apart spiritually and culturally: (1) the people's religious consciousness; (2) Irish nationalism; and (3) the question of the land (19). Writers who wish to create a national literature for Ireland, he contends, must understand that the land in Ireland will figure as prominently in any true Anglo-Irish literature as the freeing of the serfs lay behind Russian literature (22).

For centuries a predominantly agricultural country, Ireland found its history shaped to a large extent by the struggle for the ownership of land. Corkery engages in his own type of primitivism when he claims that Ireland had by the eighteenth century become a purely peasant nation, with the cabins "the custodians of its mind."[28] In 1931 he wrote that Ireland was indeed still a "peasant-ridden" country, since fifty-three percent of its population was engaged in farming or in work related to agriculture. By contrast, only six percent of the English population was so employed (Corkery, *Synge* 21). Consequently, one significant theme of Irish literature is the peasants' struggle to possess the land they worked (16).

L. M. Cullen, in his famous refutation of Corkery's concept of a "hidden" Ireland, shows that no such singular identity of outlook existed among the Irish,[29] that his concept simplifies Irish history into a "simple context of land resettlement, oppression and resentment with predictable and stereotyped relationships and situations flowing from it" (47). The poets, furthermore, were not the simple peasants Corkery represents, nor did either the mass of people or the poets live in abysmal poverty and oppression (23, 28). Maurice Goldring further challenges Corkery's authority, describing his emphasis on the social status of the "Fili" in the eighteenth century as representative of the aspirations of the educated classes in the twentieth (47).

Corkery's achievement, however, lies in his having articulated the frustration of the people of a formerly colonized nation who were still, at the time he wrote, struggling to find their own linguistic identity. The writers in a "normal" country, Corkery wrote, are "one with what they write of" (*Synge* 13). They endow the mass of people with a new significance. According to Corkery, all that an English child learns buttresses and refines his emotional nature. The literature he reads and the instruction he receives focus for him the mind of his own people. Later, he seizes all that he reads in it with an English mind; he has a national consciousness by which to estimate its value for him. The Irish child derives no such identity from literature, Corkery wrote in 1931; subsequently,

> No sooner does he begin to use his intellect that what he learns begins to undermine, to weaken, and to harass his emotional nature. For practically all that he reads is in English—what he reads in Irish is not yet worth taking account of. It does not therefore focus the mind of his own people, teaching him the better to look about him, to understand both himself and his surroundings. It focuses instead the life of another people. Instead of sharpening his gaze upon his own neighborhood, his reading distracts it, for he cannot find in these surroundings what his reading has taught him is the matter worth coming on. His surroundings begin to

seem unvital. His education, instead of buttressing and refining his emotional nature, teaches him the rather to despise it, inasmuch as it teaches him not to see the surroundings out of which he is sprung, as they are in themselves, but as compared with alien surroundings: his education provides him with an alien medium through which he is henceforth to look at his native land! . . . What happens in the neighborhood of an Irish boy's home—the fair, the hurling match, the land grabbing, the *priesting*, the mission, the Mass—he never comes on in literature, that is, in such literature as he is told to respect and learn. (14–15)

Corkery's energetic description of cultural deprivation echoes the complaint of colonized people worldwide who have accepted as their "official" language that of the colonizer; he also forcefully (if unintentionally) demonstrates the irony inherent in ascribing the importance of cultural integrity to only one gender.

We may better understand the depth of the Irish desire for cultural integrity if we consider the vehemence of the attacks upon Irish character traits. The resistance of the "native" Irish to literature written by Anglo-Irish writers resulted not only from their ignoring the land issue but also from the unfavorable stereotypes given to the Irish by artists and writers of the Ascendancy class and of the English themselves. Edward Said explains that the stereotype of the Irish flows from an English belief in "racial" superiority (*Culture* 222); moreover, a tradition of both British and European thought considered the Irish to be barbarians. Even today we hear jokes aimed at "Irish" laziness: their irresponsibility, not the poor state of their economy, for example, is said to account for high unemployment.

The early Victorian imagination invented "Paddy" who was more than the cavorting, ridiculous "stage" Irishman that had been created for English audiences in the eighteenth century. "Paddy" was by contrast both fun-loving, careless, and hard-drinking, and at the same time mercurial, bad-tempered, and easily angered. "Paddy" also meant a "tantrum," as well as being a pejorative term for "Irishman." Irish people were seen by many English as perpetually disruptive, never at peace unless they were fighting. "To get one's Irish up" was to become angry, while to "weep Irish" was to "feign sorrow." An "Irishman's hurricane" was a "dead calm," "Irish evidence" was "false witness," and an "Irish theater" was a "guardroom."[30]

We can realize the destructive nature of stereotyping through Edward Said's explanation of the power-knowledge relationship that he calls "Orientalism." This type of knowledge, he writes, " . . . means surveying a civilization from its origins to its prime to its decline—and of course, it means *being able to do that*. Knowledge means rising above immediacy, beyond self, into the foreign and distant. The object of such knowledge is inherently vulnerable to scrutiny: . . . To have such knowledge of such a thing is to dominate it, to have authority over it."[31] Knowledge gives power, he continues; more power requires more knowledge, creating an "increasingly profitable dialectic of information and control" (36). Said writes of European power over and knowledge of the Orient, but if we substitute "Great Britain" for "Europe" and "Ireland" for "Orient," we see how Said's theory clarifies much about British attitudes toward its nearest colony. Just as "Orientalism" designated the East, geographically, morally, and culturally, so did Anglo-Saxonist attitudes designate Ireland by creating a stereotype of the "Celtic" character that was to influence British attitudes and policy so deeply. Terms such as "childlike" and "different," used to describe the Irish—as well as subjugated people the world over—emphasized the spiritual and psychological distance the people of the colonizing nation felt toward the colonized. The stereotyping nation or community also has to create an image of itself as well as of the "other," in order to be able to define "otherness" (Deane, "Introduction" 12). Thus the West created the terms through which it "knew" and "recognized" the Orient, creating a discourse of power: as Foucault explains, " . . . there is no knowledge without a particular discursive practice; and any discursive practice may be defined by the knowledge that it forms."[32] If we take this argument one step further, we might conclude that Revivalists were also "colonizing" the Irish country people for their own artistic purposes—identifying what was "different" and "mysterious" about them. We might consider their attitudes to be kinder, their reasons purer, but nevertheless we must acknowledge that they sought to speak for people other than themselves, to "represent" them to the world, and to use them in order to establish a new national culture and an audience for themselves.

Anglo-Irish and English writers contributed to the unfavorable depiction of Irish peasants in the nineteenth century. Charles Lever, in *Lord Kilgobbin*, emphasized their ignorance and indolence:

Not that they were a hard-worked or a hard-working population: they took life very easy, seeing that by no possible exertion could they materially better themselves; and even when they hunted a neighbor's cow out of their wheat, they would execute the eviction with a lazy indolence and sluggishness that took away from the act all semblance of ungenerousness.

They were very poor, their hovels were wretched, their clothes ragged, and their food scanty; but, with all that, they were not discontented, and very far from unhappy.[33]

In 1849 an anonymous essayist quoted Thackeray's view of Irish deceitfulness and cynicism, their wretchedness that made them objects unworthy even of compassion. Writing of a crowd of beggars that formed around his coach in Cork, he asks: "Have they nothing else to do?—or is it that they *will* do nothing but stare, swagger, and be idle in the streets?" The reviewer concludes:

But whether this incomprehensible people can be persuaded to work for their livelihood or no, we trust that we shall hear no more of the vile cant about 'hereditary bondage and the accursed tyranny of England.' The bondage was and is no other than the bondage of obstinate ignorance, and the tyranny, the tyranny of inveterate sloth.[34]

Taking a more charitable, but still colonialist, point of view, Thomas Carlyle wrote that England was guilty towards Ireland and was reaping the full measure of fifteen generations of wrongdoing. In his essay on Chartism he described the English attitude toward Irish immigrants:

The Irish National character is degraded, disordered; till this recover itself, nothing is yet recovered. Immethodic, headlong, violent, mendacious: what can you make of the wretched Irishman? . . . Crowds of miserable Irish darken all our towns. The wild Milesian features, looking false ingenuity, restlessness, unreason, misery and mockery, salute you on all highways and byways.[35]

So many of the educated and propertied people in England opposed the desire of eighty percent of the Irish people for national self-government, not because of a single, unsolvable "Irish question," but because of a unifying assumption that the "native Irish" were alien in race and inferior in culture to the Anglo-Saxons. The assumption was developed from the reports of English adventurers and settlers in Ireland in the Tudor and Stuart periods, when the countryside was being despoiled by English and Scottish plantation and Irish rebellion, and from the notion, derived from popular theories about race and national character, that there existed a profound gulf between English and Irish character and culture.[36]

Definition of some key terms helps to elucidate cultural attitudes. "Prejudice" here involves prejudgment or premature assessment of someone or something based on insufficient evidence and motivated by national as well as social needs. "Stereotype" refers to all patterns of generalized behavior that Victorian Englishmen ascribed to all Irish men, women, and children. "Ethnocentrism" is defined as: " . . . this view of things in which one's own group is the center of everything, and all others are scaled and rated with reference to it. . . . Each group nourishes its own pride and vanity, boasts itself superior, exalts its own divinities, and looks with contempt on outsiders."[37] L. P. Curtis explains the ethnocentric response:

> Ethnocentrism characterizes that nucleus of beliefs and attitudes, cultivated and cherished by people who seek relief from some of their anxieties and fears, which make for more or less rigid distinctions between their own group (or in-group) and some other collection of people (or out-group) with the result that the former are ranked far above the latter in the assumed hierarchy of peoples, nations, or ethnic units which together make up the species of man. . . . Ethnocentric thinking flourishes in a climate of anxiety, fear, and guilt as these emotions permeate both the individual and the class or group to which he belongs, and it is reinforced by the delusion that the values or physical proximity of the out-group somehow pose a direct threat to his own way of life. (7)

Anglo-Saxonism, representing English and Victorian ethnocentrism, embraced the propositions that those of Anglo-Saxon heritage were an identifiable and historically authenticated race, that the civil and religious liberties they enjoyed had no fuller expression on earth, that they possessed superior virtues because of their inherited attri-

butes of reason, restraint, self-control, love of freedom and hatred of
anarchy, respect for law and distrust of enthusiasm, and that serious
threats were posed by impending racial deterioration. Anglo-Saxo-
nism justified imperialist expansion because it maintained that sup-
posedly "inferior" races had never had free institutions. The some-
times disruptive Parnellite activity for Home Rule in the Commons,
and the sporadic violence by the Irish Republican Brotherhood and
Land League gave Anglo-Saxonists the "evidence" they needed to
condemn the Irish as incapable of the self-control required for self-
government.

Ned Lebow, in "British Images of Poverty in Pre-Famine Ireland,"
writes:

> Students of colonialism have suggested that colonizers have attri-
> buted remarkably uniform characteristics to the peoples they
> came to dominate. With almost monotonous regularity, they de-
> scribed colonial natives as indolent and self-complacent, cowardly
> but brazenly rash, violent, superstitious and incapable of hard
> work. On the more complimentary side, they were described as
> hospitable, good-natured, and curious but incapable of prolonged
> attention.[38]

Indolence was the trait most universally ascribed to colonial natives.
Lebow concludes that colonizers projected this trait upon the colo-
nized for their own psychological and political reasons:

> By defining themselves as hard-working, thrifty, and honest, and
> the natives as indolent, superstitious, and lacking purpose, the
> colonial elite, who profited from the status quo, could shift the
> burden of responsibility for the disparity between their affluence
> and the natives' poverty from themselves to the natives. The ra-
> tionalization permitted them to counter the arguments of their
> opponents, reduce internal guilt and anxiety and accordingly en-
> joy the profits of colonial exploitation. (59)

Even Matthew Arnold was ambivalent about the Irish people's
ability to govern themselves. He opposed Home Rule in 1886 because
he doubted the political capability of the Irish, whom he considered

to be insubordinate, idle, and improvident, although he appreciated their genius and attributed their misery to unfortunate English rule. He opposed measures to give Irish peasants right of land tenure:

> The Land Bill... adopts, legalizes, formulates tenant-right, a description of ownership unfamiliar to countries of our sort of civilization, and very inconvenient. It establishes it throughout Ireland, and, by a scheme which is a miracle of intricacy and complication, it invites the most contentious and litigious people in the world to try conclusions with their landlords as to the ownership divided between them.[39]

To Arnold the Irish were sentimental and impatient; they lacked sanity and steadfastness; and they rebelled against what he described as (borrowing the phrase from historian Henri Martin) "the despotism of fact." Their endearing qualities were their sensitivity, "nervous exaltation," extravagant chivalry, and closeness to the spell of the "feminine idiosyncracy" and the secrets of natural beauty and magic. Even his admiration for the "Celtic" temperament revealed a deeply-felt cultural prejudice:

> Even the extravagance and exaggeration of the sentimental Celtic nature has often something romantic and attractive about it, something which has a sort of smack of misdirected good. The Celt, undisciplinable, anarchical, and turbulent by nature, but out of affection and admiration giving himself body and soul to some leader, that is not a promising political temperament, it is just the opposite of the Anglo-Saxon temperament, disciplinable and steadily obedient within certain limits, but retaining an inalienable part of freedom and self-dependence; but is it a temperament for which one has a kind of sympathy notwithstanding. And very often, for the gay defiant reaction against fact of the lively Celtic nature one has more than sympathy; one feels, in spite of the extravagance, in spite of good sense disapproving, magnetised and exhilarated by it.[40]

Two forms of Anglo-Saxonism are at work here: on the one hand, Arnold implies British racial superiority; on the other, he admits virtues to the Irish only insofar as they are "different" from Anglo-Saxons. Thus even the virtues of Irish people help to shore up notions of British "character" and superiority.

Many M.P.s who voted on the Home Rule Bills of 1886 and 1893 owed their limited "knowledge" of Irish history to writers who were influenced by their Anglo-Saxonist prejudice. Charles Kingsley, an Oxford historian, called the Irish "human chimpanzees" (qtd. in Curtis 84). Lord Macaulay wrote:

> The Irish, on the other hand, were distinguished by qualities which tend to make men interesting rather than prosperous. They were an ardent and impetuous race, easily moved to tears or to laughter, to fury or to love. Alone among the nations of Northern Europe they had the susceptibility, the vivacity, the natural turn for acting and rhetoric which are indigenous on the shores of the Mediterranean Sea. In mental cultivation Scotland had an indisputable superiority. (qtd. in Curtis 77)

In 1893 historian John Richard Green described his Anglo-Saxonist appreciation for Celtic character:

> The sensibility of the Celtic temper, so quick to perceive beauty, so eager in its thirst for life, its emotions, its adventures, its sorrows, its joys, is tempered by a passionate melancholy that expresses its revolt against the impossible, by an instinct of what is noble, by a sentiment that discovers the weird charm of nature.... In the Celtic love of woman there is little of the Teutonic depth and earnestness, but in its stead a childlike spirit of delicate enjoyment, a faint distant flush of passion like the rose-light of dawn on a snowy mountain peak, a playful delight in beauty.[41]

Reacting to these English ideas, twentieth-century Irish readers and audiences instinctively rejected literature and theater which they thought depicted them according to these stereotypes. Dublin audiences rioted at performances of *The Countess Cathleen, The Shadow of the Glen,* and *The Playboy of the Western World,* for they thought these plays were merely perpetuating the stereotype of the Irish as lazy, irreverent, unfaithful, violent, and irresponsible.[42]

The Home Rule debates of 1886 and 1893–94 gave Unionists fuel for their evidence against the fitness of the Irish for self-government. Although Gladstone tried to demolish convictions about the unreliability of Irish people, Lord Salisbury insisted that "incurable differences" between the Irish and English rendered the former unfit for political liberties of more "advanced" people. Home Rule was in part defeated by Anglo-Saxonist stereotypes of the Irish.

Perhaps the cruelest depiction of the Irish was artistic renderings of the stereotype with porcine and simian features. Cartoons in *Punch* and George Cruikshank's illustrations for W. H. Maxwell's *History of the Irish Rebellion in 1798* showed apelike features that designated animal instincts, slovenly women and drunken men in rebel encampments, and disorderly and foolish rebels murdering helpless children and prisoners and destroying Protestant churches. Portraits of Anglo-Irish nobles, however, revealed dignified and sober countenances.[43] Illustrations by Sir John Tenniel for *Mr. Punch's Victorian Era* also depict the Irish as apelike and animalistic. On page 23 a ragged, unruly peasant with beard, pipe, and porcine features, with cudgel raised, wears the term "Repale" on his shirt.[44] An Irishman loyal to the Union, depicted on page 161, has a more serene appearance. In Mrs. Anna Maria Hall's *Tales of Irish Life and Character*, an Erskine Nichol illustration portrays a dishevelled, disorderly Irishman with cudgel raised; the title, "Home Rule," implies that the Irish are unfit for self-government.[45]

Recent scholarship points out, however, that while *Punch* could be savage in its early years, the magazine presented a varied picture of Irish life, engaged in anti-Irish satire no more than antipolitician or anti-income tax satire, and depicted the English poor with countenances similar to those of its Irish stereotypes.[46] In fact, in early years, *Punch* sometimes adopted a resolutely pro-Irish stand (174). Nevertheless, from the mid-1840s on, *Punch* unleashed vitriolic satire on the Irish, inspired by its own less radical outlook, the rise of the extremely nationalistic Young Ireland movement that endorsed violence, and large-scale Irish emigration into Britain (175–76). English artists were not the only critics of Ireland; some of the most savage of *Punch's* satirical cartoonists were Irish or of Irish descent. Marginalization from mainstream "Englishness" may have provoked in them unusual fervor in defining the stereotype (178).

Anglo-Saxonists, however, possessed no exclusivity in cultural chauvinism. Alf MacLochlainn argues in "Gael and Peasant—A Case of Mistaken Identity?" that the Irish "national writers" adopted the same tone in comparing their own with English culture, that they too breathed the same imperialist air. They rejected the notion of British racial superiority, of course; but, instead of proposing that there was no racial superiority, they posited an *Irish* racial superiority.[47] MacLochlainn quotes from Pearse as an example of extreme Gaelicism:

> And here we have the secret of Rossa's magic, of Rossa's power: he came out of the Gaelic tradition. He was of the Gael; he thought in a Gaelic way; he spoke in Gaelic accents. He was the spiritual and intellectual descendant of Colm Cille and of Sean an Dio-mais. . . . To him the Gael and Gaelic ways were splendid and holy, worthy of all homage and all service; for the English he had a hatred that was tinctured with contempt. He looked upon them as an inferior race, morally and intellectually.[48]

W. B. Yeats, in the "Introduction" to *Representative Irish Tales,* praises the Irish peasants' shrewdness and cunning even as he attributes these qualities to the expectations of an alien gentry:

> The true peasant remained always in disfavour as "plotter," "re-bel," or man in some way unfaithful to his landlord. The knave type flourished till the decay of the gentry themselves, and is now extant in the boatmen, guides, and mendicant hordes that gather round tourists, while they are careful to trouble at no time any one belonging to the neighborhood with their century-old jokes. The tourist has read of the Irish peasant in the only novels of Irish life he knows, those written by and for an alien gentry. He has expectations to be fulfilled. The mendicants follow him for fear he might be disappointed. He thinks they are types of Irish poor people. He does not know that they are merely a portion of the velvet of aristocracy now fallen in the dust. (26)

Thus we can see how the Gaelicists, too, created an institution of superiority.

Anglo-Saxonism, nevertheless, represented the mythology of a people largely self-fulfilled in a nationalist as well as material and imperial sense. No matter how deep its divisions of class, party, and sect, England was unquestionably a nation. The Irish, struggling to achieve nationhood and a sense of cultural unity, had to confront various distortions of Irish art, including not only "Paddy" and his predecessor the "stage Irishman," but also the archaic, noble peasant. Irish artists who felt the need to reestablish Irish tradition by refuting English stereotypes of the Irish themselves unwittingly confirmed the unity and power of English culture.

Irish cultural chauvinism found spokespersons among the Revivalists, particularly those who had chosen the peasants as the embodiment of a "Gaelic" and rural ideal. In fact, the issue of the land—who was to live on it, how it was to be used—occupied an important place in the cultural debate of the Revivalist period as well as the decades following independence. Seamus Deane writes that Revivalists modified the British "Celt" into their own "Gael" and reinterpreted themselves and their countrymen ("Introduction" 13). A people's "nature" is one of culture's most precious inventions; a culture brings itself into being by an act of invention that depends on anterior, legitimating "nature" (17). Revivalists found that nature in the Gaelic ideal.

The Writers and the Country

Inspired by this Gaelic ideal, and seizing on the image of peasant Ireland, many Irish writers and politicians envisioned an agricultural society that could be created in Ireland after independence from Great Britain had been achieved. In his Saint Patrick's Day speech of 1943, Éamon de Valéra, Prime Minister of the Irish Republic, described what he perceived to be the ideal Irish society:

> The Ireland which we dreamed of would be the home of a people who valued material wealth only as the basis of right living, of a people who were satisfied with frugal comfort and devoted their leisure to things of the spirit—a land whose countryside would be bright with cosy homesteads, whose fields and villages would be joyous with the joy of industry, with the romping of sturdy children, the contests of athletic youths and the laughter of comely maidens, whose firesides would be the forums for serene old age.[49]

And W. B. Yeats, in many ways de Valéra's opposite, being a poet and Protestant rather than politician and Catholic, had earlier described his vision of the Irish landscape:

> What is this nationality we are trying to preserve, this thing that we are fighting English influence to preserve? It is not merely our pride. It is certainly not any national vanity that stirs us on to activity. If you examine to the root a contest between two peoples, two nations, you will always find that it is really a war between two civilizations, two ideals of life. First of all, we Irish do not desire, like the English, to build up a nation where there shall be a very rich class and a very poor class. Ireland will always be in the main an agricultural country. . . . Wherever men have tried to imagine a perfect life, they have imagined a place where men plow and sow and reap, not a place where there are great wheels turning and great chimneys vomiting smoke. Ireland will always be a country where men plow and sow and reap. . . . And then Ireland too, as we think, will be a country where not only will the wealth be well distributed but where there will be an imaginative culture and power to understand imaginative and spiritual things distributed among the people. We wish to preserve an ancient ideal of life. Wherever its customs prevail, there you will find the folk song, the folk tale, the proverb and the charming manners that come from ancient culture.[50]

This pastoral vision has a long history, Seán Ó'Faoláin writes in *The Irish: A Character Study;* looking backward at Irish history and culture rather than forward to some future Utopia, he claims that "The leitmotif of Gaelic society from time immemorial had been the lowing of cattle . . . Ireland's wealth was for centuries its soft rains, its vast pasturages, those wandering herds."[51] Thus, to Yeats, de Valéra, Corkery, and Ó'Faoláin, the people who best represented Ireland's true culture were those who lived and worked on the land. Still, the reader of these lines is aware that these writers are creating an agricultural, pastoral identity for Ireland that not all the Irish would be willing to accept.[52]

W. B. Yeats and J. M. Synge, who wanted to find some consciousness they could identify as "Irish," considered the "real" Ireland in the late nineteenth and early twentieth centuries to be synonymous with "peasant" Ireland. They wrote about the landscape—Yeats of Clare,

Galway, and Sligo, Synge of Wicklow, Connemara, and the Aran Is-
lands—customs, personalities, songs, stories, and expressions that
gave the locality its character and through which they could express
the people's spirit. Yeats described Howth through the lament of its
aged crazy woman, Moll Magee, and Sligo through the local song
about the "sally (willow) gardens" that he claimed an old woman of
Ballisodare had sung to him. Just as Yeats hoped to free himself from
contemporary poetic diction by turning to traditional or primitive
forms of the language, Synge also looked to the peasants to find a
theme for his art. Both wanted to create characters who would express
the native people of Ireland to themselves and to the town dwellers,
who, they believed, lacked a sense of Irish cultural unity. Synge felt
that humankind was naturally nomadic and that travelers had finer
intellectual acuity than town dwellers. Yeats rebelled against the myth
of "progress" and wrote that all that was greatest in literature was
based upon legends formed not by individuals but by nations over the
centuries. He emphasized the peasants' knowledge of folklore and
their embodiment of old ways of life, while Synge celebrated what he
called their individuality. Yeats's ideal peasant was a fisherman "wise
and simple"; Synge's was the lively, lusty peasant of Wicklow or the
west who more closely resembled an aristocrat than a "labourer or
citizen," as the wild horse more nearly resembles the thoroughbred
than the hack or cart-horse (*The Aran Islands* I, *CW* 2: 66). Yeats's
implied equation of noble and beggarman (in "The Municipal Gallery
Revisited") had sanction in tiny fiefdoms of medieval Gaelic Ireland,
where there was no intervening Gaelic middle class to come between
nobility and peasants, who shared to some extent a common culture.
Both viewed the peasants as a link with the past and the traditional
culture; their ultimate goal, of course, was to find a culture that would
provide images for literature.

"The main battle in imperialism is over land, of course," Edward Said
writes; in Ireland, the attempt to regain control of land dominated the
movement toward independence, and "Yeats cannot be severed from
this quest" (*Culture* xii-xiii, 236). To many native Irishmen, however,
Yeats's as well as Synge's peasants more nearly resembled ideals than
actualities. The term *peasantry* implies an agricultural way of life. The
peasant is usually a small-scale producer who possesses simple tech-
nology and whose primary livelihood is cultivation of the soil, although

fishing and craftsmanship may be included. Peasant communities are characterized by simple technology, subsistence production, low output, narrow range of output, and the importance of family labor.[53] Yet this emphasis on occupation obscures a more important criterion—that is, the peasant society is necessarily defined in relation to a city and did not exist prior to the establishment of preindustrial cities, when settled agriculturalists lost their political and economic autonomy.[54] They then ceased to be peasants with the advent of industrialism.

The peasant class forms part of a larger society in that what it produces is subject to the demands and sanctions of power holders outside its community, usually in an urban location (6). Many writers who analyze peasant societies emphasize structural relationships between village and city, yet the villages are not communities of autonomous small-scale producers but rather "represent the rural expression of large, class-structured, economically complex, preindustrial civilizations, in which trade and commerce and craft specialization are well-developed, in which money is commonly used, and in which market disposition is the goal for a part of the producer's effort" (5).

Far from being independent villages remote from what may be perceived to be urban corruption, peasant communities rely on the urban culture as the principal source of innovation, motivation, and prestige (5). Peasants, fascinated by the opportunities the city offers, are emotionally dependent on it. Peasant culture requires continual communication with the larger society for religious, economic, and cultural viability. Ironically, it is also the city that is the source of the peasant's helplessness and humiliation: " . . . the peasant knows he can never really count on a city man" (10). The urban society usually drains the peasant society of its economic surplus (9). Peasants have little control over the conditions that govern their lives; their leadership is normally weak and peasant revolutions rare (Foster 8). They seldom voice their own aspirations—this task falls to others, usually an urban bourgeoisie (Goldring 10). Nor is the peasant society artistically creative, although its inventiveness and vigor have been widely praised. On the contrary, the peasant's cultural forms are usually developed through imitation of urban customs. While it is true that artists often look to rural people for inspiration, the direction of influence is not evenly balanced (Foster 12). The famous accounts of peasant life, for example, required the prompting of outsiders in order to be produced. Tomás Ó Crohan wrote *The Islandman* (1929) and

Maurice O'Sullivan his *Twenty Years a Growing* (1933) after having read the autobiography of Maxim Gorky (Goldring 65). The dream of a peasant audience is therefore impossible, and, hence, the cultured but untutored peasant is someone who does not exist. Those who sentimentalize the pastoral are almost always prisoners of an urban mentality; the myth of the pastoral was, after all, created by urban dwellers.

Moreover, in creating a peasant ideal, Revivalists and Dubliners alike ignored common life of a great many peasants. Their livelihood and language, beautiful and charming to nativists, enforced on them a poor material existence and limited their cultural life (Goldring 65). This isolation resulted in shocking poverty, both material and spiritual, recorded in the biographies of peasants living in the far west and the Blasket Islands. Their writings reveal lives completely subject to their environment and range of experience so limited that they did not know what steamships were or that some people in the world are born with darker skin (63). One of the least attractive traits recorded was the Blasket islanders' believing that war was a good thing because during a bad year a cargo ship wrecked off their coast enabled the peasants to survive. Although the entire crew drowned, the islanders celebrated (64).

The Irish peasantry was dependent to a large extent on a landowning class, and while some writers of the Literary Revival praised what they believed to be the peasants' imaginative and spiritual way of life, the single most important concern of Irish peasants for centuries before independence was land tenure. The struggle for the land had cultural implications, for the landowners were often (but not always) of one religion and thought to be of an alien nation, while the workers were of another religion and believed to be the native people. These "native" people were descended from Celtic tribes who migrated from central Europe westward and northward, finally into what are now the British Isles and Ireland, as early as the fifth century B.C.E. and developed a highly stratified, well-integrated tribal society. Their way of life was both pastoral and warlike; they remained a regionalist people up to the completion of the English conquest. This pastoral regionalism was in part responsible for their inability to unite to drive away foreign invaders. So pastoral was their nature, writes Seán Ó'Faoláin, they never founded a town; the closest they came to it was the establishment of monastic settlements (38). Every Irish town that exists was founded by the Danes, Ó'Faoláin claims, who invaded in the ninth century to establish trading posts, or the Normans who invaded under Earl Strongbow during the reign of Henry II in the twelfth century.

Nor had the Irish any commercial sense or elaborate husbandry. While the Danish invasions had little effect on native life, the Norman colonists, as well as the Scottish colonists of the seventeenth century, left their character on the people to the present day. Moreover, the population of the Aran Islands was affected by its occupation for over a hundred years by English soldiers. In 1885, historian John Beddoe wrote:

> We might be disposed, trusting to Irish traditions respecting the islands, to accept these people as representatives of the Firbolg, had not Cromwell, that upsetter of all things Hibernian, left in Aranmore a small English garrison, who subsequently apostatised to Catholicism, intermarried with the natives, and so vitiated the Firbolgian pedigree.[55]

The principal effect of the Norman invasions and settlements in Ireland was the introduction of a variation of the English feudal system in which landowning families let out to tenants the land they themselves did not use in return for payment or services.

There were few viable settlements, however, until the time of Elizabeth I. The organized, long-term plantation of Ulster by lowland Scots took place during the reign of James I in the early seventeenth century. The occupation of the country was complete with Cromwell's land seizure in the mid-seventeenth century, although the settlement of land under Cromwell never approached the thoroughness of the earlier Ulster planters. The Cromwellian settlement was not so much a plantation as a transference of the sources of wealth and power—that is, the ownership of land—from Catholics to Protestants. Not a Protestant community, but a Protestant upper class, came into being; the ownership of land changed, but the people who lived on it and worked it did not. To those who were farmers by profession, the usurpation of the land was more than an economic loss: it was dispossession. One of the central questions of Irish history, and of the literature of Ireland, therefore, is the Land Question—who lives on it as opposed to who owns it. In the Jacobite War of 1690–91, when ancient Irish and Anglo-Norman Catholics, despite their previous feuds, combined against the new Cromwellian Protestant colonists, the Irishmen fought for James II because of a desire to get back the lands of which they had been deprived. Religion or personal loyalty to James had little to do with their fight.[56]

Thus the struggle for land in Ireland was not only economic but also cultural and the ownership of the land and the people's identification with locality has been a crucial element in economic, social, political, and cultural change. The universal problem faced by members of the rural population—that of getting and keeping the land—became steadily more serious in the years after the Napoleonic Wars as a result of overpopulation and the deterioration of the Irish economy. The nature of the struggle is complicated, however, and does not take the form of a simple division between Protestants and Catholics. Violence in the rural areas did not represent a collective assault by Irish "native" peasantry on the landowning class. The early 1790s saw an increase in the number of middlemen who were not Protestant gentlemen but large farmers, many of whom were Catholic.[57] Much agrarian violence in Ireland in the eighteenth, nineteenth, and twentieth centuries resulted from the struggle by small farmers and laborers against large farmers, permeating the social classes and affecting not only relations between large Protestant landlords and their tenants but also those between small holders and graziers, farmers and laborers.[58] There was a division between owners and cultivators in prefamine as well as postfamine Ireland, and among those within the farming class itself.[59]

If relations between Protestant landowners and tenants were strained, those between Catholic farmers and Catholic laborers were also strained, farmers often being accused of unfair practices, such as withholding wages, seizing property, or refusing to maintain the land they let. There were differences in attitudes toward pasture-farming, because while grazing was preferred by large farmers as long as market conditions encouraged grassland produce, greater rural population meant that additional land would be needed for tillage. Therefore, widespread hostility developed among the poor against grazing (38). Hostility against the system increased during the Famine and continued after it because graziers, both Catholic and Protestant, had benefitted from the clearances and destruction of the peasant community. Even the nationalist movements were affected by conflicts among members of the rural population, their leaders not always siding with the poorer tenant farmers.[60] Unfair agrarian practices and inequalities in land tenure clearly were not due solely to religious divisions. No clear distinction existed, moreover, between small farmers and laborers.[61] Thus the line between oppressed and oppressor cannot be clearly drawn.

Still, the urban population in late nineteenth and early twentieth-century Ireland perceived the Land Question to be a struggle largely between wealthy Protestant owners and poor Catholic peasants. Anglo-Irish writers who wished to write about, even identify with, that other, "native" Ireland, had a very wide chasm to cross, a vast ravine of suspicion, mistrust, even hatred, particularly from the urban middle class. The opposition to *The Countess Cathleen, The Shadow of the Glen,* and *The Playboy of the Western World* demonstrated that people felt that their institutions were being held up to ridicule; in addition, many Irish people did not like Ireland's representation as an overwhelmingly rural or peasant society, because new town dwellers did not want to be reminded of rural poverty. The Anglo-Irish writers' celebration of the wildness and savagery of the native Irish was too close to what the English chose as the major denigrating feature in their image of the Irish. *The Playboy of the Western World* celebrates the successful liberation of an oppressed victim from the domination of tyranny, yet to Synge's Dublin audience, Christy Mahon was another depiction of the irresponsible, violent, irreverent Irish Catholic peasant.[62] The protest against *The Playboy* reflected religious and nationalistic sentiment in a period of national revival and stemmed from the memory of an alien Ascendancy's callous treatment:

> The fault (for the riots) lies not in the native Ireland but in Ascendancy Ireland, which played the game of literature not for its own eyes, such as they have been and are, but for English eyes, not expressing Ireland to itself but exploiting it for others. Had Ascendancy Ireland treated native Ireland fairly [in literature] . . . *The Playboy,* instead of being greeted with outcry and passion, would have been taken for what it was worth. . . . It may be that he [Synge] expected a Dublin audience to look at the spectacle of the play as a purely folk audience in the West, self-contained and not conscious that their neighbor in the next seat was English-eyed, might conceivably have done, for Synge was simple about many

things, and was amorous of the honest insensibility of the folk consciousness. (Corkery, *Synge* 183)

The Irish audience greeted his play with anger and indignation because they saw him as an Anglo-Irishman exploiting English stereotypes of Ireland.

It may be that in fact the Anglo-Irish authors read the fate of their own class into that of the landless peasantry. The Land Acts enabled a new middle class to put both groups out of business and replace them with a new breed of peasant proprietors and rural bourgeoisie. Industrial society needed to replace large landowners and peasant societies with a large urbanized proletariat and middle class in order to supply both labor and markets for its products; having done so, it glorified peasant society as pure and virtuous in order to instill in the urban population the ethic of hard work and to encourage this population to find its values in antiquarianism, not in reform. Displaced people worldwide demonstrate the desire to find their own history in some antiquated ideal. At the same time, those who remained on the land became a rural bourgeoisie that did not resemble the idealized peasant. In the same way, repressive regimes first crush their victims, then find in them sources of interesting and quaint literary material.[63] In *John Bull's Other Island* (1904), George Bernard Shaw describes the upheaval in Ireland and parodies the new Catholic rural middle class. A young Irishwoman, Nora, remarks, "Youd hardly know the old tenants now. Youd think it was a liberty to speak t'dhem—some o dhem."[64] Laurence Doyle, the son of a land agent, laments that as the old landlords used and abused everything in Ireland for their own profit, the former tenants-turned-landowners are doing the same, and exploiting each other in the bargain:

> Do you think, because you're poor and ignorant and half-crazy with toiling and moiling morning noon and night, that youll be any less greedy and oppressive to them that have no land at all than old Nick Lestrange, who was an educated travelled gentleman that would not have been tempted as hard by a hundred pounds as youd be by five shillings? Nick was too high above Patsy Farrell to be jealous of him; but you, that are only one little step above him, would die sooner than let him come up the step; and well you know it.

Thus, even as the writers of the Irish Revival pushed for a nationalist literature, what they perceived to be the "real" Ireland was slipping away, or already gone. Economic changes in the countryside throughout the latter half of the nineteenth century transformed a rural proletariat into a rural bourgeoisie, and thus the "peasants" no longer existed at the time they were being "discovered" and portrayed by writers (Hirsch 1118).

Although Synge did not emphasize in his art the Irish peasants' fierce fight in the struggle for land, he did present the loneliness and tribulation in their personal lives that he experienced firsthand.[65] Denying the stereotype of the reckless, careless Irish, he wrote that the danger of the life on the islands made it impossible for the clumsy or foolhardy to survive there (*The Aran Islands* I, *CW* 2: 94); and of the western "Congested Districts" he wrote, " . . . the talk sometimes heard of sloth and ignorance has not much foundation" (*CW* 2: 340). He described the "throb of pain" that he felt when he saw the constabulary arrive on Inishmaan to evict tenants who had occupied the same land for thirty years. His glimpse of what he calls the newer types of humanity was not reassuring, "Yet these mechanical police, with the commonplace agents and sheriffs, and the rabble they had hired, represented aptly enough the civilisation for which the homes of the island were to be desecrated" (*The Aran Islands* I, *CW* 2: 88–89). The evicted tenants were the victims of anonymous owners and police who looked, to Synge, like helmetted automatons.

Synge was aware of the discrepancies in landholdings and wealth among the rural population. Dan Burke, Michael Dara, and Patch Darcy of *The Shadow of the Glen* are small tenant farmers of the southeast, or perhaps small independent holders. The economic divisions between the self-supporting landholder and those poor who held no land are represented in the Tramp's referring to Nora as "lady of the house" and Nora's own confession that in order to provide for herself in her old age and not fall victim to the fate of homeless Peggy Cavanagh, she had felt the need to marry a man "with a bit of a farm, and cows on it, and sheep on the back hills" (*CW* 3: 49). Timmy the Smith and Molly Byrne of *The Well of the Saints* are rural tradespeople able to support themselves independently as long as the local farmers require their services; Martin and Mary Doul are the destitute, landless poor. The rift between Timmy and Martin is that between tradesman and laborer struggling to survive. Old Mahon in *The Playboy of the*

Western World is a western peasant farmer eager to increase his holding by marrying his son Christy to a widow with a farm. Nevertheless, Synge's concern is not their economic or political struggle but their desire for freedom, love, and beauty.

Just as Synge drew his characters from people he knew in Wicklow and the Aran Islands, W. B. Yeats drew speakers from the peasants of Sligo and Galway. "The Meditation of the Old Fisherman" was founded (Yeats claimed) on a conversation with a fisherman in Sligo Bay (*Poems* 617). "The Lamentation of the Old Pensioner," a protest against old age and passing time, was, as we have seen, little more than a translation into verse of the words of an old Wicklow peasant. In "The Ballad of Father O'Hart" he describes a story about land-grabbing during the Penal Days (1695–1727) by an ambitious farmer, a "shoneen" or upstart imitator of the gentry from a race of "sleiveens" (rogues) who swindles a learned holy man out of his lands (*Poems* 617–18).

Although Yeats idealizes the peasants' way of life in poems like "Shepherd and Goatherd," "The Song of the Happy Shepherd," and "The Sad Shepherd," more often his peasant speakers complain of their hard way of life. Moll Magee, Crazy Jane, and Red Hanrahan suffer loneliness, ostracism, and misunderstanding. The "cursing rogue" of "The Hour Before Dawn," on the other hand, loves life even though he is reduced to sleeping outdoors, wearing rags, and stealing food.

Charges that Yeats misrepresented the Irish peasants are qualified by his choices of material for *Representative Irish Tales* and *The Celtic Twilight*, argues Mary Helen Thuente in *W. B. Yeats and Irish Folklore*, for he selected tales that revealed ignoble as well as noble aspects of peasant life (155). His major concern in *Representative Irish Tales* was the vitality of peasant life, while in *The Celtic Twilight* he elevated the peasants' imaginative life to one of visionary extravagance. The personalities of his informants were as important as their visions and beliefs (Thuente 154–55). He extolled the serious, reserved Irish peasant who was capable of deep passion. In his review of Douglas Hyde's translation of the *Love Songs of Connacht* (1893), Yeats wrote that the life of the Gael was "so pitiable, so dark and sad and sorrowful" that they had no way to express themselves but in excessive mirth or excessive lamentation.[66] Nevertheless, although given to displays of emotion, the true peasants were not like the careless buffoons of many nineteenth-century tales. In contrast to writers like Croker and Lover, Yeats sought to present the peasant as tragic and serious as well as gay and humorous (Thuente 98). In "Tales from the Twilight" (1890) he wrote:

> Irish legends and Irish peasant minds, however, have no lack of melancholy. The accidents of Nature supply good store of it to all men, and in their hearts, too, there dwells a sadness still unfathomed. Yet in that sadness there is no gloom, no darkness, no love of the ugly, no moping. The sadness of a people who hold that 'contention is better than loneliness,' it is half a visionary fatalism, a belief that all things rest with God and with His angels or with the demons that beset man's fortunes. (*UP* 1: 173)

Yeats chose material for his anthologies of Irish literature on the basis of how well he thought they depicted the peasants' lives, and his conception of the peasant in the 1880s and 1890s resembled Carleton's more than any other Irish novelist's (Thuente 108). Consequently, Yeats's anthologies of Irish literature contain a large portion of brutality, immorality, and drunkenness (Thuente 98). For example, one of the stories that appears in both Yeats's *Stories from Carleton* (1889) and his *Representative Irish Tales* (1891) is "Wild-Goose Lodge," a tale of murderous passion and revenge. Clearly, Yeats was not interested in creating or perpetuating a stereotyped ideal of the peasant.

Similarly, in spite of Synge's romanticism, he creates a countryside plagued with the problems of the world. The people in his plays are destroyed by greed, selfishness, disloyalty, impatience, and lust and are inspired by love, hope, and joy. The world they live in is harsh: careless children ignore the advice of a wise mother; a man sends his wife out onto the roads; blind people are destined to drown in the rivers of the south because they are driven from their own locality; tinkers camped beside the road must live by their wits; young men and women are forced by circumstances into unhappy marriages. They also triumph: Christy Mahon frees himself from a tyrannical father; Nora escapes her loveless marriage; the Douls are able to pursue their vision of beauty; the tinkers defeat a materialistic priest; Maurya is liberated from the destruction of the sea. Through their adversity Synge presents the nobility and the tribulations which they share with the rest of the world.

Radical Traditionalism

So, with how much authority can we describe Yeats and Synge as writers who spoke for the Irish people? As far as Yeats is concerned, Declan Kiberd acknowledges him to be one of the foremost poets of decolonization ("Irish Literature" 231),[67] while David Lloyd asserts that Yeats "devoted three decades of his life to a cultural nationalism whose object was to forge a sense of national identity in Irish subjects such that their own personal identity would be fulfilled only in the creation of the nation" (69).[68] Seamus Deane explained Yeats's aesthetic as coming from "that long line of European Romantic writers who combined a revolutionary aesthetic with traditionalist politics,"[69] identifying Yeats's theme as regeneration and release from British empirical philosophy (Yeats in "A General Introduction to My Work" calls it "the mechanical theory" which had no reality and would be replaced in two or three generations [*Essays* 518]) and urban industrial capitalism (39). Deane quotes Yeats's poem "Fragments" as illustrative of Yeats's contempt for utilitarianism. Seeking an older form of "Irishness" in order to counter materialist philosophy, Yeats chose peasant and aristocrat as kindred spirits against industrialism and utilitarianism (39), the one embodying traditional ways of life where natural and supernatural were knit together, and the other fulfilling responsibility for perpetuating the culture. Thus, for Yeats, Ireland was a revolutionary country precisely because it was traditional; it remained the only country in Europe where aristocrat and peasant *could* win out over materialism and utilitarianism, a holy land where spirits lived in every rath and hill (39, 41). To be traditionalist in the modern world is to be revolutionary:

> It is a conviction which has a true revolutionary impact when we look at the history of the disappearance from the Western mind of the sense of eternity and of the consciousness of death. It is a history coincident with the history of modern capitalism. The greasy till is, after all, spiritually empty. (49)

J. M. Synge, on the other hand, felt that the cause was lost, that the West of Ireland would become bourgeois like the East (53). He was in fact a visitor to a culture already "quaint" (56), although he may not have known it. Without losing sight of the conditions of peasant life, however, Synge aestheticized the problem of oppression, advocating reincorporation of the past into the present through art (51–52, 60), and thus saving a remnant of Ireland's cultural heritage.

Edward Said identifies the tension resulting from cultural antagonism and dependency that the Irish writers shared with those of many non-European nations (*Culture* 220). Yeats himself gives voice to this tension in his late essay "A General Introduction for My Work" when he admits that he owes his soul "to Shakespeare, to Spenser and to Blake, perhaps to William Morris, and to the English language in which I think, speak, and write, that everything I love has come to me through English; my hatred tortures me with love, my love with hate" (*Essays* 519). Colonized people find themselves unable to voice their own aspirations and experience in the colonial language; they also lose their history, recorded as it is in a nondominant language. Still, few English writers have written as well as Yeats in their own language. His work exemplifies what Deane calls "an almost vengeful virtuosity in the English language" ("Introduction" 10), an attempt to make Irish English a language in its own right—and to create a more beautiful literature in doing so—as a reaction to the loss of Irish.

Deane believes that although Yeats fell into a "blind provincialism," his attempt to escape from Ireland's colonial experience has been reproduced in other countries, that his "asphyxiating regional nativism" did not obliterate the "radically liberating elements" imitated by African, Palestinian, and South American nations (5). His recreation of himself and his community provides a model of voice and history for people deprived of both (5). Said numbers Yeats among poets of decolonization because he struggled "to announce the contours of an imagined or ideal community" (*Culture* 232); his work gave the world "a major international achievement in cultural decolonization..." (238). Claiming that capitalism (to which utilitarianism gave a special form) inevitably culminates in imperialism which dominates, classifies, and commodifies all space under the aegis of a metropolitan center (225), Said maintains that "[i]n a world from which the harsh strains of capitalism have removed thought and reflection, a poet who can stimulate a sense of the eternal and of death into consciousness is the true rebel" (228). Said identifies "Among School Children" as Yeats's call to the Irish to recognize that history and the nation are inseparable as dancer and dance (237), that his appeal in "Under Ben Bulben" to "[s]corn the sort now growing up," when colonial realities and the program of decolonization are considered, demonstrates insight and experience (238) rather than aristocratic exclusiveness.

English cultural heritage both dominated and empowered Yeats and Synge, as well as other writers of the Irish Revival, yet we can see that in the attempt to create a new national culture, both Yeats and Synge were artists of decolonization, precisely because they envisioned a transformation of the Irish spirit as well as a new government. If they aestheticized the peasants' experience, they did so in order to revolutionize all of Irish society with timeless traditions and so radically alter that society at a period of momentous change. Furthermore, they did not look to a far-off country in order to find spiritual and regenerative material for literature: they looked—Yeats primarily and Synge entirely—to their own (Deane, *Celtic* 57).

Chapter 2

"This wise and simple man": The Peasant as Noble Savage

Michael Davitt's founding the Land League in 1879 was an important Irish attempt not only to return ownership of the land to the peasantry but also to mythologize the past. The League organized the peasants' political strength, provided an ideology, and prepared the way for the transformation of the peasant by the writers of the Literary Revival of the late nineteenth and early twentieth centuries. The political myth-makers created the idea that "Celtic" Ireland had been a nation of free landowners dispossessed by English settlers. As Seán Ó'Faoláin points out (1956), however, the first people to express concern over tenants' "rights" were in fact English; the ancient Celtic landowning families probably had few notions about equality:

> At no time, however, do we form any intimate picture of the life of the lower grades, largely because both letters and society were graded upwards to a caste, and both "bards" and "chiefs" had the aristocratic outlook. . . . Not until the sixteenth century does any-body much care what happens to them [the peasants] and then it is not the Irish chiefs but the English chiefs who speak of them, in some pity and consideration (42).

Nevertheless, Land League nationalists asserted not only an ancient claim to the land but also a special virtue on the part of the country-men whose intimate relationship to the land tied them to Irish history and politics and made them a symbol for the nation's struggle. Their fight to own the land they worked paralleled Ireland's fight for inde-pendence. Moreover, their language and folklore united them with Ireland's Celtic history, and their way of life, both rural and tradi-tional, could be described as simple and uncorrupted. Thus, the Land

League's idealization of the peasants and its claim for them of an ancient heritage were both aesthetic and political.

Nationalists and Literary Revivalists, both Protestant and Catholic, desired that Ireland remain an agricultural nation (what Maurice Goldring calls "green Ireland" [71]) rather than one whose economy was founded on factory systems such as those in Great Britain. The writers of the Irish Literary Revival reacted to centralized industrialism and its attendant "progress," modernity, and commercialism by idealizing the peasants. The values of tradition, archaism, peace, and communion with nature, which were inherent in—or imposed on—the Irish peasants, were held to be in opposition to those of materialist England. Nationalists found their ideal, writes Goldring, by creating the notion of a free, hard working, and ambitionless peasantry; peasant poverty was seen as Irish, while urban poverty had been imposed by a foreign power (71). Irish nationalists rejected the English view of the Irish peasants as indigent, ignorant, and superstitious, claiming instead that they were unmaterialistic, naturally wise, and spiritual. The nationalists reversed the stereotype so that the peasants were no longer the symbol of all that was wrong in ungovernable Ireland. They became instead the embodiment of virtue: they were spiritual rather than materialistic, they belonged to an ancient race, and they lived in communion with nature.

The Irish Literary Revival and the activities of the Land League were part of the Celtic Revival, which was an attempt to revive or restore Irish or Gaelic culture to Ireland and thereby to restore national pride and international prestige and which was in turn associated with the movement for independence. The Celtic Revival was nativistic in that it constituted a conscious, organized attempt to revive or perpetuate selected aspects of the culture—in this case the Irish language, games, music, dance, and folklore—at a time when that culture was considered inferior to another—in this case, British—culture with which it was in contact.[1] What usually happens in such nativistic movements is that certain elements of the culture are selected for emphasis and given symbolic value (231). According to anthropologist John C. Messenger, revived elements of the culture come to symbolize real or imagined freedom, unity, greatness, or happiness in older times, while elements of the culture that have survived become symbols of the culture's uniqueness.[2] Irish nationalists sought to create unity of culture by developing a sense of Irish historical continuity.

Ironically, Irish writers who extolled the Irish peasantry for the same reasons the Land League nationalists did—in order to attack English bourgeois values—acquired their ideas from English Romanticism.

Part of the philosophy of the Celtic Revival was a primitivist worldview that included the idealization of earlier Irish society and contemporary folk culture. Primitivist philosophy embraces the idea that civilization is destructive:

> Central to the primitivistic position is the belief that civilization has dehumanized man and undermined his valued institutions; it has caused social bonds to disintegrate, fostered immorality, and created mental illness on a vast scale. Primitive and folk peoples, according to this view, represent man as he once was and could be or should be again were civilized society drastically reformed.[3]

Chronological primitivism embraces the notion that civilization or human life itself reached or will reach its most sublime condition at a particular time—past, present, or future.[4] Cultural primitivism, on the other hand, finds its origin in discontent with contemporary civilization or society; it is the conviction of people in a complex society that life in a simpler society is far more desirable (7) and above all "natural":

> The history of primitivism is in great part a phase of a larger historic tendency which is one of the strangest, most potent and most persistent factors in Western thought—the use of the term "nature" to express the standard of human values, the identification of the good with that which is "natural" or "according to nature." The primitive condition of mankind, or the life of "savage" peoples, has usually been extolled because it has been supposed to constitute "the state of nature" (11–12).

Cultural primitivists believe that the way of life they dream of actually exists or has existed, and that they can identify examples of it (8).

These time-honored beliefs, originating long before the Romantic period and continuing with such vigor today, provide fertile soil for a theory of the treatment of the country in literature, especially that of emerging nations. In *The Country and the City*, Raymond Williams describes Romantic nature poetry as "a way of feeling which is also a way of writing"[5]: in the words of John Clare in "Pastoral Poesy," it is "A language that is ever green." According to Williams, the Romantic "structure of feeling" dichotomized "nature against industry" and "poetry against trade" (79). He emphasizes the idea of separation which is fundamental to Romantic pastoralism: of country from city, worker from owner, rusticity from sophistication, innocence from corruption. The country supposedly represented innocence, freedom, and wholesome values—the same virtues often ascribed to childhood (297). If the country existed in a childlike state, however, then it must need guidance and protection, and those who would guide and protect came from the more "experienced" urban world. This brings us to a deeper concept of separation: "The very idea of landscape implies separation and observation" (120). In order to appreciate a landscape, the observer must view it from a vantage point somehow removed from what she observes; this standing apart implies not only aesthetic but philosophical distance. The writer of pastoral poetry as well as the "discoverer" of an ideal "primitive" culture must of necessity originate in another place, actually or spiritually. Indeed, even the "management" of land for improved agricultural methods itself implies separation—of owner and planner from land and worker.

The profoundest irony in this separation, according to Williams, is that the social process that originally allowed the development of landscapes, especially that of country houses, was the clearance system (75). It is instructive, for example, to realize that Sidney wrote the *Arcadia* in a park that had been created by clearances and eviction (22). Furthermore, land being worked is seldom valued as a landscape; indeed, when it is, the workers are not individually represented but appear as types or embodiments of labor, as in, for example, the paintings of Constable and Turner.

Nor are workers themselves involved with the land as *vista*: the average country worker is frequently indifferent to landscape's aesthetic effect.[6] In addition, love of landscape and nature unaltered by mankind was conceived in a time of reclamation, drainage, clearing of trees—the eighteenth century. Williams quotes two views of the Alps, seen as "strange, horrid and fearful crags and tracts" and "Ruins upon Ruins, in monstrous Heaps, and Heaven and Earth confounded" in the seventeenth century, and as places of "religion and poetry" (Gray) and "glorious as the Gates of Heaven" (Coleridge) in the eighteenth and nineteenth (128). Moreover, the picturesque and romantic journeys of these last two centuries came from the profits of agriculture and trade—despised by the Romantics because they necessarily altered nature and consumed the human spirit.

James Turner shows in *The Politics of Landscape* that landscape writing seldom found a place for real laborers and seldom mentions work;[7] thus the landscapes are cleared of "troublesome" natives (185). Turner recognizes, as Williams does, that landscape is an image from society, containing a social content and representing an ideal structure (xi). He discusses the metaphor of the country estate as a miniature state (87), with landlord, overseer, and peasantry as king, minister, and citizenry.[8] The self-sufficient country estate becomes a model of the national community: "Panegyric topography is thus a means of reconstructing the golden age under the benign eye of a present patron" (93). The metaphor of the country as a place apart from and governed by the city may be extended to include the British Empire, and that of the "benevolent" patron Great Britain itself.

Conceived though it was in English poetry, the pastoral provided Irish writers with an appropriate background for their own movement. In "National Drama: A Farce," Synge names landscape as the originator of art: "A beautiful art has never been produced except in a beautiful environment and nowhere is there one more beautiful than in the mountains and glens of Ireland" (*CW* III: 225). Unlike the English landscape writers that Williams quotes, the Irish Revivalists chose to leave the workers on the land, to incorporate their way of life into Irish art. They chose the details they wanted to present about the peasants' lives selectively, however, and thus they transformed both the land *and* its inhabitants into works of art.

The pastoral ideal stirred the imaginations of others in Ireland besides Land League members and nationalists. George Moore, a cosmopolitan Irishman more at home in Paris than Dublin, who had severely criticized what he called the "idiocy" of Irish life, became enamored of the cultural primitivism of the Literary Revival. He wrote:

Those who believe that dreams, beauty, and divine ecstasy are essential must pray that all the empires may perish and the world be given back to the small peasant states, whose seas and forests and mountains shall create national aspirations and new gods.

Otherwise the world will fall into gross naturalism, with scientific barbarism more terrible than the torch and the sword of the Hun.... The commercial platitude which has risen up in England, which is extending over the whole world, is horrible to contemplate. Its flag, which Mr. Rhodes has declared to be "the most valuable commercial asset in the world," is everywhere. England has imposed her idea upon all nations, and to girdle the world with Brixton seems to be her ultimate destiny. And we, sitting on the last verge, see into the universal suburb, in which a lean man with glasses on his nose and a black bag in his hand is always running after his bus.[9]

Such righteous zeal also characterized the nationalists' attitudes. Patrick Pearse wrote that the destiny of the Irish was more glorious than that of Rome or of Britain. The Gael, he said, would become "the saviour of idealism in modern intellectual and social life, the regenerator and rejuvenator of the literature of the world, the instructor of nations, the preacher of the gospel of nature-worship, hero-worship, God-worship—such...is the destiny of the Gael" (98). All this is a variant of Matthew Arnold's idea that Irish spirituality would save the English from the dire implications of their own materialism. Arnold argued this because he hoped to cement a "union of hearts" between both peoples whom he deemed essential to one another. English character needed the Celtic element in order to infuse it with energy from an "unspoiled" source (Deane, "Introduction" 12). Ironically, the subtext of this idea is covertly *Unionist* and imperialist, not nationalist at all.

Yeats, in writing of the Irish Literary Theatre in 1899, claimed that Irish plays would be different from those produced in London and Paris because Ireland's intellect was "romantic and spiritual rather than scientific and analytical" ("Plans and Methods," *UP* 2: 159). England, he said, was preoccupied by what was strong, Ireland by what was poor and weak; English poetry celebrated victory, while the Irish celebrated defeat ("The Literary Movement in Ireland," *UP* 2: 187, 196). Furthermore, the Irish peasants' dream of paradise could lead people the world over to new spirituality:

The paradise of the Christian, as those who think more of the order of communities than of the nature of things have shaped it, is but the fulfillment of one dream; the paradise that the common people tell of about the fire, and still half understand, is the fulfillment of all dreams, and opens its gates as gladly to the perfect lover as to the perfect saint, and only he who understands it can lift romance into prophecy and make beauty holy. Their paradise, Tír-nan-óg, the Land of the Living Heart, the Grass Green Island of Apples, call it what you will, created that religion of the muses which gave arts to the world; and those countries whose traditions are fullest of it, and of the sanctity of places, may yet remould romance till it has become a covenant between intellectual beauty and the beauty of the world. We cannot know how many these countries are until the new science of folklore and the almost new science of mythology have done their work; but Ireland, if she can awake again the but half-forgotten legends of Slieve Gullion, or of Cruachmagh, or of the hill where Maeve is buried, and make them an utterance of that desire to be at rest amid ideal perfection which is becoming conscious in the minds of poets as the good citizen wins the priests over to his side; of (sic) if she can make us believe that the beautiful things that move us to awe, white lilies among dim shadows, windy twilights over grey sands, dewy and silent places among hazel trees by still waters, are in truth, and not in phantasy alone, the symbols, or the dwellings, of immortal presences, she will have begun a change that, whether it is begun in our time or not for centuries, will some day make all lands holy lands again. ("The Literary Movement in Ireland," *UP* 2: 195)

Behind these convictions and the new cult of the peasant was the idealization of the primitive.

Those who wanted to revive interest in peasant spirituality found themselves at odds with the Land League's goal. Many Irish writers, including Yeats and Synge, valued the peasants for their supposed lack of materialism, their spirituality, their ties to the land, their being uncorrupted by the bourgeois mind of the urban centers. The Land League's goal, on the other hand, was to create a nation of peasant *owners*—a rural bourgeoisie. In Padraic Colum's story "Land Hunger" (1925), Catholic farmers unite against a Protestant grazier, and, by means of cattle-driving, force him to give up his lease and the landowner to sell portions of his estate to the farmers. Colum's story shows that, in his view, the Celtic Revivalists' characterization of the peasants was inaccurate, that they were potentially an eager bourgeoisie, the people James Joyce described as "a hard, crafty, matter of fact lot."[10]

While Synge's overall impression of the peasants was favorable, he also states that many were "far from admirable, either in body or mind." Acknowledging this to be an obvious fact, he explained that he writes this because it had become the fashion in Dublin "to exalt the Irish peasant into a type of almost absolute virtue, frugal, self-sacrificing, valiant, and I know not what." While there was some truth in this estimate, he continued, and while the peasant possessed many beautiful virtues, among them "a fine sense of humour and the greatest courtesy," his heart was not spotless, nor was he unacquainted with the deadly sins, even west of the Shannon. The Irish peasant, according to Synge, was neither abject nor servile, in spite of relief-works, commissions, and patronizing philosophy, nor was he altogether generous or innocent ("The People of the Glens," *CW* 2: 224, fn. 1).

Land reform, far from the ideal pastoral society of Yeats or of de Valéra, created a rural bourgeoisie striving to attain ultimately materialistic goals. Yeats, Pearse, and Hyde saw in the west the remains of a culture that had resulted from population growth in the early nineteenth century.[11] The small farmer's problem in the twentieth century was to increase the size of his holding and to ensure that the land stayed in the possession of his family. As late as 1937, Conrad Arensberg wrote that marriages of convenience were a common way of enlarging a family's holding. While familism and deference to age were crucial factors in shaping the country people's way of life, late marriage and forced emigration threatened the family and nearly turned Ireland into an old person's country.[12] Furthermore, the glorification of the past and adherence to old ways reflected only the accomplishments of older people and produced a rivalry between old and young that further threatened the security of the rural population. "The young people is no use," a man reported to Synge; "I am not as good a man as my father was, and my son is growing up worse than I am" ("In West Kerry," *CW* 2: 250). Another described his disillusion with his changed homeland: "I have come back ... to live in a bit of a house with my sister. The island is not the same at all to what it was. It is little good I can get from the people who are in it now, and anything I have to give them they don't care to have" (*The Aran Islands* I, *CW* 2: 53).

The young seldom agreed with the old on the matter of their shortcomings, and thus the rivalry between parents and offspring could be intimate and constant. Christy Mahon's rebellion, brought on by his tyrannical and ungenerous father in *The Playboy of the Western World*, characterizes the dilemma of the Irish rural populace—to depend upon one's family and at the same time desire independence. Synge's play may have been influenced by Colum's work, *The Land* (1905), in which a son rebels against the wishes of his tyrannical, land-hungry father; Synge claimed, however, to have found his plot in a story told by an old man of Inishmaan about a young man who in a fit of passion killed his father with a blow from a spade and fled to the island where he was protected by the people until he could escape. The islanders protected criminals because legal justice was associated with English jurisdiction, but more importantly because of the conviction, which Synge claimed was universal in the west, that a person would not do wrong unless under the influence of a passion "as irresponsible as a storm on the sea" (*The Aran Islands* I, *CW* 2: 95). Their impulse may also have been due to understanding the frustration caused by dependence, well into adulthood, upon a parent.

Still, Synge's vivacious peasants as well as Yeats's mystical country people of "The Celtic Twilight" were in many ways very different from the peasants Arensberg and Colum described. The writers of the Literary Revival chose to create a vision of Ireland in which those who live and work on the land are more closely in touch with national consciousness than urban dwellers. To Yeats the peasant represented Irish genius uncorrupted by the materialism of modern, urban life. To Synge the peasant was spiritually, if not economically, free, and should be left alone to live in the traditional way; above all, Synge praised the peasants' self-sufficiency. The cult of the Irish peasant as a repository of ancient wisdom and natural virtue found its origins in the English Romantic movement of the nineteenth century, an important aspect of romanticism being the return to nature—the desire to find the spiritual within the natural or to achieve a union of real and unreal, tangible and mysterious. Antiquarianism, which had helped foster English Romanticism and the great vogue for folklore studies in the nineteenth century, generated Irish folklore studies as well

(Thuente 38). A mood of Romantic naturalism from the mid-eighteenth century included the cult of scenery, the child, the peasant, and the savage. Among these, the Noble Savage is a free and wild being who draws directly from nature virtues that raise doubts as to the value of civilization itself because they are virtues that were previously thought to be held only by civilized persons. Thus, the impulse toward antiquarianism stemmed directly from global imperialism.[13]

The assumption that an idyllic society once existed and can be brought to life again grew out of the fundamental desire to believe that human beings can return to Eden if they will only abandon materialism and pride. The ideal is the recovery of lost virtue or innocence. The Golden Age, a related notion, represents belief in a time in which a culture or society achieved its greatness, perhaps in unity, influence, or the arts. The relationship between the ideal of a Golden Age and a Noble Savage stems from rejection of the notion of "progress" and affirmation of belief in archaic values. The Golden Age is to the ancient world what the Noble Savage is to the modern: each represents a protest against evil presumed to be incidental to human progress and looks yearningly from what is believed to be contemporary corruption to an imaginary primal innocence.[14]

Pastoral literature, among the earliest forms of poetry, involves the contrast between simple, rural life and some more complex civilization.[15] Elizabethan England and eighteenth-century Europe—as well as twentieth-century America—desired greater simplicity because of dissatisfaction with "sophisticated" ways of life. Sir Philip Sidney describes such an idyllic country (in *The Countess of Pembroke's Arcadia*, 1590) populated by shepherds who live in scattered houses among fields and who tend orchards that produce "the most taste-pleasing fruits" and gardens of "delicate green" with thickets, fair ponds, and beds of flowers. Their happiness stems from their modest desires, their abundant good temper and natural artistic ability, and their lack of ambition and materialism. These traits are fostered by a naturally beautiful environment:

> This country Arcadia, among all the provinces of Greece, hath ever been had in singular reputation, partly for the sweetness of the air and other natural benefits, but principally for the well-tempered minds of the people, who (finding that the shining title of glory so much affected by other nations doth indeed help little

to the happiness of life) are the only people which, as by their justice and providence, give neither cause nor hope to their neighbors to annoy them; so are they not stirred with false praise to trouble others' quiet, thinking it a small reward for the wasting of their own lives in ravening that their posterity should long after say they had done so. Even the muses seem to approve their good determination by choosing this country for their chief repairing-place, and by bestowing their perfections so largely here that the very shepherds have their fancies lifted to so high conceits as the learned of other nations are content both to borrow their names and imitate their cunning.[16]

Both the pastoral and the Golden Age are expressions of instincts and impulses deeply rooted in the nature of humanity, for, able to imagine an ideal world, human beings desire to believe in it.

The conception of a Golden Age of rustic simplicity, however, does not involve the whole of pastoral literature but rather that pastoral expression of the yearning for escape, even if only in imagination, to a life of simplicity and innocence from the unhappiness and anxiety of the "sophisticated" and ambitious urban world. The Romantic sees in the peasant a picture of primitive virtue, which he or she prefers to the studied, cultivated ways of the educated populace; however, although Romantics may find in the peasant an image of one who embodies the "natural" ideals of their imagination, they may detest the pastoral as ultimately insincere because it stems from a literary tradition created by urban dwellers. When Wordsworth subtitles *Michael* "a pastoral," for instance, his use of the term is ironic, for he does not present an idyllic rural life but the story of a shepherd's difficult struggle to keep his land and family together. The Romantic rescues the peasantry from their depiction as happy, unself–conscious shepherds who spend leisurely days singing their own verses, heedless of the future, and transforms them into Noble Savages who are not without their troubles, which are usually caused by encroaching "civilization."

The Noble Savage who possessed an innate sense of justice and a simple way of life certainly predates Romantic and even Elizabethan literature. Rejecting the sophistication and hierarchy of Rome, Tacitus, in *Germania*, praised what he saw as the self-sufficiency and egalitarianism of the Gauls:

In every household the children, naked and filthy, grow up with those stout frames and limbs which we so much admire. Every mother suckles her own off-spring, and never entrusts it to servants and nurses. The master is not distinguished from the slave by being brought up with greater delicacy. Both live amid the same flocks and lie on the same ground till the freeborn are distinguished by age and recognized by merit. The young men marry late, and their vigour is thus unimpaired. Nor are the maidens hurried into marriage; the same age and a similar stature is required; well-matched and vigorous they wed, and the offspring reproduce the strength of the parents.[17]

Furthermore, the innocent primitive was prey for the corrupted, "civilized" intruder. In "Of Coaches," Montaigne wrote that native American societies had been contaminated by European explorers who were in no way superior to the tribes they adversely influenced, and who were in fact inferior to them as well as to the Europeans' own ancestors:

> I am very much afraid that we have very much precipitated its declension and ruine by our contagion; and that we have sold it our opinions and our arts at a very dear rate. It was an infant world, and yet we have not whip'd, and subjected it to our discipline, by the advantage of our valour and natural forces; neither have we won it by our justice and goodness, nor subdu'd it by our magnanimity. Most of their answers, and the negotiations we have had with them, witness, that they were nothing behind us in pertinency and clearness of natural understanding.... But as to what concerns devotion, observance of the laws, bounty, liberality, loyalty, and plain dealing, it was of use to us, that we had not so much as they; for they have lost, sold, and betray'd themselves by this advantage. As to boldness and courage, stability, constancy against pain, hunger and death, I should not fear to oppose the examples I find amongst them, to the most famous examples of elder times, that we find in our records on this side of the world.[18]

"Primitive" tribes displayed more virtue than Europeans because they were still governed by "natural" laws, Montaigne continues in "Of

Cannibals," and laments that Europeans had not discovered them in older, "better" times when Europeans were more capable of valuing them and justly governing them than were the people of contemporary times (169).

Noble Savages obtained knowledge from experience, not from books. Similarly, they possessed a natural religion derived from contact with nature rather than from theological teaching. Anchorites who abandoned civilization in order to worship God in the solitude of nature anticipated the Romantic attitude. Nature provided the meeting ground between humankind and God, or between humankind and the spiritual or supernatural, which could never be reached in civilized surroundings. The English Romantics associated nature with innocent wisdom and perpetuated the ideal of the natural innocent. For William Wordsworth, "One impulse from a vernal wood" carried greater moral impact than the instruction of teachers. In "Frost at Midnight" (1798) Samuel Taylor Coleridge's speaker expresses his desire that his child should "wander like a breeze" among lakes and mountains, to "see and hear / The lonely shapes and sounds intelligible / Of that eternal language, which thy God / Utters, who from eternity doth teach / Himself in all, and all things in himself." Coleridge's lifting the natural up to the supernatural, and Wordsworth's finding supernatural significance in common things, both derive from the idea that innocence, intuitive wisdom, and even the true spirit of poetry lie in primitive simplicity. Percy Bysshe Shelley wrote that the impulse to create art came from the interaction of humankind with nature, and that the savage ("for the savage is to the ages what the child is to years") expressed emotions inspired by his surroundings. Poetry indeed was timeless and universal, being "connate with the origin of man."[19] Much of Romantic poetry, including the *Lyrical Ballads*, descends from the Noble Savage ideal.

While the Golden Age was based on belief in a glorious time long past, when people had been stronger, braver, and more just than those of contemporary times, Noble Savages lived on, in remote areas of the known world. They might be tied to the land on which they had been born, yet they were free of ambition, anxiety, and dependence on others. Their traditional way of life kept them in touch with old values and with nature, and while they lacked amenities, their lives were purer than that of the urban dweller, for they were not materialistic or acquisitive. Physical activity made them courageous, strong, naturally handsome. Innocent of the political intricacies that plagued "civilized humankind," they were unself-conscious, honest, and sincere, yet also accomplished, versatile, and self-sufficient. Their spirituality, based on the mythic past, had nothing of pious sentiment. Sharing the sensibilities of the artist, they created natural poetry—songs and stories that told of pure emotion, joy and loss, triumph and tragedy. Their way of life was not idyllic, however, for it was threatened by corrupted "civilization."

Lest we chuckle at the naïveté implicit in these notions, we should remember that thousands of people tramp abroad yearly in search of romantic ideals. Goldring identifies this phenomenon in relation to Ireland: few tourists are lured anywhere entirely through advertising; they go in search of mythologies that are not imposed from outside but that they themselves foster and bring along with them (8). In the early 1970s idealistic young English people emigrated to Ireland in order to find a more "spiritual," less materialistic, "natural," and "uncorrupted" life, as D. H. Lawrence went to the American Southwest, young Australians emigrated to New Zealand, and Americans—having failed to find a "spiritual" way of life on communes—looked to Canada and Mexico—nations considered to be less "sophisticated" and "corrupt" than their own.

Yeats, influenced by Romantic pastoralism, believed that the "Celtic" ethos existed among the Irish peasants and was the enduring basis for unity of Irish culture. Folk belief of the west of Ireland held a mystic appeal for Yeats and enabled him to link folklore with theosophy, because, he thought, true Celtic nature was in contact with the occult. He sought the spirituality of the peasants and began his folklore studies in an attempt to link folk belief with the occult (Thuente 35, 141). Madame Blavatsky, founder of the Theosophical Society (1875), taught that all religions owed some common beliefs to secret doctrine that had been preserved in oral tradition. Yeats, too, preferred oral tradition to the written accounts of myth (Thuente 43). The west of Ireland, he felt, was a place of inarticulate power in which psychic memory was attached to certain areas remote from the "ordinary" (Anglo-Saxon) world. He wrote:

> I learned from the people themselves, before I learned it from any book, that they cannot separate the idea of an art or a craft from

the idea of a cult with ancient technicalities and mysteries. They can hardly separate mere learning from witchcraft, and are fond of words and verses that keep half their secret to themselves. ("What is 'Popular Poetry'?" *Essays* 10)

They were in touch with the spiritual, mystical world of the ancient Celts because they lacked formal education which would have made them forget the old ways. The unwritten tradition, Yeats maintained, binds the unlettered to the beginning of time and the foundation of the world (6). He thus used folk-belief and legend, but not Catholicism, to create his myth of the spiritual, visionary peasantry.

The peasants' heritage united them with the history of Ireland and the history of the world. Folklore ("natural magic") expressed the world's ancient religion and the worship of nature ("The Celtic Element in Literature," *Essays* 175–76); therefore, the peasant's imagination, steeped in fairy lore and legend, offered the richest sources for understanding the past:

> Folk-art is, indeed, the oldest of the aristocracies of thought, and because it refuses what is passing and trivial, the merely clever and pretty, as certainly as the vulgar and insincere, and because it has gathered into itself the simplest and most unforgettable thoughts of the generations, it is the soil where all great art is rooted. Wherever it is spoken by the fireside, or sung by the roadside, or carved upon the lintel, appreciation of the arts that a single mind gives unity and design to, spreads quickly when its hour is come.[20]

Like Synge, Yeats believed the peasants to be superior to the urban middle class and free like "unbroken horses, that are so much more beautiful than horses that have learned to run between shafts."[21] He praised the "quick intelligence, the abundant imagination, the courtly manners of the Irish country people" (7). By virtue of their mythopoeic imagination they constituted an ancient and a natural aristocracy. The old stories, if they could be perpetuated, would make Ireland once again a "Holy Land" of the imagination, as it had been before the coming of the Graeco-Roman and Judeo-Christian civilizations (12–13).

While Yeats created the myth of the Irish peasant possessed of natural virtue and ancient memory, Synge too saw them in a reverent, almost mythic way. He claimed to put aside idealism and to accept the country people as they were:

> Adieu, sweet Angus, Maeve and Fand,
> Ye plumed yet skinny Shee,
> That poets played with hand in hand
> To learn their ecstasy.
>
> We'll search in Red Dan Sally's ditch,
> And drink in Tubber fair,
> Or poach with Red Dan Philly's bitch
> The badger and the hare.
>
> ("The Passing of the Shee," CW 1: 38)

Nevertheless, he believed that their traditions and fundamental differences from urban dwellers gave them insight. He felt that they represented a link with a more virtuous time and that their folklore endowed them with wisdom. Synge wrote that both the wildness and vices of the Irish peasants were due, like their virtues, to the extraordinary richness of their nature. He recognized not only the fragility but also the harshness, brutality, and vitality of their way of life, and described these qualities in the accounts of the fight after a horse race in West Kerry, when four men fought on the shore until the tide came in ("In West Kerry," CW 2: 275), and of the "profuse Gaelic maledictions" from some fishermen to the crew of a steamer that passed too close to their nets (The Aran Islands IV, CW 2: 151). He employed vigorous, often brutal diction (in The Playboy, The Tinker's Wedding, and The Well of the Saints) in order to convey these ideas about the peasants' way of life and to react against what he considered to be the morbid, unhealthy tendencies of art in his time.[22]

Synge described the peasants as recklessly brave, intelligent, and, above all, unself-conscious. Peasant Gaelic was full of beauty, he wrote: the islanders who told stories were full-voiced and dramatic (TCD 4393, 4382). They rode their Connemara ponies at a desperate gallop with only a simple halter and stick, with nothing to hold on to (The Aran Islands I, CW 2: 79), and expressed their vitality in their vigorous dancing:

The lightness of the pampooties (leather shoes that helped island-
ers keep their balance on rocky terrain) seems to make the danc-
ing on this island lighter and swifter than anything I have seen
on the mainland, and the simplicity of the men enables them to
throw a naïve extravagance into their steps that is impossible in
places where the people are self-conscious. (*The Aran Islands* IV,
CW 2: 153)

Their kindliness and merry-making, absent from the towns, made him
think of the life described in the ballads of Scotland ("In West Kerry,"
CW 2: 256). Yet the peasants were also full of riot and severity and
daring, and they bewildered him with their talk of wonderful events,
always detailed, picturesque, and interesting. The islanders, he wrote,
though pure and spiritual, had all the healthy animal blood of peas-
ants and delighted in broad jests and deeds (*The Aran Islands* I, *CW* 2:
102 n. 1). At the same time, the peasants were in their own way
accomplished and well-schooled. They were naturally courteous and
artistic, and their way of life made them courageous and versatile:

It is likely that much of the intelligence and charm of these people
is due to the absence of any division of labour, and to the corre-
spondingly wide development of each individual, whose varied
knowledge and skill necessitates a considerable activity of mind.
Each man can speak two languages. He is a skilled fisherman, and
can manage a curagh (traditional fishing canoe of Aran) with
extraordinary nerve and dexterity. He can farm simply, burn kelp,
cut out pampooties, mend nets, build and thatch a house, and
make a cradle or a coffin. His work changes with the seasons in a
way that keeps him free from the dulness that comes to people
who have always the same occupation. The danger of his life on
the sea gives him the alertness of a primitive hunter, and the long
nights he spends fishing in his curagh bring him some of the
emotions that are thought peculiar to men who have lived with
the arts. (*The Aran Islands* III, *CW* 2: 132–33)

Synge praised the beauty of the islanders' clothing, which he said
was more colorful than any European costume (TCD 4385). The island

men, he wrote, were fresh-looking as sea gulls, while the women's red bodices and petticoats made them look like tropical seabirds. He suggested a possible link between the wild mythology accepted on the islands and the strange beauty of the women, both of which were haunting and majestical. For Synge, island women embodied the natural elements and composed their emotions in accordance with those elements.

> Many women here are too sturdy and contented to have more than the decorative interest of wild deer, but I have found a couple that have been turned in on themselves by some circumstance of their lives and seem to sum up in the expressions of their blue grey eyes the whole external symphony of the sky and seas. They have wildness and humour and passion kept in continual subjection by the reverence for life and the sea that is inevitable in this place. (*The Aran Islands* III, CW 2: 143 n. 1)

Synge the primitivist thus explains the islanders' virtue as in part created by their living so close to nature.

Like Yeats, Synge too saw in the Irish peasantry a Celtic aristocracy. He wrote of the tinkers, farmers, and fishermen: "These strange men with receding foreheads, high cheek-bones, and ungovernable eyes seem to represent some old type found on these few acres at the extreme border of Europe, where it is only in wild jests and laughter that they can express their loneliness and desolation" (*The Aran Islands* III, CW 2: 140). They lived like the earliest sailors: "It gave me a moment of exquisite satisfaction to find myself moving away from civilisation in this rude canvas canoe of a model that has served primitive races since men first went on the sea" (*The Aran Islands* I, CW 2: 57). He compared them with an aristocracy, not of blood but of ability, writing that "shrewd observation, and naïve reasoning" were common to both learned men of the age of Geoffrey Keating and to peasants of modern times ("The Poems of Geoffrey Keating," CW 2: 358). Their primitive and beautiful poetry was filled with "the oldest passions of the world" (*The Aran Islands* II, CW 2: 112). Their fullness of life grew from their contact with nature in the place of their origin: "All day in the sunshine in the glens where every leaf sparkles with peculiar lustre, and where air, foliage and water are filled with life, one has inevitable sympathy with vitality and with the people that unite in a rude way the old passions of the earth" (Notebook entries "[People and Places]," *CW* 2: 199).

Locality—central to traditional poetry—must also inform contemporary writing, or so thought the authors of the Irish Literary Revival. Verses, Yeats wrote, should hold the color of one's own climate and scenery, for love of the land had enabled the Irish to create the most beautiful literature of a whole people. He went so far as to claim that Ireland possessed a history more filled with imaginative events and legends than that of any other modern country, and that these stories surpassed all but the ancient Greeks' in wild beauty. In Ireland as in Greece there was no mountain not associated with some event or legend, while political events had made the Irish love their country ever more deeply. Thus, artists must become impatriated through geography as had the old Gaelic storytellers (*seanchaí*) and should master the history and legends and "fix upon their memory the appearance of mountains and rivers and make it all visible again in their arts" ("Ireland and the Arts," *Essays* 205). Yeats's ambition for the Abbey Theatre was to bring upon the stage what he believed were the deeper thoughts and emotions of Ireland—loyalty, heroism, love of the land. It must be a folk theater because literature had its roots in folklore and should be fashioned for artists who understood the necessity of recreating Ireland's heroic past, and for "a few simple people who understand from sheer simplicity what we understand from scholarship and thought" ("The Theatre," *Essays* 166). These "simple people" were the peasants as he imagined them to be—intuitively wise, endowed with a rich memory, and imbued with ancient folklore, without which poetical passages could not be understood, for high poetical style was not ostentatious and stemmed from variations upon old cadences and customary words ("Certain Noble Plays of Japan," *Essays* 227–28).

A poet, Yeats wrote in 1893, must have access to symbols, types, and stories embedded in folk imagination: "No conscious invention can take the place of tradition, for he who would write a folk tale, and thereby bring a new life into literature, must have the fatigue of the spade in his hands and the stupor of the fields in his heart" ("The Message of the Folk-lorist," *UP* 1: 288). "Folk" meant to Yeats the largely illiterate people of the countryside—peasants, tinkers, fishermen; Shakespeare's and Keats's knowledge of folklore had made them far greater, in Yeats's opinion, than Shelley who had only mythology. Irish authors should exploit native traditions and choose Irish subjects, as William Carleton had done. In "By the Roadside," the last prose piece in *The Celtic Twilight* (1893), Yeats expressed his appreciation of the popular imaginative tradition: "There is no song or story handed down among the cottages that has not words and thoughts to carry one as far, for though one can know but a little of their ascent, one knows that they ascend like medieval genealogies through unbroken dignities to the beginning of the world" (*Mythologies* 138–39). By 1902, he was able to write that he had "not yet lost the belief that some day, in some village lost among the hills or in some island among the western seas, in some place that remembers old ways and has not learned new ways, I will come to understand how this pagan mystery hides and reveals some half-forgotten memory of an ancient knowledge or of an ancient wisdom" ("Away," *UP* 2: 275).

For Yeats, the peasants' folklore was more than a link with the "Celtic" past, important for political purposes. Poets must come into contact with images and symbols from myth and legend, for artists themselves did not create; they remembered images of past greatness (*New Island*, 43), stored in a universal memory—the "fibrous darkness" from which all ideas emanated. The imaginative stories and songs that united people to their localities were expressions of universal themes: "The root-stories of the Greek poets are told to-day at the cabin fires of Donegal...." (*UP* 1: 284). Folklore was the living continuation of the same Irish mind that produced the sagas of the past (Thuente 24). Furthermore, the great myths of Ireland were not only expressions of the nation's history; they also belonged to the collective memory of the world, the "Spiritus Mundi" of Yeats's "The Second Coming." In his essay "Magic" (1901), he describes his theory of psychic processes and the collective memory.

(1) That the borders of our mind are ever shifting, and that many minds can flow into one another, as it were, and create or reveal a single mind, a single energy.

(2) That the borders of our memories are as shifting, and that our memories are a part of one great memory, the memory of Nature herself.

(3) That this great mind and great memory can be evoked by symbols. (*Essays* 28)

The supremacy of imagination was derived from "the power of many minds to become one, overpowering one another by spoken words and by unspoken thought till they have become a single, intense, unhesitating energy" (36). Barbaric and semi-barbaric people receive the invisible beings, spirits, and far-wandering influences more visibly and obviously, and more easily and fully than contemporaries could, for city life deafens the ear and kills the separated, self-moving mind that makes the soul less sensitive. The winds that made contemporary humankind shiver uneasily and move near to the fire had much greater power long ago (41).

For Yeats, primitive imagination was more powerful because of belief in magic and folklore. Music and poetry, which originated in the sounds enchanters made to help them charm and spellbind themselves as well as others, should rediscover this power. While contemporaries praised the perfected individual life, primitives praised the one mind that was the foundation of all perfection. Visions resulted from "buried memories," possessions of some supernatural artist. Symbols held the greatest of all power, Yeats believed, whether they were consciously or unconsciously used by the masters of magic, or half consciously used by the successors of magicians—poets, artists, and musicians. Yeats wrote in 1893 that he sought "powerful emotion" and "noble types and symbols" in the character of the peasantry ("Old Gaelic Love Songs," *UP* 1: 295) and that "there is no passion, no vague desire, no tender longing that cannot find fit type or symbol in the legends of the peasantry or in the traditions of the scalds and the gleemen" ("The Message of the Folk-lorist," *UP* 1: 295). The Great Memory associated symbols with events, moods, and persons. Yeats wrote:

> Whatever the passions of man have gathered about, becomes a symbol in the Great Memory, and in the hands of him who has the secret it is a worker of wonders, a caller-up of angels or of devils. The symbols are of all kinds, for everything in heaven or earth has its association, momentous or trivial, in the Great Memory. . . . ("Magic," *Essays* 50)

Imagination always sought to remake the world according to the impulses and the patterns in that Great Mind and Great Memory. What was called romance, poetry, intellectual beauty, was only the signal that the supreme Enchanter was speaking of what has been and shall be again. Each individual soul shared its history with that of the world and manifested some universal and historical truth. Tradition was a living thing with roots in every human consciousness and an analogue in an Other World. Yeats wrote: "To the greater poets everything they see has its relation to the national life, and through that to the universal and divine life: nothing is an isolated artistic moment; there is a unity everywhere; everything fulfills a purpose that is not its own; the hailstone is a journeyman of God; the grass blade carries the universe upon its point" (*New Island* 174). Images from tradition would affirm the unity of Irish culture and be part of a deeper culture underlying all societies: "The Irish peasant and most serene of Englishmen are at one. Tradition is always the same. The earliest poet of India and the Irish peasant in his hovel nod to each other across the ages, and are in perfect agreement" (*New Island* 204).

The remarkable similarity between Yeats's "Great Memory" and Carl Gustav Jung's "Collective Unconscious" has been examined in detail by James Olney in *The Rhizome and the Flower*.[23] In brief, Jung proposed the existence of two layers of the unconscious, a personal layer and an impersonal, or transpersonal, layer. The latter was not dependent upon personal experience and was entirely universal, its contents being found everywhere.

> There are present in every individual, besides his personal memories, the great 'primordial' images . . . the inherited powers of human imagination as it was from time immemorial. The fact of this inheritance explains the truly amazing phenomenon that certain motifs from myths and legends repeat themselves the world over in identical forms.[24]

The personal unconscious stands for the subjective psyche; the collective unconscious for the objective: " . . . the collective unconscious is anything but an encapsulated personal system; it is sheer objectivity, as wide as the world and open to all the world. There I am the object of every subject, in complete reversal of my ordinary consciousness, where I am always the subject that has an object. There I am utterly one with the world, so much a part of it that I forget all too easily who I really am."[25]

The primordial images of the Collective Unconscious comprise the most ancient and universal "thought forms" or patterns of thought. They resemble feelings as much as thoughts, and, although they cannot be truly personified, they lead their own independent lives. Jung calls them "archetypes" or "dominants" of the unconscious, upon which the greatest thoughts of mankind shape themselves. Their origin is in the repeated experiences of humanity: "The archetype is a kind of readiness to produce over and over again the same or similar mythical ideas. Hence it seems as though what is impressed upon the unconscious were exclusively the subjective fantasy-images aroused by the physical process. Therefore we may take it that archetypes are recurrent impressions made by subjective reactions" (*Two Essays* 68). The archetypes are mythological images from the legacy of ancestral life, ruling powers, gods, images of the dominant laws and principles, and regularly occurring events in the soul's cycle of experience. Insofar as these images are more or less faithful replicas of psychic events, their archetypes—general characteristics—also correspond to certain general concepts for physical phenomena. Archetypal images may be regarded as the effect and deposit of experiences that have taken place, but they also appear as the factors causing such experiences. The concept is equivalent to the idea of soul, spirit, or God.

According to Jung, the universal parallelism between mythological motifs is evidence that the archetypes are mythological images from the legacy of ancestral life. Myths are psychic phenomena that reveal the nature of the soul: "Primitive man impresses us so strongly with his subjectivity that we should really have guessed long ago that myths refer to something psychic" (6). The psyche contains all the images that have ever given rise to myths. Primitive people do not invent myths but rather experience them as original revelations of the preconscious psyche and involuntary statements about unconscious psychic happenings; they are not allegories of physical processes. The myths, Jung claims, are the psychic life of a tribe that decays when it loses its mythological heritage.[26]

The Irish peasants as Yeats and Synge created them embodied the collective memory of the nation and the timeless memory of the world; their imagination was necessary for the preservation of Irish culture. Free from materialism and ambition, they lived close to nature and in the old ways. Although they might be illiterate, their songs and stories told around the fireplace gave them knowledge that was superior to that which they could learn from books. Although they might be tied to the land on which they were born, their self-sufficiency and individualism gave them freedom. They belonged to an ancient aristocracy both because they were descended from the "Celts" of Ireland's Heroic ("Golden") Age and because they possessed the ancient folklore. Yeats specifically attempted to link the peasants' imagination with ancient Ireland (Thuente 143). Synge wrote that all art is a collaboration between the artist and the speech of the common people ("Preface" to *The Playboy of the Western World*, CW IV: 53). Only the peasants could provide the poet with images that affirmed the unity of Irish culture and described a deeper experience that underlay all culture.

Nevertheless, both Yeats and Synge knew that relief-works and middle-class values were changing the Irish peasants' way of life, and they feared that folklore—so important for Irish culture—would be lost as well. It was Ireland's misfortune, Synge wrote, that nearly all the characteristics giving color and attractiveness to Irish life were bound up with a social condition near to penury ("In Connemara," CW 2: 286). Synge associated "progress"—materialism and modernity—with death of the culture. He wrote that among the farmers and fishermen, nearly everyone—man or woman—was interesting and attractive, and his initial reaction was dread of reform that would in any way lessen their individuality while promising improvement in their well-being: "The thought that this island will gradually yield to the ruthlessness of 'progress' is as the certainty that decaying age is moving always nearer the cheeks it is your ecstasy to kiss" (*The Aran Islands* I, CW 2: 103). Progress deprived the peasants of their language and the unwritten literature which was as full and distinguished as that of any European people (*The Aran Islands* II, CW 2: 116). Progress also destroyed the mystery of their lives.

> It is hard to believe that those hovels I can just see in the south are filled with people whose lives have the strange quality that is found in the oldest poetry and legend. Compared with them the falling off that has come with the increased prosperity of this island is full of discouragement. The charm which the people over there share with the birds and flowers has been replaced here [Inishmore] by the anxiety of men who are eager for gain. (116)

When the peasants came into contact with sophisticated life they became ashamed of their own. Synge wrote that his friend whom he calls "Michael" (Martin McDonagh) wanted to be photographed in his Sunday clothes from Galway instead of his native homespuns (which better became him in Synge's view) because they connected him with the primitive life of the islands (*The Aran Islands* III, *CW* 2: 134).

Yeats distrusted progress in the form of land distribution to the peasants which transformed them into independent farmers. Integral to his vision was the reciprocal respect between aristocrat and peasant, derived from mutual "contact with the soil." Through this contact and self-conscious artifice, the aristocrat could recover the innocence and simplicity that were the peasants' natural virtues. Thus the aristocrat must learn from the peasant. Three types had created all beautiful things: aristocrats, a beautiful way of life; country people, beautiful stories and beliefs; and artists, all the rest ("Poetry and Tradition," *Essays* 251). All three were necessary for the creation of a unified culture. Poets themselves—poets of the people—had first created the traditional life of the Irish countryside.

> The life of the villages, with its songs, its dances and its pious greetings, its conversations full of vivid images shaped hardly more by life itself than by innumerable forgotten poets, all that life of good-nature and improvisation grows more noble as he meditates upon it, for it mingles with the Middle Ages until he no longer can see it as it is, but as it was when it ran, as it were, into a point of fire in the courtliness of kings' houses. He hardly knows whether what stirred him yesterday was that old fiddler, playing an almost-forgotten music on a fiddle mended with twine, or a sudden thought of some king that was of the blood of that old man, some O'Loughlin or O'Byrne, listening amid his soldiers, he and they at the one table, they too, lucky, bright-eyed, while the minstrel sang of angry Cuchulain, or of him men called 'Golden salmon of the sea, clean hawk of the air.' (*Explorations* 205–6)

Scholars have written that indeed one of the richest parts of Irish heritage was the *seanchas* or traditional lore of the countryside, orally transmitted throughout centuries by *seanchaí*, or bards. The lore embraced all that was held in popular memory—family history, wars, festivals, customs, and many other things.[27] The Irish peasantry, Yeats wrote, should not lose "the imagination that is in tradition" before it has found "the imagination that is in books" ("The Literary Movement in Ireland," 1899, *UP* 2: 187). Here, Yeats laments the coming of materialism and progress. Furthermore, Yeats believed that the folklore of the Irish countryside preserved remnants of ancient doctrines, the wisdom of which was desperately needed by a materialistic modern world (Thuente 43).

During Spenser's time the country people had lived the life that made Theocritus and Virgil think of shepherd and poet as one, Yeats wrote ("Edmund Spenser," *Essays* 373). He tried to transform this life into mythology in "Shepherd and Goatherd," in which shepherd, aristocrat, and artist all become the hero. In this dramatic dialogue, the shepherd and goatherd meet when the former, lost in his poetic thoughts, allows his sheep to stray on the rocks of the goatherd's demesne. Both praise a local man, a hero killed in a war: "He that was best in every country sport /And every country craft, and of us all /Most courteous to slow age and hasty youth, / Is dead" (*Poems* 142). He had been a shepherd who threw away his crook and abandoned the pipes he played among the hills, expressing their loneliness—"the exultation of their stone." This aristocrat-shepherd-artist was familiar with the old ways and kept his ancient house as it had been in his father's lifetime. The old goatherd praises the young shepherd, also a poet: "You sing as always of the natural life, /And I that made like music in my youth / Hearing it now have sighed for that young man / And certain lost companions of my own" (144). Experience has taught the goatherd the ways of the natural and the supernatural. The shepherd replies: "They say that on your barren mountain ridge / You have measured out the roads that the soul treads / When it has vanished from our natural eyes; / That you have talked with apparitions." His thoughts have found supernatural pathways. The shepherd urges him to "Sing, for it may be that your thoughts have plucked / Some medicable herb to make our grief / Less bitter." They resolve to cut their rhymes into strips of "new-torn bark." Shepherd and goatherd represent youth and age, natural and supernatural, wisdom that transcends the temporal, and spiritual rebirth: "The outrageous war shall fade; / At some old winding whitethorn root / He'll practise on the shepherd's flute, / . . . Knowledge he shall unwind / Through victories of the mind (145)." They are both artists and countrymen praising a national hero. Thus country people, peasants, heroes, and artists are joined by their consciousness of their heritage.

Just as Yeats's myth of the Irish peasant is partly an expression of feudal or archaic class sensibilities, but also partly an expression of genuine idealism, similarly his rebuke of the new Catholic middle class is more than a manifestation of social prejudice. Yeats contrasted the noble peasant with the modern middle class—to the detriment of the latter—believing that cultural unity could be strengthened only by infusing the peasants' spiritual sensibility into the urban middle class. He defined middle class as an "attitude of mind more than an accident of birth" ("Irish Language and Irish Literature," *UP* 2: 241) and described social position in terms of opposition to the utilitarianism of the spirit which he identified with England. He called the middle class notion of "getting on in life" timid; "At Galway Races" makes clear that brave men—horsemen—were spiritual companions of the poet: "Hearers and hearteners of the work / Aye, horsemen for companions" (*Poems* 97). All this was true "Before the merchant and the clerk / Breathed on the world with timid breath." Yeats emphasized middle-class timidity, not social status.

Yeats associated lack of worldly success with improvement in moral character just as Romanticism equated success with moral vulgarity. The "new ill-breeding" involved commitment to arduous utilitarianism and prudential morality. Middle-class weakness lay in rising above the tradition of the rustic, without first learning that of the cultivated life, and in fear born of ignorance and superstitious piety. Immediate utility was everything to the middle class, and thus their real poverty was spiritual. The country people, who made beautiful stories and songs, were in danger of being spiritually corrupted by middle-class values.

The poet, peasant, and aristocrat were indissolubly and organically linked because they had nothing to do with the commercial bourgeois world, and the aristocracy became the means of holding onto hope for unity of culture in the face of increasing mercantilism. In "Coole and Ballylee, 1931" (*Poems* 243), Yeats laments that a spiritual aristocracy which believed in tradition and ties to the land were the last of their breed. The symbols of aristocracy—the books, sculptures, pictures—are not material symbols of leisure or useless intellectual cultivation, but of dedication to a tradition. Thus, their lives present models for the rest of society to follow. The hero, like the aristocrat, commits to the people, expecting no reward. Yeats's "aristocracy" is a mental or cultural elite in which wealth and power are not valued for their own sake but for the nation's cultural unity. The aristocracy serves as an example, with the gifts that govern a people and preserve tradition, and the hero serves through self-sacrifice, to save his people's lives and land.

Yeats condemned aristocracies indifferent to tradition or responsibility.

> The poet must always prefer the community where the perfected minds express the people, to a community that is vainly seeking to copy the perfected minds. To have even perfectly the thoughts that can be weighed, the knowledge that can be got from books, the precision that can be learned at school, to belong to any aristocracy, is to be a little pool that will soon dry up. A people alone are a great river; and that is why I am persuaded that where a people has died, a nation is about to die. ("The Galway Plains," *Essays* 214)

The peasants were thus more important than aristocrats for Ireland's cultural unity. In order to show the Irish aristocracy what it should aspire to, Yeats compared it to another, greater aristocracy, that of the Italian Renaissance, in "To a Wealthy Man who promised a second Subscription to the Dublin Municipal Gallery if it were proved the People wanted Pictures" (*Poems* 107). In the first stanza the wealthy Dublin aristocrat degrades himself by sharing the values of the utilitarian and calculating middle class. The speaker contrasts him with Duke Ercole, Guidobaldo, Duke of Venice, whose great vision for his country was exemplified by his patronage of the arts, proof of the "exultant heart." The aristocrat should be free of self-serving motivations and does not need the voice of the middle class in order to act. The poem represents an attempt to purify life by offering higher, more ideal models for imitation. The Irish aristocracy can survive only by imitating those greater than itself.

In the same way, the great house in "Upon a House shaken by the Land Agitation" (*Poems* 95) is a symbol of the spiritual aristocracy that serves to guide the nation toward its realization of cultural unity.

Aspiring ideals should transcend the local historical situation such as the 1909 Land Act that forced large landholders to sell parts of their estates to peasants and to reduce rents.[28] The peasants' houses were "Mean roof-trees" that would become sturdier for the fall of the great houses, but the peasants could never hope to achieve the "gifts that govern men." While they were essential to the preservation of Irish culture, they had to be guided by the aristocrats, who would in turn be taught by the poets. Thus the peasants must simply *be*, in order that their way of life might survive; the aristocrats would lead them, and the poets would praise both of them. The Land Act created a class of peasant owners that Yeats feared would abandon the country people's heritage without learning the values of cultivated people and in so doing would hasten the destruction of the traditional ways of life, both those of peasant and aristocrat. Yeats's "aristocratic" poetry offered images that simultaneously criticize meaner values and provide noble goals to aspire to. Not a reversal of his earlier commitment to the importance of locality and peasant culture, the poetry elaborates on one aspect of that poetic commitment.

W. J. McCormack describes Yeats's invention of a romantic tradition for the peasant and aristocrat as spurious.

> To see Ireland, or even parts of Ireland, as 'primitive' was a task greatly eased by the success of Protestant Ascendancy. For a start, the middle classes were evidently dismissed from the discussion by the polarized sectarianism of nineteenth-century Ireland. Second, the antique dignities and guilts which the myth of Protestant Ascendancy laid upon the landowning class rendered the invocation of medieval and feudal sources all the more plausible—one of Yeats's more ridiculous fictions was that in which he converted Augusta Persse's (Lady Gregory's) evangelical upbringing into a feudal apprenticeship. (294)

For Yeats, the poet's task in the Irish Literary Revival had little to do with accurately reflecting or criticizing sociological realities but had much to do with creating and recreating archetypal or ideal images which should direct and shape history and society. Poets who cared about Irish culture, Yeats wrote in "The Municipal Gallery Re-visited," knew that everything they did or said "Must come from contact with the soil" where everything grew strong. The sole test was the "Dream of the noble and the beggarman" (*Poems* 321), not the images dreamt by noble and beggar, but the poet's ideal image, his myth.

Of course, the ferocity of Yeats's attacks on the middle class is based on his being a product of this class: he was anti-middle class in the most middle-class way; that is, he identifies himself with the Ascendancy, the class immediately above his own, as the Ascendancy did with an aristocracy.[29] Like all middle-class people, he lived his dream life through aristocratic imagery, and like many essentially urban people, he idealized the life of the country. Declan Kiberd explains that "An Irish Airman foresees his Death" best emphasizes the poet's understanding of the phenomenon of postcolonial middle-class success ("Irish Literature" 268). The semi-aristocratic airman sees his own imminent extinction in the fate of the landless poor of Kiltartan: "No likely end could bring them loss / Or leave them happier than before" (*Poems* 135). He can do nothing for them; they can do nothing for him, for the new middle class had victimized them both.

> In the fate of Kiltartan's landless poor, Robert Gregory reads his own, for both will be common victims of the new nationalist regime. The peasant, like the landlord, is mythologized by the new middle class which, at that very moment, is putting both other groups out of business. Every repressive regime first crushes its victims; and, having safely contained them, it sentimentalizes them and reduces them to the status of merely literary material. The myth of a timeless peasantry, like the conceit of a noble aristocracy, is a middle-class invention, purveyed by the *arrivistes* who were seizing the positions of power and influence in Ireland's cities and towns. And in the writings of the impeccably middle-class W. B. Yeats, these conjoint conceits found a trusty celebrant. (268)

Consider that "The Irish Airman" precedes "The Fisherman" in *The Wild Swans at Coole* and that the speaker in the latter poem recognizes that his ideal audience—whether J. M. Synge, an Irish peasant, or Yeats's ideal self—"does not exist."

Those who dream of the Noble Savage want to create a social ideal because they need to believe that somewhere (usually in some remote place) people live simply and naturally. Dissatisfied with their own culture and education, desiring communion with nature and a "simple" way of life, which they associate with wisdom and peace, they try to change their own identity in terms of the dream. The irony remains that they carry these states inside them: looking to "primitive" or "quaint" cultures merely verifies (solidifies) their myths for themselves. Yeats and Synge created their myth of the Irish peasant in the Romantic tradition that their readers might continue to believe in national culture and the imaginative power of the ideal.

Chapter 3

Natural and Supernatural

The pastoral ideal inspired the imaginations of writers long before the industrial age. The need to believe that a simpler age once existed in which people were less anxious and troubled by complexities of their world and the belief that this lost innocence or tradition can be recovered, is deeply rooted in art and culture and has both religious and secular significance in the story of Eden and Utopian literature. The countryside provides an artistic setting in which the author may work out ideas about human desire, identity and society, life and death. The seasons are metaphors for birth, growth, maturation, and decay. Sowing or planting time symbolizes hope and desire, while the harvest represents fulfillment or maturity. Separation of individual from community takes on greater significance in the country, for isolation there is both mental and physical: individuals are divided not only by misunderstanding and alienation, as are lonely people of the towns, but also by distance and weather. In Ireland, the very mist and mountains become symbols for isolation. Furthermore, loneliness in rural people comments ironically on primitivist philosophy and the values of pastoral romance.

Nature held an important place in Celtic tradition. Daily and annual patterns had meaning beyond the temporal one: the fourfold division of the day into morning, afternoon, evening, and night paralleled the annual passing of the seasons. Certain tasks were assigned for specific parts of the day, and different times possessed particular virtues or vices. Morning dew, for example, was virtuous, while midnight was a time of danger because supernatural powers dwelt near isolated places. The Celtic year was divided according to the round of agricultural life rather than to exact movements of the sun.[1] Many antique practices were related to livestock and milking. The luck of the herd was linked to certain flowering bushes, especially whitethorn and rowan, and white May blossoms brought the promise of milk through

summer, while marsh marigolds promised rich butter.[2] At the same
time, history and tradition endowed the landscape with spiritual sig-
nificance.

W. B. Yeats and J. M. Synge embraced the Romantic distrust of
the middle class and the city and the endorsement of the peasantry
and the country. Disliking what they believed modernity meant for
Ireland—the dehumanizing machine age, the loss of spirituality, the
destruction of tradition, the concentration of people into cities—they
criticized what they regarded as the materialism of the new (largely
Catholic) middle class and its lack of respect for art. Yeats lamented
the loss of the old order of peasant and aristocrat, while Synge re-
sented the imposition of the culture of eastern Ireland on that of the
west. Because Ireland was a predominantly rural and agricultural
country, its traditions were those of country people and were likely
to be preserved by them, if the traditions were to be preserved at all.
For Yeats, the virtue of the peasants lay in what he saw as instinctive
wisdom, understanding of nature, and the supposed ability to see and
hear the supernatural beings around them, which made them superior
to the "rational," materialistic, and calculating middle classes. His
country people are isolated, symbolic figures like Red Hanrahan the
wandering poet, Crazy Jane the mad peasant woman, beggars, and
fools.[3] As Thuente shows in the "Foreword" to Yeats's *Representative
Irish Tales*, his interest in peasants began with the study of fairy lore,
yet he soon turned to stories of the peasants themselves as superior
material for literature. Synge, on the other hand, rejected the impor-
tance of Irish fairy lore so carefully studied by Yeats and Lady Gregory
because he believed that the character of Ireland was to be found in
the country people themselves and in their way of life, not in legends.
He wrote that the new religion of the modern world was love of the
beauty and mystery of nature, which Synge believed had arisen just
as religion in the dogmatic sense had died (*CW* 2: 351). He believed
that the peasants' superiority lay in their dependence upon nature for
their livelihood and their freedom from the artificialities of the civiliza-
tion of eastern Ireland. For Yeats and Synge, the natural and super-
natural worlds were entwined. The peasants provided a link to simple
spirituality and to the natural world of colors and shadows, changing
seasons and seclusion.[4]

Folklore, the literature of the folk, was for Yeats and Synge imagi-
nation at its most unrestrained. Both were nationalists who held at the

same time idealistic and traditional views about the peasants, seeing the country people of Ireland as a noble peasantry possessed of a primitive life-force and an ancient cultural heritage superior to the corrupted modern way. They sought to incorporate into their own work this heritage of vitality (Bradley 80), which they contrasted with the dehumanized, colorless context of urban life. Yeats wrote that Irish folklore would give the new century its most profound poetic symbols. In "The Lake Isle of Innisfree," for example, County Sligo becomes an idealized, rural place that beckons from the "deep heart's core" (*Poems* 39) to the speaker who seeks to escape from the gray and uninteresting city. For Yeats, the west of Ireland was less an identifiable place than a country of the mind, a place where he could transcend the modern world. Although Synge recognized that local conflict, the constrictions of provincial life, and the greed and corruption of the east threatened peasant culture, he believed he could still find in the west of Ireland an innocence and lack of self-consciousness that he equated with spiritual vitality.

In "The Celtic Element in Literature," Yeats explains the "celticist" ideas that underlay concepts of natural magic. Writing of Matthew Arnold's *The Study of Celtic Literature,* Yeats describes the idea that Celtic passion for nature stemmed more from a sense of natural mystery than natural beauty.

> Once every people in the world believed that trees were divine, and could take a human or grotesque shape and dance among the shadows. . . . All old literatures are full of these or of like imaginations, and all the poets of races who have not lost this way of looking at things could have said of themselves, as the poet of the *Kalevala* said of himself, "I have learned my songs from the music of many birds, and from the music of many waters." (*Essays* 174–75)

Yeats goes on to write that the Celtic belief in "natural magic" is part of the ancient religion of the world.

Yeats and Synge sought to incorporate into their work that pastoral tradition of Irish lyric poets, whose constant motif was the open air, the hunt, changing seasons, love, animals, food, and drink (Ó'Faoláin 33). The Celtic poets observed nature carefully and recorded its sounds and colors.

Tonight the grouse is not asleep
above the high, stormy, heathery hills,
clear and sweet the cry of her throat,
sleepless among the streams.

(35)

A little bird
Has let a piping from the tip
Of his shining yellow beak—
The blackbird from the yellow-leaved tree
Has flung his whistle over Loch Laigh.

(37)

The lyricists carefully described details of the landscape in order to convey the harshness of winter and the beauty of summer.

The eagle of brown Glen Rye gets affliction from the
    bitter wind;
great is its misery and its suffering, the ice will
    get into its beak.[5]
. . . .
All the sweetness of nature was buried in black
    winter's grave,
and the wind sings a sad lament with its cold plaintive cry;
but oh, the teeming summer will come, bringing
    life in its arms,
and will strew rosy flowers on the face of hill and dale.

In lovely harmony the wood has put on its green mantle,
and summer is on its throne, playing its string-music.

(87)

Animals and places are individually named.

The grouse in Cruachan Cuin,
The otter whistling in Druin da Loch,
The eagle crying in Gleann na bFuath,
The laughter of the cuckoo in Cnoc na Scoth.

(Ó'Faoláin 33)

Specificity of location and love of the landscape, important themes in Irish lyrics, necessitated such attention to detail. Stags roam in a particular wood in these poems; blackbirds, thrushes, and linnets sing and twitter; the mountain stream whispers a song in the rushes; and the wind moans in specific mountain valleys. Through these lyrics the poets describe a love of walking, the outdoors, woods, and hills, which persists in the Irish literature of every century. The Celts, writes Ó'Faoláin, kept their idea of a heaven free of time but deeply rooted in place (32). They celebrated nature without even a trace of pantheistic belief (36): what was important was what they themselves could see.

Yeats's early poetry is filled with the mystery, beauty, and terror of the natural world that he found in Romantic poetry and in folktales. Born, he wrote, in a time when traditional memory still flourished in Ireland, he describes the transcendence of the immediate, physical world through stories of the supernatural. In "Ireland Bewitched" (1899) he writes:

> When one talks to the people of the West of Ireland, and wins their confidence, one soon finds that they live in a very ancient world, and are surrounded by dreams that make the little round fields that were the foundations of ancient houses (forts or forths as they call them), a great boulder up above on the hillside, the more twisted or matted thorn trees, all unusual things and places, and the common crafts of the country always mysterious and often beautiful. (*UP* 2: 167)

This beauty and mystery, however, threatens the mortal world. "The Unappeasable Host" (*Poems* 58) presents the reader with feelings of terror and delight. The winds have shaken the speaker's heart with desire that cannot be fulfilled; this desire, however vague, appears more beautiful than religious devotion, yet the fairy lack human sympathy ("a heart fallen cold") and fill the speaker with foreboding ("And hear the narrow grave calling my child and me"), for those taken by them often die. The fairy, according to Irish legend, adopt the form of whirling wind; Yeats writes that the peasantry know better than to mistake the fairy for wind ("Irish Fairies, Ghosts, Witches, Etc.," 1889, *UP* 1: 134). The power of nature is clear here: the winds are "desolate" and cry over the sea and the west of Ireland. Frank Kinahan

demonstrates the connection between Yeats's occult and folklore inter-
ests and writes that they led "by different ways into the same ancient
grove,"[6] that the visions Yeats evoked by using magical symbols had
been described to him in the stories told by Irish cottagers who were
ignorant of magic. Believing his studies in magic to be part of a folk-
lore that was generations old (17), Yeats could draw from these
sources in order to create poetry firmly grounded in Irish tradition.
Peter Smith maintains that Yeats's letters prove that he believed in
fairies and had developed a sophisticated theory of fairy lore reminis-
cent of his ideas about *Spiritus Mundi*; Yeats wrote, "The fairies are the
lesser spiritual moods of that universal mind, wherein every mood is
a soul and every thought a body."[7]

The poems in the early section of *The Wind Among the Reeds* (1899)
all concern the desire for transcendence and human interaction with
nature and with pagan spirits. The natural world of these poems has
an Irish topography; the spirits are drawn from Irish folklore. More-
over, Faeryland coexists with and invades the temporal world with a
forceful, even menacing power (Smith 156).

In his late essay "A General Introduction for My Work" (1937),
Yeats reiterates the significance of location in mythology and tradition,
which had always been important in his work, for natural and super-
natural were knit together (*Essays* 518). The dead stayed where they
had lived, sought no region of blessing or punishment, but retreated
into the "hidden character" of the neighborhood. He writes that to the
wise peasants the green hills and woods round about are filled with
never-fading mystery, which modern science can never defeat. The
peasants, who lived close to nature, thus became a poetic device for
Yeats who wanted to write of a life apart from the modern world.
When an aged country woman told him the mountains made her think
of the goodness of God, he concluded that God was nearer to her than
He was to the people of the cities. The peasants' Catholic spirituality
and reverence appealed to Yeats's sense of mystery and tradition: their
religion and customs had kept them from modern, empirical thought
that denied transcendence. He proposed that Europeans might find
something attractive in a Christ posed against a background not of
Judaism but of Druidism, not shut off in a dead history but "flowing,
concrete, phenomenal" ("A General Introduction for My Work," *Es-
says* 518). He wrote: "I will not of a certainty believe that there is
nothing in the sunset, where our forefathers imagined the dead follow-

ing their shepherd the sun, or nothing but some vague presence as little moving as nothing" ("Enchanted Woods," *Mythologies* 63). Natural beauty was a "gateway" to the spiritual world (63–64).

The pagan powers were not far from the peasants, either, because the very country places the people visited were the settings of stories about the Sidhe and legendary figures. Northward in Ben Bulben, "famous for hawks," a white door is believed to swing open at sundown, allowing wild unchristian riders to rush forth upon the fields ("Drumcliff and Rosses," *Mythologies* 90). Drumcliff was known to be a place of omens while both Drumcliff and Rosses were haunted. In letters to Katharine Tynan in 1887, Yeats had written that all the peasants at the foot of Ben Bulben knew the legend of Dermot and Grania and knew that Dermot haunted the place where he died (*Collected Letters* 1: 37) and that going for a walk was a continual meeting with ghosts (41). The members of a local Sligo family, called Kirwan or Hachett, were rumored in peasant stories to be descended from a man and a spirit and to be notable for their beauty ("Kidnappers," *Mythologies* 74). Stories abounded of the Sidhe who carried off infants and then returned them to the living. "Kidnappers" tells of Sligo residents taken by the Sidhe; hardly a valley or a mountainside lacked a story of someone stolen by a fairy. For example, an old woman who lived near Hart Lake had been stolen in her youth. When after seven years she returned, she had no toes, for she had danced them off.[8]

Because of their closeness to the supernatural, the peasants could appreciate poetry as the materialistic urban classes could not. Yeats wrote that the peasants could still see enchanted fires ("William Blake and the Imagination," *Essays* 114) and that they were not surprised by miracles ("Cuchulain of Muirthemne," *Explorations* 10). Traditional poets had been able to write more profound and lasting poetry because they knew the folk-beliefs; contemporary poets had to learn to exploit the mystical relationship with nature which they shared with the peasants.

Yeats defined inspiration as the ability to see the permanent and characteristic in all forms ("Blake's Illustrations to Dante," *Essays* 120). The Celtic source in literature gives its sense of the mystery of nature, of passionate turbulence, reaction against the despotism of fact: "Once every people in the world believed that trees were divine, and could take a human or grotesque shape and dance among the shadows; and that deer, and ravens and foxes, and wolves and bears, and clouds and pools, almost all things under the sun and moon, and the sun and moon, were not less divine and changeable" ("The Celtic Element in Literature," *Essays* 174). The makers of the Sagas had less of the old way than the poet of the Kalevala, for they lived in a more crowded and complicated world, while he learned his songs from the music of many birds and many waters (175); they were learning the abstract meditation that lures men from visible beauty, and were unlearning, Yeats wrote, the impassioned meditation that brings men beyond the edge of trance and makes trees, beasts, and dead things talk with human voices. The old Irish and old Welsh had less of tradition than the makers of the Kalevala, but more than the makers of the Sagas (175). The Irish "natural magic" was of the ancient religion of the world, the ancient worship of nature and the certainty of all beautiful places being haunted (176). The belief in a supernatural stemmed from contemplation of nature.

> Men who lived in a world where anything might flow and change, and become any other thing; and among great gods whose passions were in the flaming sunset, and in the thunder and the thundershower, had not our thoughts of weight and measure. They worshipped nature and the abundance of nature, and had always, as it seems, for a supreme ritual that tumultuous dance among the hills or in the depths of the woods, where unearthly ecstasy fell upon the dancers, until they seemed the gods or the godlike beasts, and felt their souls overtopping the moon; and, as some think, imagined for the first time in the world the blessed country of the gods and of the happy dead. They had imaginative passions because they did not live within our own strait limits, and were nearer to ancient chaos, every man's desire, and had immortal models about them. (178)

Poets like Keats, Shakespeare, and Virgil "looked at nature in the modern way, the way of people who are poetical, but are more interested in one another than in a nature which has faded to be but friendly and pleasant, the way of people who have forgotten the ancient religion" (178).

For Yeats, the peasants' experience was embodied in the conflict of natural and supernatural, which could at any moment create new myths ("The Celtic Element in Literature," *Essays* 185). In *The Secret*

Rose (1897), a series of stories about this conflict between the physical and spiritual worlds, he sought to create a mythology out of folklore. In "The Heart of the Spring," an old man discovers through meditation and isolation the way to the spiritual realm. He has given up everything in his search for what he calls the Great Secret, and longs for a life that would fill centuries, not "fourscore winters," to be like the ancient gods. His reverent and incurious servant boy fears the Sidhe who linger near the monastery at night. He begs his master not to fast or to beckon to the beings who dwell in the waters of Lough Gill or among the hazel trees and oaks, for he believes the old man to be weak and is concerned for his physical health. The boy himself hopes for a peaceful manhood, a cottage, and a family, but the old man hopes that the moment when he will hear the Song of the Immortal Powers is at hand, for a fairy has told him of it, and he desires to become like the immortal beings themselves. He instructs the boy to pile green boughs outside the door, fresh rushes on the floor, and roses and lilies on the table, for he is going to enter the kingdom of youth.

As the boy performs his tasks, the landscape takes on a magical appearance: the lighted lamp smells of flowers; the rocks seem to be carved of precious stones; Sleuth Wood appears to have been cut from beryl; the waters shine of pale opal; roses glow like rubies; lilies have the dull luster of pearl. Everything, in fact, takes the appearance of imperishability, except a single glowworm whose faint flame burns on sturdily among shadows, moving aimlessly, "the only thing that seemed perishable as mortal hope" ("The Heart of the Spring," *Mythologies* 175). The boy arises an hour after dawn to prepare his master's boat, for he believes the journey will be a mortal one. Everything seems to overflow with the music of birds: "It was the most beautiful and living moment of the year; one could listen to the spring's heart in it" (176). Finding the old man dead, the boy regrets that his master had not striven for the Christian heaven. At once a thrush alights on one of the boughs and begins to sing; perhaps it is the old man's soul, and natural and supernatural are one, as the old man believed.

Still, his marvelous transformation represents the same irony we find in "Sailing to Byzantium": while the old man wished for eternal youth in palaces of marble, he in fact achieves a natural form; while the "aged man" of the later poem wishes to be embodied as a work of art, he must turn back to the natural world in order to sing his song.

The speaker of "Into the Twilight" urges his heart ("Out-worn heart, in a time out-worn") to leave the troubles of the world as well as its moral decisions ("Come clear of the nets of wrong and right") and to rejoice "in the grey twilight" and sing in "the dew of the morn" (*Poems* 59). He wants to go to the beautiful, mysterious land "where hill is heaped upon hill," for the "mystical brotherhood"—the sun, moon, hollows, wood, river, and stream—is victorious over despair and death, and the heart will find solace because the twilight and dew are kinder and dearer than love and hope. In "The Hosting of the Sidhe" (55), the fairy call anyone who looks upon them away from his earthly pursuits ("the deed of his hand," "the hope of his heart") and entice him to follow them to the Other World. "The Moods" (56) reminds us of humankind's mortality and nature's cycle of birth and death, contrasted with the everlasting emotion and life of the Sidhe, whose "fire-born moods" never fade. In these poems, human beings (usually country people, because the fairy inhabit the countryside and because in Yeats's view the country people were the only ones besides artists whose way of life was traditional and spiritual enough to be imbued with the supernatural) are tempted by supernatural powers to abandon their earthly desires and mortal ambitions ("the hope of his heart"). At the same time, they abandon ideas of good and evil ("the nets of wrong and right"), responsibility, and action ("the deed of [his] hand"). By embracing the fairy, they relinquish moral choice.

To desire and pursue immortality, youth, and beauty is not, however, to attain them, whatever sacrifices are incurred. In "The Song of Wandering Aengus" (*Poems* 59–60) the legendary speaker grows old wandering in search of a beautiful woman of the Sidhe. He leaves at dawn—the time, according to legend, when the veil between this world and the unseen is very thin (Rees 92). He goes to the hazel wood (apple trees and hazel trees were rich in associations with the Otherworld [90–91]), because of some inexplicable longing ("Because a fire was in my head") and wanders through "hollow lands and hilly lands" in search of unattainable beauty which he does not understand. As time passes, the light grows and shimmers: when he leaves home, the "moth-like stars were flickering out"; the little silver trout he catches becomes a "glimmering" girl who fades through "brightening air." The speaker, named for the god of love, pursues her not because he is under a magical spell but because of his own free will. Although he has now grown old with wandering, he refuses to give up his quest. He will find her, and will gather the fruit of magical nature, "The silver apples of the moon, / The golden apples of the sun."

In other variants of the story, the woman visits Aengus night after night and plays to him on a lute but eludes him when he reaches out to her. She takes the shape of a swan, not a fish. Aengus promises that if he can stay with her he too will take the form of a swan every other year and human form the remaining years (Jackson 93–97) and in some versions of the story is granted his request. In his 1899 note to this poem, Yeats tells of a folk belief of Galway that attributed to the Sidhe the power to take the shape of fish and to swim in the sea. Yeats found his sources in a Greek folk song and a story told to him by an old man of Gort who said that he had seen a beautiful woman in Inchy Wood at about eight in the morning: "And I followed her and looked for her, but I could never see her again from that day to this, never again" (*Variorum Poems* 806). Yeats will not allow his Aengus to achieve his desire, as did the Aengus of the folktale, because he wants to show that desire for something beautiful and yet unattainable transcends reason and practicality. Aengus is old, but he prefers to wander and to gather spiritual treasures rather than to stay in one place. In order to retain his vision of beauty, he pays the price of eternal, unsatisfied desire.

Just as the Sidhe call mortals away from earthly matters, the voices of the natural world—audible in the songs of birds, in the wind, among hills, in shaking boughs, in the tides—call to unsatisfied humankind who must live with the knowledge of mortality. The speaker of "The Everlasting Voices" (*Poems* 55) begs the voices to be quiet ("O sweet everlasting Voices, be still") for to look upon the world itself is to realize that one will grow old and die, while the longing for youth, beauty, and wisdom never fades: "Have you not heard that our hearts are old." Although the voices belong to the natural world, they tell of the immortal one. Longing and desire were themes in Yeats's poetry all his life, as was the romantic motif of wandering in search of beauty or wisdom.

In "The Withering of the Boughs" (79–80), Yeats again employs a technique of the Irish lyricists. In this poem, the natural and supernatural worlds converge: the moon murmurs to the birds, and the man speaks to the moon. The speaker asks the moon for his "merry and tender and pitiful words," for the road was unending and he cannot find a place to rest. When he does, he falls asleep upon "lonely Echtge of streams," which may be Slieve Aughty (Sliabh Echtge, the Mountain of Echtge, a fairy goddess [631]). He dreams of the Country of the Young, where the moon drifts and the pale foam gleams, swans fly with golden chains, and a king and queen wander, transformed by a magical song. The boughs wither because he had told them his hopeless dream of immortality and beauty.

Nature, mystical powers, and the Sidhe are beautiful and majestic, but also dangerous, for they call people away from earthly comfort and such imperfect love as mortals are able to feel. While the natural and supernatural powers promise spiritual transformation, they also threaten disappointment, disillusion, and loss of individuality. In "The Madness of King Goll" (16–18), the powerful, influential, wealthy speaker (like Aengus, Goll is legendary) rules a rich kingdom and commands fighting men as well as the respect of "every ancient Ollave" (learned man) for his ability to restrain the "Northern cold"—the Fomorah, or powers of death and darkness, cold and evil, that come from the north (616). Like the speaker of "The Song of the Wandering Aengus," King Goll searches for something he cannot explain. He abandons his kingdom to wander in fens and on the shore because within his "most secret spirit grew / A whirling and a wandering fire." Now he wanders in the woods, companion to birds, deer, and wolves, and the leaves—both those in the trees and the dry ones at his feet—refuse to hush their old song. The supernatural never ceases to call to him through the natural world. Goll follows a sound, "a tramping of tremendous feet," possibly of fairy, that draws him and sings of "some inhuman misery"—he does not say what he desires, for he does not know—and of Orchill, a sorceress who "shakes out her long dark hair." While he sang his mournful, plaintive song, his desire (the "whirling and the wandering fire") was quenched, "with sound like falling dew." Now, however, the stringed instrument is torn and still, and he is destined to continue wandering in the woods and hills in all seasons, still searching for whatever he wants.

Emblematic of the outcast, King Goll wanders, singing, in the woods, driven mad because greatness—riches, power, or wisdom—cannot satisfy the desire for life and beauty. Still a member of society, "The Man Who Dreamed of Faeryland" (43–45) is nevertheless consumed by the same frustrated desire to find the spiritual world. He experiences no happiness in love, prosperity, or fame, and no peace in death because the creatures of the natural world—the fish, lugworm, knotgrass, and, finally, worms—sing to him of a country where Time cannot mar lovers' vows or turn the green leaf brown, where exultant fairy dwell in magical surroundings, and where "old silence" bids the enchanted men and women who live there to rejoice. The man achieves a measure of worldly success but never finds peace or comfort, for the songs of the supernatural reach him as he contemplates the natural world. Notably, the objects that convey to the dreamer his visions of the Other World—dead fish, lugworms in mud, knotgrass, worms in the grave—are all repulsive, increasingly so throughout the four stanzas, and may represent the state in which the man finds himself (Kinahan 66). At the same time, he grows increasingly strange throughout the lyric and appears to be a special sort of victim of the Sidhe: although not carried away by them, the man can never find peace, happiness, or love in this world. One folklore tradition maintains that the fairy "take a perverse delight in preventing mortals from finding happiness in love" (Kinahan 71). The man who dreamed appears to be one of these, and to suffer far more from the fairies' "glamoring" than does Aengus, whose all-consuming pursuit of the Sidhe woman does not leave him as dismally unhappy.

The supernatural is as threatening as it is beautiful. "The Stolen Child" (18–19) tells of the attractiveness and also the danger of the powers that call to human beings. The fairy sing to the human child of dancing on the strand and chasing the fish in the streams, creating a vision of beauty that is part of the natural world and at the same time promises release from anxieties and cares and from the cycles of birth and death which are also part of the natural world. The child must abandon the familiar world in order to become part of the fairy realm and so gain release from mortality. While they call to him to leave this world full of care, they fill the natural one itself with anxiety, for they lean from the ferns and whisper to the trout, giving him "unquiet dreams." The child must leave not only the sorrow and unhappiness of the world but also its peace and comfort. He will never again hear the lowing of the calves on the warm hillside nor the singing kettle on the hearth, nor see the brown mice bob "round and round the oatmeal chest." The child must abandon earthly happiness in order to follow those who promise immortality.

Yeats found his sources for "The Stolen Child" and "The Man who Dreamed of Faeryland" in Irish folklore—Croker's *Fairy Legends*

(1825), Carleton's *Traits and Stories of the Irish Peasantry* (1830) and *Tales and Sketches, Illustrating the Character, Usages, Traditions, Sports and Pastimes of the Peasantry* (1845), and Lady Wilde's *Ancient Legends* (1888) (Kinahan 69). Although found in different collections (*Crossways* [1889] and *The Rose* [1893]) these poems are allied, as Kinahan lucidly argues, not only because of their common sources, but because together they create a "poetic atlas" of Sligo. Slewth Wood, Rosses, Lissadell, Toberscanavan (shortened in the poem to "Scanavin"), and Lugnagall are key places in Sligo and Glen Car and Dromahair are immediately across the border in Leitrim (66). When Yeats writes as a poet of place, that place is almost always Ireland, and Sligo within Ireland, with its heritage of folklore. In addition to their being firmly grounded in the country of Yeats's youth, both poems center on mortals trapped between the ethereal beauty of the Other World and the potential happiness of this one. Both dreamer and child could have found earthly happiness or peace if not for the seductive pull of fairy. Like "The Madness of King Goll" and "The Hosting of the Sidhe," these two poems present not a dichotomy between perfect and imperfect worlds, nor a longing for a life removed from this, but "an exegesis of the woe that too great a longing for perfection must engender" (Kinahan 76).

Here we might ask the question of how comfortable Yeats was with what he believed to be the power of magic as well as how much these poems reflect the consequences of moral choice. One of the distinguishing characteristics of the man in "The Man who dreamed of Faeryland" is the obsessiveness of his inner life (Smith 194). The beings in the natural world who sing to him do so of his own condition; clearly, dreaming is insufficient, as it leads to despair. Although the occult lures people away from materialistic pursuit, it also draws them from nobler ones, and, moreover, the pursuit of pleasure may itself be seen as amoral. If Faeryland represents desire, then the imagination creates it, just as imagination is necessary for the creation of art. Faeryland is not a realm of art, however, for those who dwell there are not creative, given as they are to love and pleasure. Subsumed in beauty, they may be emblematic of art but do not create it. We learn from later work (especially the Byzantium poems) that this impulse to be subsumed into art results in turning back to nature (not magic) for images, and hence Faeryland does not represent creation. Moreover, the qualities of the natural world that lead to the impulse to create art—the struggles between good and evil, life and death, love and hate—are absent from Faeryland, which is thus shown to be hollow.

The barrier between the physical and spiritual worlds vanishes in the *Stories of Red Hanrahan* (1897; revised in 1905) where natural objects take on magical characteristics. Hanrahan, a peasant "hedge schoolmaster" who is also a poet and mystic, travels between these worlds.[9] The introductory story draws on the folkloristic motif of the peasant card game on Samhain Eve with old men who possess other-worldly powers.[10] Upon receiving the message that his sweetheart, Mary Lavelle, has promised to marry him following the death of her mother, Hanrahan tries to hurry out to go to her at once. The old men try to stop him with invitations to stay and celebrate with them; marriage will leave him little time for sport, they argue. Hanrahan rebuffs them, saying that if Mary does not find a husband, her lands will go to someone else, and hurries toward the door, where an old man who has been sitting and mumbling strangely to himself stops Hanrahan and compels him to play a game of cards. Hanrahan plays, mesmerized, while the old man shuffles the cards, seeming to create rings of fire in the air with his hands. The only things visible in the room are his hands and the cards. Suddenly a hare jumps from the cards and then a pack of hounds, and they run around the room and then out the door. Hanrahan follows them in his dream-like state. He comes to a great shining house where grand women offer him the things the old man had mumbled about—pleasure, power, courage, knowledge—but he cannot accept what they offer, and he falls asleep, awakes alone, and stumbles back to the village one year later on Samhain Eve. Mary Lavelle has lost her land and emigrated, and he never sees her again.

Hanrahan, in the stories that follow, seeks for love, for the spirit of Ireland, for youth, and for Tír nan Óg. "The Twisting of the Rope" sees him tricked by magic out of a prospective marriage. In "Hanrahan and Cathleen" he learns that love of Ireland and anger at her oppressors can never be appeased. His imprecation ("Hanrahan's Curse") against age itself brings the old men of the village against him. In "Hanrahan's Vision" he sees a procession of fairy men and women come out of Ben Bulben's side through the white square door and ride through the valleys. The mist takes the appearance of waves of the sea washing the mountains. Welcomed as a poet wherever he goes, Hanrahan never ceases his wanderings. He knows that there are great secrets locked in the mountains and lakes but he cannot discover them for all his wandering. Birgit Bramsbäck has pointed out that harpers and bards were so highly esteemed in Ireland—in real life as well as in ancient literature—and had so much influence that during Queen Elizabeth's time laws were passed that prohibited nobles from keeping them. The English disapproved of gamblers as well, and it is interesting to note that Hanrahan possesses magical knowledge of card-playing (*Folklore and W. B. Yeats* 106–7). When Old Winny Byrne of the Cross-Roads, whose wits were stolen on Samhain Eve, passes him, singing of youth and beauty, he follows her willingly. He dies, dreaming that she has become a beautiful Sidhe woman who has carried him off. From Irish folklore Yeats adopted the themes of transfiguration, wandering in search of wisdom or beauty, the love of solitude and the open air, and love itself. His wandering ballad poet is a spokesman for the people who still believed that certain places, inhabited by spirits, can exercise power over the minds of people. Like King Goll and the man who dreamed of fairyland, Hanrahan understands the bitterness of frustrated desire; unlike them, he is able to glimpse the spiritual world he seeks, for he is a poet, the true bearer and harmonizer of culture, who mediates between aristocrat and peasant.

In "The Twisting of the Rope" (1892) and "Hanrahan's Vision" (1896) we find different versions of the lyric that was to evolve into "The Happy Townland." Published as "The Rider from the North" in 1903, the poem demonstrates a view of the Other World as a place of joyful celebration that can be entered by human beings without the consent of fairy. Linda Revie demonstrates that Yeats borrowed his theme from "An Maidrín Rua" ("The Little Red Fox"), a folk ballad, and possibly Katharine Tynan's poem "The Little Red Fox."[11] In the Gaelic folk ballad, the fox, representing the peasants who composed the story, escapes its hunters, who would have been looked upon as Anglo-Irish landlords. In an English variant of the ballad, "The Little Red Fox," however, the animal is caught by "strong farmers," gentrified peasants or small landholders who do as the English do—oppress the landless people (113–18). The narrator of Tynan's poem reveals ambivalence about the fox, approving of the chase but relieved that the animal escapes. Revie points out that Tynan's narrator suggests someone of dual loyalties, such as a landowning farmer, sympathetic to the peasants' cause but wanting to keep them in their place (121). Strong farmers, as we have seen, had been peasants but became owners who changed the character of rural Ireland, especially after the Wyndham Act of 1903 enabled more farmers to become landowners. Yeats's earlier versions of "The Happy Townland" include no strong farmer; the first appears in 1903, and he is pointedly excluded from the Happy Townland.

The poem unites aristocrats and peasants in a townland that has become a mystical place of bounty and celebration:

> Boughs have their fruit and blossom
> At all times of the year;
> Rivers are running over
> With red beer and brown beer.
> An old man plays the bagpipes
> In a golden and silver wood;
> Queens, their eyes blue like the ice,
> Are dancing in a crowd.

The heart of the "strong farmer" would break in two out of desire to be part of this courageous, happy world where men express high emotion through battle, where the souls of heroes reside: " . . . all that are killed in battle / Awaken to life again."[12] The poem celebrates heroic courage and the abandonment of common life for the Other World:

> It is lucky that their story
> Is not known among men,
> For O, the strong farmers
> That would let the spade lie,
> Their hearts would be like a cup
> That somebody had drunk dry.

The peasants have achieved nobility through their hard work and preservation of tradition, including the desire to find the Land of the Ever-Living. To pursue immortality and heroism is noble, yet to leave the fields and the homeland is bitter:

> *The little fox he murmured*
> *'O what of the world's bane?'*

The sun was laughing sweetly,
The moon plucked at my rein;
But the little red fox murmured,
'O do not pluck at his rein,
He is riding to the townland
That is the world's bane.'

The poem presents the joy of action and life in the Other World with the sorrow felt by those who contemplate mortality. In addition, the poem represents Yeats's political conviction that a new Irish society should be forged from the cultures of aristocrat and peasant. The strong farmer's economic aspirations prevent him from entering the heroic world.

The three parts of society Yeats deems praiseworthy—the aristocrat, peasant, and poet—are present in *The Countess Cathleen;* however, the peasants are not presented in a noble light. Yeats bases his play, written primarily from the aristocratic perspective, on the story from *Irish Fairy and Folk Tales* called "The Countess Kathleen O'Shea" (originally a French folktale, the story was translated into English; even in the French version, the setting is Ireland [Bramsbäck, 15–16]) in which the beautiful and generous Cathleen is robbed by evil spirits disguised as merchants so that she is unable to save the local people who are selling their souls to the devil in order to keep from starving. She sells her own soul to the devils for gold with which she endeavors to save all the people. After she dies, God declares the transaction to be null, for Cathleen's action is motivated by generosity.

To the basic plot of the self-sacrificing aristocrat, Yeats adds the characters of Aleel the bard (Kevin in the 1892 version), who brings romantic love (as compared with Cathleen's Christian love), and Oona, Cathleen's foster mother, who possesses loyal devotion. Cathleen is the most heroic character, but Aleel is more complex and ultimately more interesting, for he is in love with the woman he serves, and is troubled by visions of hell (in the version of 1892, it is Oona who sees these visions). The earlier version ends with Oona's rebuke to anyone else who would keen her mistress, for she says she loved Cathleen the best, and her resolve is to die after Cathleen is buried, because she has seen a vision. In the later versions Oona expresses her wish to die because she has seen a vision of passing time and destiny— a darker vision than that in the play of 1892.

The years like great black oxen tread the world,
And God the herdsman goads them on behind,
And I am broken by their passing feet.[13]

Cathleen's self-sacrifice has not rid the world of evil.

The play opens with a scene inside the peasant cottage of Mary and Shemus Rua. Mary and her son Teigue, hearing the hen flutter, speculate fearfully on what has caused her to do so; Teigue says that he has heard of walking ghosts and disfigured spirits appearing to the local people. These peasants are not the interesting ones Yeats describes in "Ireland Bewitched," nor are they wise like the peasants who know better than to think that passing fairies are merely wind. The Irish landscape in this play has none of the mysterious beauty of the early poems. The peasants of *The Countess Cathleen* are fearful, suspicious, and opportunistic. Their fears are well-grounded, for Teigue sees horned owls with human faces in the bushes, and soon the messengers of Satan come to buy souls. The peasants (except for Mary) are easily persuaded to sell their souls for gold in order to survive, for their souls mean little to them. Furthermore, tradition means little to them. Shemus Rua, hearing Aleel's harp, declares that the poet is "mocking us with music" (13), and later refers to him as a fool (25). Aleel, however, responds wisely that "Who mocks at music mocks at love" (23). Shemus and Teigue blaspheme openly, stating that God and the Mother of God are asleep and cannot hear their prayers (9). And Shemus describes his search for food:

I'm in no mood to listen to your clatter.
Although I tramped the woods for half a day,
I've taken nothing, for the very rats,
Badgers, and hedgehogs seem to have died of drought,
And there was scarce a wind in the parched leaves.

(9–11)

Throughout the progress of the play, the peasants increasingly take on the role of chorus and lose their individuality; they also learn that they are unworthy of Cathleen's sacrifice and try to convince her not to make it. In Scene 1, Teigue, Shemus, and Mary have the central part in the conflict, with Cathleen merely making an appearance, followed by the entry of the wicked merchants and Shemus and Teigue's conversion. In Scene 2, Cathleen meets Shemus and Teigue, who tell her of the merchants' business, and her steward, who informs her that her garden has been robbed. Here she resolves to have no joy or sorrow of her own for the rest of her life (77). After Aleel's vow of love in Scene 3 (87–89), she encounters the merchants whom she immediately suspects of being demons. In Scene 4, which was added in the ninth version of the play, the nameless peasants act as chorus, revealing the extent of their ignorance and distance from the poet Aleel: while they talk about gold, he sings of his impetuous and sorrowful love. Shemus and Teigue appear again in their own house in Scene 5, where the merchants have gathered to buy souls, and where Mary lies dead, having refused to sell hers. The peasants who enter are like the nameless, faceless members of the chorus of Scene 4, although toward the middle of the scene some of them turn from the merchants because a damned woman has screamed with pain inflicted for her having said the name of God. After Cathleen offers her soul for five hundred thousand crowns, the peasants beg her not to sacrifice herself for them, and when she does, their choral-like voices praise her as "the great white lily of the world" (163). Shemus and Teigue have no speeches after the early part of the scene; Cathleen, Aleel, and Oona take over the major part of the action. At the end, the peasants are merely part of a mountainous and stormy landscape. Aleel the poet-visionary comes from Gaelic or what Yeats might call Celtic tradition, while the devils who try to take Cathleen's soul are clearly patterned on Christian myth. She knows (and Oona fears) that Aleel is a pagan because in a dream he sees someone walking who had "birds about his head" (83). Although Cathleen possesses greater moral strength, Aleel is free from the devils' threat, for his soul can never be purchased by them; indeed, he cannot even give it away when he grows tired of it, for Cathleen possesses it (139–43). He inspires fear in the devils because as a lover he is free of damnation and redemption, and as a poet he sees visions of the Other World and supernatural powers which are greater than they are. As Peter Smith points out, we may consider Yeats's Faeryland to be a country of imagination, but this does not elucidate the play (162). The fairies, neutral in the war between good and evil, neglect the Christian values that Cathleen represents and that the merchants and some of the peasants invert. *The Countess Cathleen* represents an escape *into* responsibility, as Oisin's choice is an escape *from* it (Smith 171). A three-way struggle between good, evil, and the fairies is played out (160), with good only the partial victor, for the drama ends with Oona's dark vision and Aleel unsaved. Aleel the artist remains the most interesting character because he represents the tension between moral choice and the pursuit of love and beauty.

If Yeats casts aspersion on Irish peasants in *The Countess Cathleen*, he presents at least one in a nobler light in his play of 1894, *The Land of Heart's Desire*. Less fortunate (or perhaps more fortunate from an escapist viewpoint) than Red Hanrahan, and unable to be content as the wife of a peasant farmer, Mary Bruin finds an old book in the thatch that Maurteen Bruin, her father-in-law, claims to have been written by his grandfather. Bridget, Mary's mother-in-law, is vexed because Mary would rather read than work; Maurteen asserts that his grandfather also derived no good from the book, "Because it filled his house with rambling fiddlers, / And rambling ballad-makers and the like" (183). The book tells of Princess Edain's journey to the Land of Faery, which Mary envisions as happier and more beautiful than the world she knows. It is a place:

> Where nobody gets old and godly and grave,
> Where nobody gets old and crafty and wise,
> Where nobody gets old and bitter of tongue.
>
> (184)

That she repeats three times the phrase "Where nobody gets old" indicates what she really fears about the natural world. Her mother-in-law's continual nagging drives her into the power of the fairies. Yeats uses the folkloristic belief that May Day posed special danger for newly married brides and that certain precautions must be observed in order to ward off the fairies. Although Maurteen Bruin believes that Mary dreams that she has seen someone outside, when there is nothing but wind, he reprimands her about forgetting to place a branch of quicken wood before the door; as soon as she does so, a child runs up and takes it away. In an earlier version, the charm is to throw primroses before the door, but when she does, the wind blows them away (185–87). Twice she transgresses custom by giving milk to a "little queer old woman dressed in green" (188) and fire to a "little queer old man" who in the earlier version is also dressed in green (191).

Mary resembles the fairy people already, for as her husband Shawn describes her, she is pale and her hair is like a "cloudy blossoming" (192). The fairy child who enters the house in spite of the priest's (Father Hart) being there sings the fairy song, just as Mary has repeated her desire for a world where no one grows old, bitter, or wise (in other words, a timeless world).

> The wind blows out of the gates of the day,
> The wind blows over the lonely of heart,
> And the lonely of heart is withered away.
>
> (200)

The child promises to take Mary where she will be happy.

> You love that young man there,
> Yet I could make you ride upon the winds,
> (Run on the top of the dishevelled tide,)
> And dance upon the mountains like a flame,
>
> (202)

and yet there is much to hold her to this world as well. Although she tells Father Hart that she is weary of "a kind tongue too full of drowsy love, / Of drowsy love and my captivity," clearly Shawn and Mary love each other, for he tells her that all her troubles are his and that Bridget nags her only because she has forgotten her own youth (192). Mary responds that Shawn is "the great door-post of the house," herself "the branch of blessed quicken wood" that would hang upon the post, bringing good luck (192–93). Shawn and Mary make poetic love-talk, with Shawn regretting that he cannot give his wife more freedom, and Mary responding that she would destroy the world to see Shawn smile (193). His wish is to create a world for her of fire and dew, "With no one bitter, grave or over-wise, / And nothing marred or old to do you wrong" (193). She answers that "Your looks are all the candles that I need" (193). Shawn's speech then becomes quite lyrical as he describes her romantic dreams and her pride.

> Once a fly dancing in the beam of the sun,
> Or the light wind blowing out of the dawn,
> Could fill your heart with dreams none other knew,

But now the indissoluble sacrament
Has mixed your heart that was most proud and cold
With my warm heart for ever.

(194)

At this moment the fairy child sings in the wood and Mary knows
she is in danger of being carried off, not because she cannot stop
herself, but because secretly she wills herself to be taken away. She is
afraid because the mortal world she would leave is not entirely bad.
Although Bridget nags her, Shawn loves her and Maurteen is kind to
her, telling her that they in fact live the best life available to them: they
have love, friendship, and a hundred acres of good land. The best of
life, to Maurteen, is

To watch the turf-smoke coiling from the fire,
And feel content and wisdom in your heart.

(190)

Maurteen's vision of the best life is naïve, homey, comfortable, while
Shawn's is romantic and physical.

Beloved, I will keep you.
I've more than words, I have these arms to hold you,
Nor all the faery host, do what they please,
Shall ever make me loose you from these arms.

(208)

The fairy child who comes to fetch Mary reveals that she is "older than
the eagle-cock," who is "the oldest thing under the moon" (203), and
that she has been reborn many times. Birgit Bramsbäck points out that
the eagle occurs in a poem in the story "Red Hanrahan's Curse," again
as "the oldest thing that knows of cark and ill" (*Mythologies* 243). The
association of the child with the eagle-cock emphasizes her dangerous
qualities and the unpurged state of her soul (Bramsbäck 87–88).

Still, it is the child who tells Mary of her greatest loss in leaving
the mortal world. Like the solemn-eyed child in "The Stolen Child"
who must leave familiarity and comfort, Mary must lose all "clinging
mortal hope" (*Variorum Plays* 207). The life she goes to may be better
for her than for the solemn-eyed child, since Mary is a proud woman

who is filled with dreams of freedom, youth, and eternal joy even before she hears the fairy song which promises that she will ride the winds and "dance upon the mountains like a flame" (202). In Yeats's earlier poems, the speakers often question whether the mortal or immortal world is preferable (in "The Stolen Child," for example); in his later poems, however, the human world is usually superior to the superhuman (in, for example, "Sailing to Byzantium," "Vacillation," "The Circus Animals' Desertion"), for suffering leads to ennoblement.

Smith argues that Faeryland in this play is both possible and desirable (181), and certainly the fairy child's description of a woman many years married would cause anyone of romantic temperament to flee; if Mary stays, she will

> grow like the rest;
> Bear children, cook, and bend above the churn,
> And wrangle over butter, fowl, and eggs,
> Until at last, grown old and bitter of tongue,
> You're crouching there and shivering at the grave.[14]

Even Maurteen's reminding her of the prosperity a hundred acres would bring and Father Hart's admonition to remember her duties sound hollow and materialistic beside the Child's promise of a place where "joy is wisdom, time an endless song" (*Plays* 45). Still, the old tensions work on the reader's sympathies: while the occult lures mortals away from drudgery and materialism, the pleasures of Faeryland do not promise ennoblement. The Child, after all, admits that the fairies are obedient "to the thoughts / That drift into the mind at a wink of the eye" (*Plays* 45) and so cannot know anything about lasting love or devotion, good or evil (they are "clear of the nets of wrong and right" ["Into the Twilight," *Poems* 59]). Still, although she hesitates to leave it, Mary Bruin cannot accept mundane peasant life. Less interested in fairy lore than in using that lore to express the longings of the soul (Thuente 103), Yeats gives the victory in this play to the realm of desire and imagination.

While Yeats created new mythologies from old folk motifs and legends, Synge wrote plays derived from his experience on the Aran Islands. Like Yeats he was a traditionalist, but he was far more a primitivist, for he celebrates in his prose and drama the peasants' way of life, which he believed to be more virtuous and meaningful than the "civilization" of eastern Ireland. Yeats the folklorist was interested in folk belief and stories that could link the modern poet with timeless tradition; Synge the primitivist focused on the stories of the peasants' lives. Magic for him was the beauty of the landscape, the physical attractiveness of the hardy people, and a way of life close to nature. Always interested in natural history, he experienced in the Wicklow mountains the hypnotic influence of mists and shadows that he believed were the origin of local superstitions and beliefs ("Autobiography," *CW* 2: 10). He rejected, however, sentimental notions of the pastoral; like the Irish lyricists, he recognized that nature was both rejuvenator and destroyer. Peasants who looked daily upon the natural world looked also upon their own fate.

Synge's account of his stay on the islands forms a detailed, if somewhat idealized, picture of life there. He had the poet's ear for dialect, and wrote that he caught the real spirit of the island in some old fragments of melody or in the intonation of a few sentences when he listened to the men talking of tides, fish, and the price of kelp in Connemara (*The Aran Islands* I, *CW* 2: 74). He also had an artist's eye for color and described tableau-like scenes that reinforce his conviction that the peasants' ancient way of life was superior to that of urban dwellers. An old man in one of the houses where he stayed told him stories as they sat in the kitchen in the evening, while the family drew round on their stools and the daughter of the house in her "wonderful red garments" spun on her wheel (48 fn.). He describes a girl, about fourteen years, sitting on a heap of straw near the doorway of her cottage where a ray of sunlight fell on her. Synge wrote that her figure in her red dress and the straw formed a curious relief against the nets and oilskins and created the impression of exquisite harmony and color (130).

In Inishmaan, Synge wrote, one is forced to believe in sympathy between man and nature (75) and the inability of the people to distinguish between the two (128). He wrote:

Their minds have been coloured by endless suggestions from the sea and sky, and seem to form a unity in which all kinds of emotion match one another like the leaves or petals of a flower. (102 fn.)

Miracles abound for the people: rye becomes oats, storms rise up to keep away evictors, and cows isolated on lonely rocks bring forth calves (128). Wonders, such as thunderstorms and rainbows, are expected (129). At a funeral, the thunder sounding a death peal of extraordinary grandeur seemed in concord with the faces, stiff and drawn with emotion. When the storm passed, the people's expression changed to one of friendly interest in each other. According to Synge, the supreme interest of the island lay in the strange concord that existed between the people and the impersonal, powerful impulses of the natural world (75 fn.). They depended on the sea for their livelihood, and even their knowledge of the time depended on the direction of the wind, for they told time by the passing of light on the floor; nearly all cottages were built with two doors opposite one another, the more sheltered of which lay open all day to give light to the interior. When the wind was too strong, this door was closed, and so no light was admitted (66). Everything they did and, indeed, all that they felt was affected by the weather and the sea.

Synge felt himself transformed by the world around him.

> ... I was wandering out along the one good roadway of the island, looking over low walls on either side into small flat fields of naked rock. I have seen nothing so desolate. Grey floods of water were sweeping everywhere upon the limestone, making at times a wild torrent of the road, which twined continually over low hills and cavities in the rock or passed between a few small fields of potatoes or grass hidden away in corners that had shelter. (49)

A week of fogs that swept over the island left him with a profound sense of exile and desolation: when he walked he saw nothing but a mass of wet rock, surf, and tumultuous waves (72). On the other hand, the Atlantic storms were so dramatic that he was shocked when he first saw one arise and noted that the overwhelming power and beauty of Atlantic storms affected him as beautiful music might affect some mythical person who possessed a sophisticated appreciation of music in spite of never having heard any, or as the sight of a corpse might affect one who knew nothing of death (97–98 fn.).

The immense suggestion from the world of inarticulate power made him tremble long after the storm had passed. The tremendous power of nature led him to morbid musing that if he were to die there, no one outside the island would know until after he was buried. He talked with no one through days of rain and tempest, but gave himself over to dreaming of his roving years in Europe. The raging winds, he said, chanted a cadence to his "inner powers."

> Have I not reason to join my wailing with the winds, who have behind me the summer where I lived and had no flowers and the autumn with the red leaves of the forest and never gathered any store for the winter that is freezing at my feet? I have wandered only some few thousand miles yet I am already beyond the dwelling place of man. (110 fn.)

The birds took up one plaintive note and passed it on to one another along the cliff, "a sort of an inarticulate wail, as if they remembered for an instant the horror of the mist" (74). The birds exist between rational man and inanimate nature, and voice the sinisterness that reflects the islanders' relation with the sea. Their cry of horror at the mist echoes the people's cry of horror at their brutal treatment by the elements. The folk were less affected by the storm than Synge was, but after a few days their voices sank in the kitchen, and their talk of pigs and cattle fell to a whisper, as if they were telling stories in a haunted house (72). Synge also felt the power of nature and the anguish of human helplessness before it. The "profound ecstasy of grief" he had heard expressed in the funeral keen contained not merely sorrow for the dead but also the whole passionate rage that every native of the island possessed.

> In this cry of pain the inner consciousness of the people seems to lay itself bare for an instant, and to reveal the mood of beings who feel their isolation in the face of a universe that wars on them with winds and seas. They are usually silent, but in the presence of death all outward show of indifference or patience is forgotten, and they shriek with pitiable despair before the horror of the fate to which they are all doomed. (75)

This is the cry of humankind who looks upon nature and is reminded of one's own destruction. Synge went to the pier at nightfall in order to understand those who do their work after dark. "The sense of solitude was immense," he wrote. "I could not see or realise my own body, and I seemed to exist merely in my perception of the waves and of the crying birds, and of the smell of seaweed" (129–30). After a voyage to the south island he wrote:

> The black curagh working slowly through this world of grey, and the soft hissing of the rain gave me one of the moods in which we realise with immense distress the short moment we have left us to experience all the wonder and beauty of the world. (139)

Individuality and humankind itself seemed to dissolve in the mist and sea.

The climate of the islands, however, produced some spectacular beauty as well as mist, fog, and rain. He wrote of the dreamy tone that comes with the rocking of the waves (94), of lying on the rocks for hours, companion to cormorants and crows, of the "intense insular clearness" of Ireland which allowed him to observe every ripple in the sea and sky, the crevices in the hills beyond the bay (53). Even when the sea was shrouded in gray and rain threatened, the thin clouds threw a silvery light on the sea and an unusual depth of blue on the Connemara mountains (68). When the gray cleared, the sun shone with luminous warmth that made the whole island glisten with the splendor of a gem, and filled sea and sky with a radiance of blue light (73). His descriptions resemble those of the Irish lyricists.

> Bars of purple cloud stretched across the sound where immense waves were rolling from the west, wreathed with snowy phantasies of spray. Then there was the bay full of green delirium, and the Twelve Pins touched with mauve and scarlet in the east. (110)

Yet these days, so different from the storms and mists, did not invite him to think of rejuvenation, as the storms and gray, overcast days taught him to dwell on mortality.

In this lonely world where human beings were so dependent on nature, artifacts possessed extreme significance; Synge may be suggesting that in this subsistence economy, things have more personality than people.

> Every article on these islands has an almost personal character, which gives this simple life, where all art is unknown, something

of the artistic beauty of mediaeval life. The curaghs and spinning-wheels, the tiny wooden barrels that are still much used in the place of earthenware, the home-made cradles, churns, and baskets, are all full of individuality, and being made from materials that are common here, yet to some extent peculiar to the island, they seem to exist as a natural link between the people and the world that is about them. (58–59)

In *Riders to the Sea* (CW 3: 1–27) the natural and supernatural are interrelated, and even very mundane activities are endowed with significance—replenishing turf, stitching, making a rope halter or bread, or changing an old shirt for a new one. At the same time, objects interconnected with life seem to prophesy disaster. The white boards from Connemara intended for Michael's coffin are used for Bartley's. The new rope that hangs on a nail by the white boards also comes from Connemara and is being reserved for Michael's funeral. Cathleen saves the rope from being eaten by the pig with the black feet, which Bartley tells her to sell to the pig-jobber. The rope then becomes a halter for Bartley's fateful ride.

Familiar articles of peasant life become symbolic of disaster. A knife bought from the man who tells the family about the seven-day walk to Donegal from the Connemara coastline is used to open Michael's clothes. Nora's stitching becomes evidence of possession and also of Michael's impending disaster: through her altered stitches, his identity is established. Her sewing thus foreordains his fate. Nora gives Maurya the stick that Michael brought from Connemara, one of the objects Maurya says the young leave behind for the old (3: 13). She uses it in order to make her way to the well where she sees the apparition of Michael on the gray pony, which leaves her unable to bless Bartley. Flannel from Galway is used to determine whether the shirt in the bundle is made of the same material. Maurya poked the coals away from the cake and then failed to give Bartley his bread (product of the fire). The cake (bread) then becomes food for the builders of Bartley's coffin.[15]

The primitive, organic culture of the island is based on the small world surrounded by the larger—the hearth surrounded by kitchen, cottage, island. The kitchen as center of both work and communication is at the middle of the "cognitive map," the islanders' territory (76). The symbol of the hearth, the fire, is never entirely extinguished. The kitchen houses both men's objects (nets, oilskins) and women's (spin-ning-wheel, turf loft) and the objects from the outside (rope, knife, and boards). The threshold line between the family and cottage and the outside is dangerous and exposed, the big world having both physical and psychological ramifications for the islanders, since economic con-ditions require that men like Bartley must go to Galway in order to continue to support their families. Kilronan is the center of primitive culture; Galway and Dublin call enticingly and dangerously, as the east threatens the islanders: the people from the big world enter as bailiffs and police. Thus the mercantile world threatens, invades, and desecrates the island. Economic conflict further divides the two worlds, as agents controlled market prices (77).

From inside the cottage, the center of their world, the women hear the threatening wind and sea. The doorway marks a boundary between the small and larger worlds of *Riders to the Sea*. When the wind blows the door open, the big world invades the small. Objects mark the distance from the doorway: the spring well, site of Maurya's vision, is another boundary line that Bartley crosses. Beyond that lie the pier, the shore, the green head, the white rocks, and still farther, the sea. Next come Connemara and Galway, place of origin of the white boards, the new rope, the stick, the knife, the flannel, the young priest who is ignorant of the sea, the pig-jobber who will likely cheat Nora, the hooker which is coming in from the east and will presum-ably bear the island men away, the black hags (birds) which are the only mourners for Michael. Galway's fair beckons ominously to Bartley. Still beyond lies Donegal, "the black cliffs of the far north," the distance to which is measured in time: seven days are required to walk there from "the rocks beyond," the Connemara coastline. The women listen from inside the cottage to the roaring of the sea in the west, to Bartley passing on the pony, to someone crying out near the shore. They are unable to battle the sea or protect themselves against the grief that is their inheritance. The wind blows open the door, the big world invading the small.

Nora, Cathleen, and Maurya continuously use symbols of the dark night in their speech: the cliffs of the north, the hags of the sea, the knot on the bundle of Michael's clothes, the night, and the feet of the pig are all black, the color of evil and death (Messenger, *Inis Beag* 106). The pig is the central symbol of death, for in Irish mythology the pig was an eater of corpses.[16] This one has been eating the new coffin rope and will soon be sold for slaughter: both references link him with death. Maurya rakes the fire aimlessly until it is almost extinguished; since the fire was traditionally symbolic of human life, the prosperity of the house and farm were closely associated with it. If anyone in the house were ill, the fire would not be allowed to die down.[17] Synge uses this folkloristic motif to foreshadow the tragedy: an audience unaware of the traditional belief would still understand the symbolic relationship between fire and life, both of which may be extinguished.

Maurya's children are careless of precautionary rules that protect the natural world from the supernatural. The play's action may fall about November 11, for Maurya looks ahead, after Bartley's death, to the long nights after Samhain (Skelton, *Writings* 45). Cathleen transgresses the feast customs at the beginning by kneading cake and spinning in violation of festival rules. Bartley carelessly puts on the flannel shirt formerly owned by the drowned Michael. A common belief that the departed still own whatever property they possessed in life, and that others' taking possession of such property constitutes injustice, dictates that no one else should use such property.[18] Thus, Nora's giving Maurya Michael's walking stick for her journey to the well demonstrates the girl's indiscretion. One aspect of the departed which Bartley would do well to heed is the desire of the dead to draw the living away from this world (15). Similarly, it is unlucky for a traveler to return for something forgotten, as Bartley returns for the rope (Ó Súilleabháin, *Irish Folk Custom* 31). Not returning a blessing was even more dangerous, for even compliments were harmful unless returned with the precautionary words "God bless you" (Messenger, *Inis Beag* 102). Bartley, who presumably knows something of the sea, ignores the warnings of wind and tide: the southwest wind and eastern tide create two surf masses that collide loudly and produce dangerous weather conditions.

The young in *Riders to the Sea* are foolish, in contrast to Maurya's depth of understanding. Grief has taught her wisdom; she knows that human beings, and especially an only son, are more important than horses. She gives a vital clue to her spiritual condition and a premonition of the disaster that will soon overtake her household when she prophesies that by nightfall she will have no son left her in the world. She knows the young priest is ignorant of the sea; indeed, throughout the play, he is always referred to as "young," and hence, inexperienced. She knows he is wrong not to stop Bartley and to trust that God would not leave her without a son. Her remark that in the big world the old bequeath things to the young, while on the island the young leave things behind for the old (3: 13), expresses her understanding more poignantly: while the islanders are dependent upon the mercy of the elements, more of them might survive if they heeded the wisdom of age, if the young would abandon their foolish security and pride; that is, if they would stop being young. Maurya's only concern is for Bartley, not for the physical welfare of the family, and she is so grief-stricken that she forgets the blessing of leave-taking. Maurya warns him not to go, telling him that the wind was raising the sea and there was a star up against the moon (3: 9). He ignores her pleading, hurrying with his work, eager to go to the boat and the fair, which he has heard will be a good one for horses. His concern is that the family will be hard pressed with only one man working and orders Cathleen to do the work normally undertaken by men—including striking a hard bargain for the pig. He is sure he will not be needed to dig a grave for Michael, for his mother's nine-day seaside vigil resulted in nothing, and so he eagerly grasps at the opportunity the fair offers. Cathleen sides with him, insisting that the life of a young man is to be going out on the sea and that no one wants to listen to an old woman who repeats herself (3: 11).

Bartley has learned nothing from the deaths of his brothers. Nora and Cathleen are naïve and unable to understand what is happening to them. Even at the end, Cathleen tells the man who brings in Bartley's body that her mother is getting old and broken, and remarks to Nora that an old woman will soon be tired from anything she will do. Nora merely attributes her mother's courage in watching for Michael nine days and her passivity at Bartley's tragedy to favoritism for Michael (3: 25). Far from being a weak woman, however, Maurya, although she is old, is both remarkable and strong, as we see from her final, eloquent affirmation of life and individuality (3: 25–27). Nora has not been able to accept Michael's death with the courage Maurya displays after Bartley's; she remarks that it is a pitiful thing when there is nothing left of a man who was a great rower and fisher but a bit of an old shirt and a stocking (3: 17).

The details of the story come from Synge's experiences on the Aran Islands. The articles Bartley picks up before he heads off to the sea—Michael's shirt and his own purse and tobacco—are articles found on a man washed ashore in Donegal. For three days the people of the island tried to fix his identity, which was determined by his sister who pieced together all she could remember about his clothes, purse, his tobacco box, and stockings. In the end there seemed little doubt it was her brother, whose name was Michael. She said, "please God they'll give him a decent burial," then began to keen slowly to herself. The drowned man's mother had stood on the shore as Maurya stares out to sea, looking out and weeping. To Synge, the sister represented a type of the women's lives upon the islands (*The Aran Islands* III, *CW* 2: 136), where the loss of a single man was a slight catastrophe to all except the immediate relatives, because (Synge believed) very often all the working men of a household died together at sea (137).

The theme of the coffin boards used to bury someone for whom they were not intended comes also from *The Aran Islands*. A woman died of typhus, and as no boards could be found to make a coffin, a man gave up the boards he had kept for two years to bury his mother, who was ill but still alive (158). In one of his Aran notebooks Synge recorded his observation of a steamer that seemed to grow "like a living thing" as it drew near to the island, just as the steamer in *Riders* seems to loom in Bartley's life (TCD 4384). After the funeral of a young man, Synge wrote that he realized that he was talking to men who were under a judgement of death: "I knew that every one of them would be drowned in the sea in a few years and battered naked on the rocks, or would die in his own cottage and be buried with another fearful scene in the graveyard I had come from" (*CW* 2: 162). Grief for the death of a person under forty is deep and prolonged on the islands (Messenger, *Inis Beag* 94); a common folk remark is that "It's not often the old are taken."[19] The idea for Maurya's apparition might have come from a story a woman told in which, when horses were being herded toward a boat, a woman saw her son, who had been drowned some time before, riding on one of them (*The Aran Islands* IV, *CW* 2: 164), or from another story he collected in which a young woman who had been taken by the fairies returned to tell the people that four or five hundred of the fairies rode on horses, and she herself rode a gray horse behind one of them (*CW* 159).

The crucial lines of Maurya's speech at the end of *Riders to the Sea* may come from a letter written in Irish by Martin McDonagh, a friend of Synge's from Inishmaan, on February 1, 1902: " . . . that it is a sad story to tell, but if it is itself, we must be satisfied because nobody can be living forever." *Riders to the Sea* was written later that year.[20]

In his letter Martin also says that Seaghan (Sean) his brother "must be satisfied." Rage against shortened life and tragic death was ineffectual. Martin displays the same philosophical acceptance that Maurya does.

Nora Burke, in *The Shadow of the Glen*, will not be satisfied with philosophical acceptance. She demands from life what Maurya knows can never be hers—love and companionship. Maurya is a tragic figure who opens her heart to the world and blesses her sons, giving them individuality and achieving it herself while accepting the limitations life has imposed. Nora possesses an impetuous, energetic personality, but in the end chooses to immerse herself in the natural world which in *Riders to the Sea* and *The Shadow of the Glen* is destructive of life, and to relinquish individuality. In doing so she escapes both fear and loneliness and gains a measure of freedom.

In *The Shadow of the Glen*, the shelter protects human individuality, yet it is also the sterile denial of life while the outside is vital, amoral, and instinctual. Michael Dara and Dan Burke remain powerful and safe inside the shelter but are the least sympathetic, heroic, or imaginative characters. The mist is the entity into which humankind dissolves, like the sea in *Riders*.[21] Human disintegration is associated with the coughing and choking sheep who live in the rain and fog: Patch Darcy dies raving in the white formlessness. Just as the sea transforms Michael, the great rower and fisher, into a memory, leaving nothing but a plain shirt and stocking, the mist transforms Darcy, once a great shepherd who could walk through five hundred sheep and not miss one of them, into a madman.[22] Synge describes the effect of the mountain mists in his essay "In Wicklow."

> The daylight still lingered but the heavy rain and a thick white cloud that had come down made everything unreal and dismal to an extraordinary degree. I went up a road where on one side I could see the trunks of beech trees reaching up wet and motionless—with odd sighs and movements when a gust caught the valley—into a greyness overhead, where nothing could be distinguished. Between them there were masses of shadow, and masses of half-luminous fog with black branches across them. On the other side of the road flocks of sheep I could not see coughed and choked with sad guttural noises in the shelter of the hedge, or rushed away through a gap when they felt the dog was near them.

Above everything my ears were haunted by the dead heavy swish of the rain. (*CW* 2: 192)

This is the world that has engulfed Darcy and will engulf Nora and the Tramp.

Loneliness plagues the characters of this play as well as those of *Riders to the Sea.* Nora Burke laments to the Tramp her sense of loss at Patch Darcy's death: " . . . and it's very lonesome I was after him a long while . . . and then I got happy again—if it's ever happy we are, stranger—for I got used to being lonesome" (*CW* 3: 39). In doing so she echoes the words written to Synge by his friend from Inishmaan, John (Seaghan) McDonagh, the brother of Martin: " . . . it is lonely we were the time you left, for a long while, but now we are getting out of it, when we are used to being lonely" (Kiberd, "J. M. Synge" 62, and *Synge* 207). Throughout this play, loneliness is a theme that Nora and the Tramp explore. Old Dan Burke was always cold to her, day and night, and so Nora surmises that coldness in him might not be a sign of death after all. The Tramp muses on her living alone, that not two living souls would ever see her candle in the window. The cottage sits so far back in the hills that only a small path leads up to it and an ass and cart would be drowned in the rain water. Nora and the Tramp both suffer loneliness: she lives virtually alone in the back hills while he wanders by himself. Nora remarks, when she leaves to call Dara, that even a corpse is better company for the Tramp than nothing and no one. She later foretells a lonely old age for Michael and for Dan.

Nora yearns for emotional satisfaction. Although she was hard to please as a child, a girl, and a woman, she settles for Dan Burke because he owns property which she believes will shield her against poverty in her old age (*CW* 3: 49). She now regrets her marriage: although she has not met the fate of Peggy Cavanagh, who is forced to tramp the roads, neither does she have a family like Mary Brien, who is younger than herself (51). Fear of poverty and old age made her choose Dan, and now she is dissatisfied.

I do be thinking in the long nights it was a big fool I was that time, Michael Dara, for what good is a bit of a farm with cows on it, and sheep on the back hills, when you do be sitting, looking out from a door the like of that door, and seeing nothing but the mists rolling down the bog, and the mists again, and they rolling up the bog, and hearing nothing but the wind crying out in the bits of broken trees were left from the great storm, and the streams roaring with the rain? (49)

She thinks of passing time, the winter and summer, the fine spring, the young growing behind her and the old passing, and realizes that she has spent a long time on the back hills meditating on the meaning of life. Rebelling against her unhappy match, she resembles the wilful mountain ewes that Dara cannot control. Clearly, he is no match for her: as she muses on loneliness and romantic longings, he imperviously counts out the money he thinks Dan has left to her. Darcy, a great shepherd like those reared in Glen Malure and Glen Imaal (47), could have been a suitable match for her. That she was married might have been one of the reasons he went mad; loneliness and the impersonal landscape obscured in mist drove his wits away.

Fear also plagues the characters in *The Shadow of the Glen*. The Tramp is afraid to touch Dan's corpse because of the curse he laid on Nora. Michael Dara is unashamed to admit his fear of the dead (45) and grows uneasy at the mere mention of mad Darcy. The Tramp was so afraid of Darcy's raving that he feared for his own sanity, and, instead of seeing whether he could help the man, he ran to the town to get drunk, believing that the voice he had heard was supernatural, "queer talk, you wouldn't believe at all, and you out of your dreams" (39). His courage did not return until he learned that the strange voice was Darcy's, yet he tells Nora that he is not easily made fearful, as a tramp must not be. He then asks her for a needle to protect him from spirits, saying as he moves uneasily, "there's great safety in a needle, lady of the house" (41).[23] Nora, on the other hand, demonstrates her fearlessness in admitting him to the house and later in going out into the woods to live.

Declan Kiberd in *Synge and the Irish Language* shows that in this play Synge affects a dramatic presentation of a wake, during which it was customary to discuss topics of current interest, as Nora and the Tramp discuss Darcy's death (168–70). A common feature of wakes was playing imitative and courtship games, such as "doctoring" and "Downey." In the former, a man asks a girl to marry him in order to cure his sickness, but she rejects him and herself becomes the patient, while in the latter a man nicknamed Downey feigns death in order to monitor the sorrow of his friends who are keening him; just as he is to be buried, he awakens and asks for a drink. Those who have not mourned him sufficiently are attacked with a strap or rope.[24] The plot of *The Shadow of the Glen* is a variant of these games, for Nora and Dara arrange their own match, yet she rejects him for the Tramp. In fact, marriages were often arranged at wakes. Financial considerations having been paramount in many rural Irish matches (Kiberd, *Synge* 172), Dara discusses Dan's legacy to Nora. Dan, like Downey, sits up and asks the startled Tramp for a drink, and he threatens to attack Nora and Dara with a stick. The play represents a mock-wake, for not only is Dan still alive, but his faults rather than his virtues are recalled (174). The audience is entirely on Nora's side, for Dan reveals himself to be the kind of man she says he is. Her planning a marriage on what she supposes is the day of his death is overhasty and irreverent, yet it is forgivable because she has always had to turn to others for companionship. While Nora, the Tramp, and Dara praise Darcy, Dan reveals his callousness by cursing him (*CW* 3: 43). Although Darcy has been dead a year, Nora speaks more respectfully and lovingly of him than of Dan, implying that Darcy and not Dara was her true love. The Tramp praises Darcy's prowess as a shepherd to Dara, who cannot deny the truth. Nora regards the Tramp with noticeably greater respect after he speaks well of Darcy (47). Nora and the Tramp distinguish themselves with their love of talk and, presumably, communication: he remarks that she is "a grand woman to talk" (43), and she agrees to go with him because of his "fine bit of talk" (57). Dan is a poor talker and a worse listener: he chides the Tramp for his "blathering about the rain" (43), and, as Kiberd points out, repeats in mockery the words that passed with such vitality between Nora and the Tramp (*Synge* 173).

After the first performances of Synge's play, *The United Irishman* published "In a Real Wicklow Glen," proclaiming that its play, in which the woman stays with her husband, was more "nationalistic." Arthur Griffith accused Synge of borrowing his plot from a Greek tale, the "Widow of Ephesus," but Synge claimed to have collected the tale from Pat Dirane on Inishmaan (*CW* 2: 70–72). In this tale a tramp goes to a lonely country house in which a woman waits alone after her husband—as she thinks—has died. She offers the tramp tea, spirits, and a pipe, as Nora does, and then goes to tell the neighbors of her husband's death. As in the play, the husband reveals himself and his plot to the stranger, who keeps his secret. The woman returns to the cottage with a young man who goes to the bedroom to sleep, he says. The woman follows him, and the husband and tramp find them in bed together. In the play, Nora and Dara try to entice the Tramp to sleep in the bedroom so that they can make plans for their marriage. Dara is surer of Nora's assent than he has reason to be. In the story the husband beats the young man with a club; in the play Dan Burke invites Michael Dara to stay with him. The tramp in Dirane's story is an onlooker who narrates the tale; in the play he becomes a major figure, verifying Darcy's virtues, and convincing Nora to leave the shelter and go to live in the glen.

Furthermore, many of the motifs Synge uses in the play are recorded in his notes and essays about his walks in the Wicklow glens. Among the people who live in the scattered cottages of Wicklow, Synge found many whose personalities demonstrated the influence of their particular locality. They lived for the most part beside old roads and pathways where scarcely one person passed in a day, and looked out "all the year on unbroken barriers of heath." Heavy rains caused the thatch to drip, and terrible storms bowed the larches. After a night's rain the valley was "a riot of waterfalls" with sheets of water everywhere (TCD 4396). Winds howled through the narrow glens with the roar of a torrent, breaking at times into silence that increased mental tension. "At such times," Synge wrote in "The Oppression of the Hills" (1905), "the people crouch all night over a few sods of turf and the dogs howl in the lanes" (CW 2: 209). In "An Autumn Night in the Hills" (1903), he described his walking in a Wicklow glen when heavy rain and a thick white mist made everything seem unreal and dismal: trunks of beech trees reached wet and motionless into the grayness overhead, and between were masses of shadow and half-luminous fog with black branches across them (CW 2: 192). At sunrise, however, the almost supernatural radiance brings everyone out into the air with the joy of people who have recovered from a fever. This climate, Synge concluded, acting on a dwindling and lonely population, caused or increased a tendency to nervous depression, and made common "every degree of sadness" from mournfulness to insanity (209). After Nora's lamenting her unsatisfying life, Dara suggests that she sounds like the men who have spent "a great while on the back hills" (CW 3: 49).

Patch Darcy's fate may have been suggested to Synge by a tale he collected from an old man in Wicklow in which a young lad who was reaping in the glens had gone mad and lost his way. In the morning the people found footprints, but nothing was known until they found his body on the mountain half-eaten by crows. The informant assured Synge that when he was a lad the young had been robust, but now the country people were "lonesome and bewildered" and no one knew the cause of their ailment (*CW* 2: 209–10). The play informs us that the cause is isolation and shows us that the price of natural beauty can be too high.

Nora's romanticism and her shepherd-hero also come from folklore which Synge collected in the glens. He overheard a tinker rebuke a shepherd for boasting of his prowess, for the herd had been after sheep from his boyhood but had never attained the skill of shepherds reared in the mountains.

> Those men are a wonder, for I'm told they can tell a lamb from their own ewes before it is marked, and that when they have five hundred sheep on the hills—five hundred is a big number—they don't need to count them or reckon them at all, but they just walk here and there where they are, and if one is gone away they'll miss it from the rest. (228)

Synge borrowed the tinker's words for Nora's respectful description of Patch Darcy.

The Irish countryside in the work of Yeats and Synge thus became a setting for the working out of ideas about literature and society. Their landscapes do not resemble those of pastoral idylls, for while their landscapes are spectacularly beautiful and magical, they are also remote, dangerous, and haunted. Closeness to nature enabled the Irish rural people to communicate with the spiritual world, but their lives are far from contented, peaceful, or happy. Natural cycles remind them of mortality, and sinister supernatural forces threaten. Yeats and Synge both celebrate the rural way of life, but they also present the loneliness, confusion, and fear that are part of it. Their work reveals quite different purposes, for while Yeats's undisguised lyricism emphasizes the connection of the natural world to folkloristic motifs, Synge focuses on direct experience of the peasants' difficult lives. For both writers, the relationship between the people and nature is complex and dynamic and extends deep into the mysterious, and sometimes dangerous, spiritual realm.

Chapter 4

The Peasant and Love

If the countryside provided a setting for the working out of ideas about self and society, it also provided a setting for love and romance, a necessary part of the pastoral ideal. The fundamental conventions of courtly love poetry are the ennobling power of love, the elevation of the beloved above the lover, and the conception of love as unsatisfied and increasing desire. In pastoral romance, the woods or countryside represented safety and freedom for the lovers. Modern Anglo-Irish writers drew images and motifs from traditional Irish love poetry, which was both pastoral and romantic, but also tragic, principally because of separation from the loved one and because of fear of death. While the woods represent safety and solace, they also remind the lovers of their own mortality. The speakers in Irish love poems praise the beauty of the natural world but also lament the passing of seasons which will bring them closer to old age. Thus the pastoral setting creates an ironic contrast, for while it represents safety and freedom from the "civilized" world, it also represents mortality. Birth and blossom, death and decay become important metaphors in love poetry.

Nora Burke laments in *The Shadow of the Glen:*

> Isn't it a long while I am sitting here in the winter, and the summer, and the fine spring, with the young growing behind me and the old passing. (*CW* 3: 49)

Passion seems lost to her, the consequence of marriage for economic reasons: she felt she had to choose Dan Burke in order to have a home and security, and found herself married to an old man who could not share her love, "wheezing the like of a sick sheep close to your ear" (*CW* 3: 57). Christy Mahon and Pegeen Mike imagine their life together, but neither they, nor any of Synge's or Yeats's peasant characters or poetic speakers, experiences lasting married love. In this, Yeats and Synge follow a tradition of Irish love poetry. The speakers in Irish love poems seldom, in fact, praise the virtues of married love. Only an old man and woman (Martin and Mary Doul of *The Well of the Saints*), who cannot see each other, remain together. The theme of much Irish love poetry, the reality of growing old—rather than romantic idealism—becomes a major concern in Yeats's and Synge's writing.

Love itself is insufficient: inevitably society or the outside world interferes with the lovers in their creation of an ideal world, as the bishop does when he comes between Crazy Jane and Jack the Journeyman in *Words for Music Perhaps*. Sometimes the lovers themselves lack the virtue or courage that love demands: duty and bravery are also necessary, as Nora Burke, Christy Mahon, and Crazy Jane discover. Romantic love is threatened by a harsh world of human treachery, pride, ambition, adversity, greed, and especially old age and fading beauty.

Yeats and Synge develop the theme of the lover's lamenting the loss of the loved one and of youth which makes love possible. They found sources in Douglas Hyde's translations of the songs and poems ascribed to the Irish poet Anthony Raftery (1784?-1835) and of the love songs from Connacht, published in 1893.[1] A frequent motif in the songs Hyde translated is the jealousy of those in heaven—the saints, prophets, and bishops, even God himself—of the lovers who openly express their pleasure in being with one another. In the song entitled "Úna Bhán" ("Fair Una"), the lover contrasts his beloved, to her advantage, with life in heaven:

> O Una, O maiden, O friend, and O golden tooth,
> O little mouth of honey that never uttered injustice,
> I had rather be beside her on a couch, ever kissing her,
> Than be sitting in heaven in the chair of the Trinity.[2]

The lover in Irish folk songs repeatedly vows: "I had rather be beside you than in the glory of Paradise" (quoted in Kiberd, *Synge* 126). The song "Nancy Walsh," translated by Hyde, also declares that the lover prefers life with the woman to life in heaven:

> A girl beyond comPARE, a pretty girl lives THERE,
> By Geata-mor the FAIR one is dwelling;

Such cheeks, like roses RARE, the dead would rise to STARE,
I'd rather be with HER than in heaven.[3]

J. M. Synge's poem "Dread" (1906–8) incorporates this notion of the deprived deity:

Now by this window, where there's none can see,
The Lord God's jealous of yourself and me.

                                                    (CW 1: 40)

Christy Mahon expresses this sentiment in his speech to Pegeen in which he says that the Lord God is lonely in his splendor:

It's little you'll think if my love's a poacher's or an earl's itself when you'll feel my two hands stretched around you, and I squeezing kisses on your puckered lips till I'd feel a kind of pity for the Lord God is all ages sitting lonesome in his golden chair. (CW 4: 147)

In Synge's poem "Is it a Month?" (1907–9, CW 1: 52), Paradise seems "but a wreck" in comparison with the body of the speaker's beloved, and stars grow "wilder" and "wise" with the "splendour" of her eyes; and in *The Playboy of the Western World*, heaven becomes a veritable prison which houses lonely souls:

If the mitred bishops seen you that time, they'd be the like of the holy prophets, I'm thinking, do be straining the bars of Paradise to lay eyes on the Lady Helen of Troy, and she abroad pacing back and forward with a nosegay in her golden shawl. (CW 4: 149)

Such images are irreligious; they affirm life and confirm the lover's belief that the living woman is superior to promises of heaven.

Another frequent motif from Irish love songs that Synge used was the praise of the beloved who is called a "knowledge-star" or "star of knowledge." These celestial motifs evoke images of the sky and dawn, brightness or light, as metaphors for love's inspiration. In "Father Leeam" the image refers to religious understanding or devotion: "And is it not happy for the flock who are under his shield / If they believe the Star of Knowledge" (Hyde, *Raftery* 83). The speaker in the poem "Oh, Youth Whom I Have Kissed," longing for a tryst with her lover, employs the image of the star with the promise of a meeting:

> Oh, youth whom I have kissed, like a star through the mist,
>   I have given thee this heart altogether,
> And you promised me to be at the greenwood for me
>   Until we took counsel together.
>
>   (Hyde, *Love Songs* 103)

The image is used in its commoner context as a symbol of the beloved, together with images from nature which describe her beauty, in the poem "Breedyeen Vesey":

> If you were to see the Star of Knowledge
> And she coming in the mouth of the road,
> You would say that she was a jewel at a distance
> Who would lift mist and enchantment.
> Her countenance red, like the roses,
> And her eye like the dew of harvest,
> And her thin little mouth, very pretty,
> And her neck like the colour of the lime.
>
>   (Hyde, *Raftery* 227)

In *The Playboy of the Western World*, after Christy has become the hero of the village and the gallant lover Pegeen desires, his speeches echo the celestial image from Irish love poetry ("star of knowledge") and words of devotion ("holy Brigid" and the "infant saints"):

> Amn't I after seeing the love-light of the star of knowledge shin-uing from her brow, and hearing words would put you thinking on the holy Brigid speaking to the infant saints. . . . (CW 4: 125–27)

Pegeen learns to speak eloquently to Christy, although before his arrival she shows little inclination or talent for what the Widow Quinn calls "poetry talk." However, she possessed a vivid imagination before she met Christy, if what she describes to him of her daydreams is true:

And myself a girl was tempted often to go sailing the seas till I'd marry a Jew-man with ten kegs of gold, and I not knowing at all there was the like of you drawing nearer like the stars of God. (CW 4: 151)

Christy's imagination is also inspired by his love:

Isn't there the light of seven heavens in your heart alone, the way you'll be an angel's lamp to me from this out, and I abroad in the darkness spearing salmons in the Owen or the Carrowmore. (CW 4: 149)

The significance of Hyde's translations of the love songs he collected in Connacht and the Songs Ascribed to Raftery lies in their influence on the language of Anglo-Irish literature. In a book review of October, 1893, Yeats praised the translations, saying they were better than either Walsh's or Mangan's poetry ("Old Gaelic Love Songs," UP 1: 295). Hyde, Yeats wrote, had made available to the public "that beautiful English of the country people who remember too much Irish to talk like a newspaper." Yeats also praised the commentary on the poems, describing it as "almost as much a fragment of life as are the poems themselves" (292).[4] Of the poem "If I Were to Go West," Yeats wrote, "The whole thing is one of those 'thrusts of power' which Flaubert has declared to be beyond the reach of conscious art" (294). He lamented that the time when these songs were commonly sung among the people had passed away:

As for me, I close the book with much sadness. These poor peasants lived in a beautiful if somewhat inhospitable world, where little had changed since Adam delved and Eve span. Everything was so old that it was steeped in the heart, and every powerful emotion found at once noble types and symbols for its expression. But we—we live in a world of whirling change, where nothing becomes old and sacred, and our powerful emotions, unless we be highly-trained artists, express themselves in vulgar types and symbols. . . . Yet perhaps this very stubborn uncomeliness of life, divorced from hill and field, has made us feel the beauty of these songs in a way the people who made them did not, despite their proverb:

"A tune is more lasting than the song of the birds,
A word is more lasting than the riches of the world."

We stand outside the wall of Eden and hear the trees talking together within and their talk is sweet in our ears (295).

Yeats saw that Hyde's book signified the advent of a new power into literature:

I find myself now, as I found myself then, grudging to propaganda, to scholarship, to oratory, however necessary, a genius which might in modern Irish or in that idiom of the English-speaking country people discover a new region for the mind to wander in. In Ireland, where we have so much to prove and to disprove, we are ready to forget that the creation of an emotion of beauty is the only kind of literature that justifies itself. ("Samhain: 1902," *Explorations* 93)

The English spoken by native Irish speakers in the west, Yeats argued, was the only good English spoken by any large number of Irish living at that time; therefore, the new literary idiom should come from them, for literature must be founded on the speech of the common people (94).

Love in these songs of Connacht involved not only joy at the sight of the beloved and celebration of youth and beauty but also dissatisfaction, sorrow because of separation, and unfulfilled desire. These songs are characterized by light-heartedness and mirth, even extravagant celebration, but also melancholy. The singers celebrate not only the local beauty and the individual, secret love, but, soliloquizing alone in the woods, they also pine for the lost lover who has emigrated. So profound is the grief of the lover that all contemplation of peace with God, all hope of happiness and the power of love to ennoble the lover, all comfort in the family or home, are forgotten. The poems tell more of grief, melancholy, and contrition of heart than of gaiety or mirth. The poem "If I Were to Go West" laments simply and gently the loss of love and takes images from nature to describe the lover's sorrow:

If I were to go west, it is from the west I would not come,
On the hill that was highest, 'tis on it I would stand,
It is the fragrant branch I would soonest pluck,
And it is my own love I would quickest follow.

My heart is as black as a sloe,
Or as a black coal that would be burnt in a forge,
As the sole of a shoe upon white halls,
And there is great melancholy over my laugh.

My heart is bruised, broken,
Like ice upon the top of water,
As it were a cluster of nuts after their breaking,
Or a young maiden after her marrying.

(Hyde, *Love Songs* 5)

The melancholy lover goes on to compare his love with the color of blackberries (a common image in Irish poems), and to declare that he will leave his town, which no longer holds any joy for him, only blame and spite, and to denounce love itself and to prophesy unhappiness for his beloved who has given herself to a man who does not understand her (Hyde, *Love Songs* 7).

The sorrow of love is the theme of "Long Am I Going," which has two speakers, a man and a woman:

'Tis a pity without me to be married[5]
    With the bright treasure of my heart,
On the brink by the great river
    Or at the nearer ditch by its side.
Company of young women,
    It is they who would raise my heart,
And I would be a year younger
    If I were married to my desire.

(Hyde, *Love Songs* 25)

On the halls of this great house
    Resides and does be my white love,
Altogether (?) (*he is*) my knowledge-star;
    What I am sure of is that he is not to be got;

I would think his kiss sweeter
   Than the b'yore and the sugar white; [6]
And, unless I get you to marry,
   What I think certain is that my heart will not be whole.

(27)

The woman laments that the garden is a wilderness and all fruit spoiled for her because she desires a man she cannot have (27). Perhaps the saddest of the love songs is spoken by a woman whose lover has crossed the sea:

My grief on the sea,
   How the waves of it roll!
For they heave between me
   And the love of my soul!

Abandoned, forsaken,
   To grief and to care,
Will the sea ever waken
   Relief from despair?
   . . . .
On a green bed of rushes
   All last night I lay,
And I flung it abroad
   With the heat of the day.

And my love came behind me—
   He came from the South;
His breast to my bosom,
   His mouth to my mouth.

("My Grief on the Sea," Hyde, *Love Songs* 2931).[7]

Another convention of Irish love poems was the comparison of the beloved with legendary queens (Deirdre or Helen), with the declaration that the beloved was more beautiful. Raftery tells of Mary Staunton, who lived on a quay in Galway and was considered to be extremely beautiful. In the song she is called "a lovely POSY lives by the ROADWAY," a "sky-woman" who kindles light from her bosom when she walks, "the Star of Monday," who is more beautiful than Deirdre or Helen. Her cheeks are like roses growing among lilies, her mouth melodious with songs, her waist narrow and chalk-white, her countenance like roses, her hair shining like the dew, "her two breasts equal-round over against her heart." She appears like harvest dew and is compared with apple-blossom (Hyde, *Raftery* 321–25).

Raftery sang even more gloriously of the Posy Bright of Ballylee, a peasant woman who was the most beautiful in the west of Ireland for a hundred years. She too is a "sky-woman," and those who see her find that words are insufficient to praise her beauty and her manners (325). She lived in Ballylee near Gort Inse-Guaire. "I never saw a woman as handsome as she, and I never shall till I die," said an old man to Lady Gregory. An old fiddler who claimed to remember her remarked, "Mary Hynes was the finest thing that was ever shaped. There usedn't to be a hurling match in the county that she wouldn't be at it, and a white dress on her always. Eleven men asked her in marriage in one single day, but she would not marry any one of them. There were a number of young men sitting up drinking one night, and they fell to talking about Mary Hynes, and a man of them stole away to go to Ballylee to see her, and when he came to the Bog of Cloone he fell into the water and was drowned" (327). Another old man said, "The strongest man that we had, and that Shawn O'—, he got his death on the head of her, going across the river in the night hoping to see her." An old woman declared that the sun and moon were not so fine as she, and that all praised her courtesy highly (327–29). She was a "jewel-woman," the fairest in the world, fairer than Deirdre, Venus, or Helen, a "Star of Light, O Sun of Harvest" (333).

Hyde tells us that she welcomed blind Raftery with a hundred welcomes. Raftery followed Mary Hynes to her house and although he, being blind, could not see her beauty, he could write a song about her.[8] Yeats also collected the story of Mary Hynes, who was believed to be the most beautiful woman the west of Ireland had ever produced. She lived in Ballylee, and her story was told for sixty and more years after her death. Yeats heard the story of the men drinking in Kilbecanty and the one who died in Cloone Bog as he attempted to learn the truth of the tale. Another man, the strongest in the countryside, named John Madden, died while trying to cross the river at night to get to Ballylee to see her. Yeats wrote that because of their generous spirits and their love of beauty, "These poor countrymen and countrywomen in their beliefs, and in their emotions, are many years nearer to that old Greek world, that set beauty beside the fountain of things, than are our men of learning" ("Dust hath closed Helen's Eye," *My-thologies* 28).

In "The Tower" Yeats incorporates this theme of the power of the legend to inspire the poet's song about beauty he cannot see. One of the images the speaker summons is that of Mary Hynes. Yeats's treatment of her, however, is much different from Raftery's, for in Yeats's version the song itself—art—confers the glory on the woman rather than her providing inspiration for the song ("So great a glory did the song confer"). Not her face but the song (poetry and music) drove the men mad who sat drinking and toasting her, and caused one man to drown "in the great bog of Cloone" (*Poems* 195).

Yeats is less respectful of Mary Hynes than Raftery is, for he does not celebrate her manners, kindness, or beauty, but rather the song that drove men mad and the legend that created the song. In other words, art (lyric poetry and stories) inspires the men so strongly, not what they see with their own eyes. He wants to question the poet, "beauty's blind rambling celebrant," and the drowned man whose wits were driven astray by the song ("The man drowned in a bog's mire, / When mocking muses chose the country wench" [*Poems* 197]), for they know secrets the speaker wishes to know about love, the heart, the legendary history of the countryside. Mary Hynes in Yeats's poem is "A peasant girl commended by a song, / Who'd lived somewhere upon that rocky place" (*Poems* 195). The few who remembered her had "greater joy in praising her" not because of her fine manners but because of the power of the song to influence men:

> Remembering that, if walked she there,
> Farmers jostled at the fair
> So great a glory did the song confer.
>
> (195)

Those who praised her were maddened by the poet's rhymes, or else were driven mad by their own words of praise ("And certain men, being maddened by those rhymes, / Or else by toasting her a score of times,"), and declared that they must "test their fancy by their sight"—measure the dream against the reality. Theirs is a disastrous decision, for the reality is transformed by the dream and can never be measured. Furthermore, they cannot test their dream because they have lost their senses and are unable to perceive the tangible world:

But they mistook the brightness of the moon
For the prosaic light of day—
Music had driven their wits astray—.

(195)

They do not know that, once inspired by the music and the legend, they can never look upon the physical world in the same realistic ("prosaic") way, for poetry has inspired them ("Music had driven their wits astray—") and their efforts to "test their fancy" end in disaster: "And one was drowned in the great bog of Cloone" (195). The pursuit of a dream destroys the pursuer.

The dream vision of beauty or a life full of happiness or inspiration informed the Irish poetry of love, and it was this that Yeats and Synge incorporated into their writing. Yeats praised Synge's delight in language, which made him resemble the great writers, and his preoccupation with individual life and with what was lasting and noble, that came to him from listening to old stories in the cottages, not from books. It was Synge who demonstrated that the dialect in Hyde's translations could become a powerful new literary idiom. Yeats wrote that the only literature the Irish country people possessed were their songs, full of extravagant love, and their stories of kings and of kings' children ("Preface to the First Edition of *The Well of the Saints*," *Essays* 303). Every writer who was part of a great tradition has had his dream of an impossibly noble life, and the greater he is, the more does it plunge him into some beautiful or bitter reverie:

Mr. Synge, indeed, sets before us ugly, deformed or sinful people, but his people, moved by no practical ambition, are driven by a dream of that impossible life. That we may feel how intensely his Woman of the Glen dreams of days that shall be entirely alive, she that is "a hard woman to please" must spend her days between a sour-faced old husband, a man who goes mad upon the hills, a craven lad and a drunken tramp; and those two blind people of *The Well of the Saints* are so transformed by the dream that they choose blindness rather than reality. He tells us of realities, but he knows that art has never taken more than its symbols from anything that the eye can see or the hand measure. (304)

Synge's characters, wrote Yeats, are preoccupied with the dream of this impossible life, and of greatness of love. Their emotional subtlety stems from this dream that they might transcend their surroundings to find their own desire. The attainable is not part of his plays; moreover, the characters themselves—like everyone caught up in great events—do not know why they act as they do:

> She (Nora Burke) feels an emotion that she does not understand. She is driven by desires that need for their expression, not "I admire this man," or "I must go, whether I will or no," but words full of suggestion, rhythms of voice, movements that escape analysis. In addition to all this, she has something that she shares with none but the children of one man's imagination. She is intoxicated by a dream which is hardly understood by herself, but possesses her like something half remembered on a sudden wakening. . . . For though the people of the play use no phrase they could not use in daily life, we know that we are seeking to express what no eye has ever seen. (305)

Nora Burke's longing for a life of greater richness and excitement suggests pathos and melancholy. She faces a situation extremely harsh and severe—her husband is setting her out on the road, without food, shelter, or protection. The motif is common in Irish poetry: in the aristocratic songs, the protagonist was a noblewoman, wife of a chief or prince; but in the peasants' love songs, she might be any woman unhappily wed. The husband is hard and cold; he fails to satisfy her; she strikes out against the marriage, which was usually arranged by the parents. She wishes for her husband's death so that she can escape with her lover. One common feature of the songs is the argument between the aged husband and the restless wife, in which he invariably loses patience and vows to cast her out on the roads without food or clothes (Kiberd, *Synge* 127).

Donal O'Sullivan collects two folk songs that relate the tale of a young woman married to an aged man. The first ends with the woman freed from her burden:

> By prayer and entreaty and threat they did worry me
>   To be wed to the gaffer my youth denied,

On leaden feet to the priest they did hurry me,
  With a heart stone dead while the knot was died.
I like not his gait nor the rheumy red eyes of him,
His furry grey brows, the groans and the sighs of him,
I long for a young man, to lie and to rise with him,
  Who would kiss and caress me at morning-tide!
. . . .
Last night as I lay between waking and sleeping
  I heard that my wretched old man was dead;
I leapt from the pillow, my gratitude heaping
  On the man in the ditch who had done the deed.
They made up their story while still there was breath in him,
  'Twas the bay mare that kicked him—that was the death
    of him,
Go, take to the young man this news that is best for him—
  In the grave at Kilcockan my wretch is laid! [9]

The second song contains elements similar to the plot of *The Shadow of the Glen*. The woman, wishing for her husband's death, dreams of going off with her young lover. Believing her husband to be dead, she makes preparations for his wake, only to return to find him alive:

I went off to Cork to get whiskey to wake him,
Tobacco and snuff, and a coffin to make him.
I then started homeward and—as I'm a sinner—
There was my old man a-cooking his dinner!

(76)

O'Sullivan quotes Conrad Arensberg (*The Irish Countryman* 1937) on the important custom of the arranged marriage in Irish rural society and speculates that few marriages between an elderly man and young woman would have been contracted, since the principal object in such a union would be perpetuation of the family line. During the eighteenth century, however, incidents of matches between people "'misgraffed' in respect of years" (O'Sullivan 72) took place, and so the songs—which help to disprove Arthur Griffith's claim that Synge borrowed his plot from Greek rather than Irish sources—came into being. In point of fact, the situation described in the play is universally applicable, since people in nearly every place and time have been known to marry for economic reasons, whether or not the match was "arranged."

In *The Shadow of the Glen*, Synge presents dramatically the story of the young wife caught in a loveless, arranged marriage. To this he adds the theme of Patch Darcy's madness brought on by isolation and perhaps by the knowledge that he can never have Nora, for she is already married.

The women of Ireland, Synge wrote, could look forward to a life much different from that which was described in their love poetry. The greatest merit which the men of Aran could see in a woman was that she should bring them many children:

> The direct sexual instincts are not weak on the island, but they are so subordinated to the instincts of the family that they rarely lead to irregularity. The life here is still at an almost patriarchal stage, and the people are nearly as far from the romantic moods of love as they are from the impulsive life of the savage. (*CW* 2: 144)

These are not the sentiments of romance heard so clearly in the songs ascribed to Raftery or in those collected by Hyde. Women of Aran expected unhappiness and dissatisfaction.

> The maternal feeling is so powerful on these islands that it gives a life of torment to the women. Their sons grow up to be banished as soon as they are of age, or to live here in continual danger on the sea; their daughters go away also, or are worn out in their youth with bearing children that grow up to harass them in their own turn a little later. (*The Aran Islands* II, *CW* 2: 108)

Men seemed to fare little better than women. The unmarried man was not valued for himself, but rather as a potential husband. An islandman told Synge:

> . . . Listen to what I'm telling you: a man who is not married is no better than an old jackass. He goes into his sister's house, and into his brother's house; he eats a bit in this place and a bit in another place, but he has no home for himself; like an old jackass straying on the rocks. (121)

This sentiment is repeated in *The Playboy* by Michael James, father of Pegeen, when he hears that she is determined to marry Christy and not Shawn:

> What's a single man, I ask you, eating a bit in one house and drinking a sup in another, and he with no place of his own, like an old braying jackass strayed upon the rocks? (*CW* 4: 157)

Synge may also be drawing here from the mockery of poet Brian Merriman in *The Midnight Court* (c. 1780) because he is thirty years old and unmarried.

The loveless rural marriage of *The Shadow of the Glen* was contracted because of necessity. Pat Dirane's tale of the unfaithful wife emphasized the husband's ruthless cunning, while Synge emphasizes the sterility of rural Irish life (Watson 78). Nora's only hope of escape is little better than her marriage: Michael Dara is cowardly and greedy. One suspects that he too is little capable of satisfying her. As G. J. Watson makes clear, Michael Dara in the final version of the play is the weak and somewhat comical forerunner of Shawn Keogh. In earlier drafts, Dara is a "fine handsome man," very sure of himself. The change in his personality darkens the tone and shows more poignantly Nora's predicament. Dara's greed and Dan Burke's bitterness contrast with Nora's humility, loneliness, and sense of mortality. The hopeless reality is contrasted with her dreams of love and fulfillment.

Nora Burke leaves the "civilized" world that promises her nothing. Yeats's Crazy Jane, a countrywoman by her description of her surroundings, faces a loveless old age, but her way of dealing with her loneliness is to curse the world and to refuse to respect social convention. Many of Yeats's poetic speakers, both in the early poems and the later ones, are beggars and old men and women (Moll Magee, the Old Mother, the Old Pensioner, Father O'Hart, Father Gilligan) whose age has reduced them to a state of poverty and rags, and of spiritual or emotional deprivation. Yeats transformed the Crazy Jane of legend into an old hag for whom sexual love and desire have become the meaning of life.[10] Like the woman of popular tradition, Jane gives her virginity to a lover who is gone but whose memory she cherishes. The poems resemble ballads in their simple diction and unequivocal facing of tragic emotion. Although the tone of "Crazy Jane and the Bishop" may resemble that of "The Ballad of Moll Magee," who laments her lost child, husband, and youth, the theme is quite different. Moll asks the children to pity her and to desist from throwing stones, while Jane feels no remorse for anything, only anger that her beloved was banished, and she asks for no pity.

The Crazy Jane cycle of literature, about a poor maniac girl who becomes mad as a result of her lover's leaving her, extends about one hundred fifty years, beginning with Matthew Gregory Lewis's "The Ballad of Crazy Jane" (written between 1793 and 1801). "Crazy Jane" appeared on broadsides and in popular song chapbooks for half a century. A chapbook published in 1813 by Sarah Wilkinson describes Jane as seventeen, beautiful, and very poor. Jane falls in love with her brother-in-law, Henry, surrenders her virginity to him, and says farewell to peace for her lifetime. Henry goes to London and the West Indies, while Jane, alone, discovers she is pregnant and aborts her child. She goes mad and lives two years more as a maniac, wandering in places where she had met Henry. After her death he returns, repentant, and commits suicide on her grave, and is buried beside her under a yew tree. Various theatrical versions of the story remained in popular tradition for a century, until it died away toward the close of the nineteenth century. Wilkinson's epitaph for Jane reads:

> Traveler, stop, whoe'er thou art,
> Shed a tear ere thou depart;
> For here, releas'd from care and pain,
> Lies Love's sad victim, Crazy Jane.[11]

In a play by Charles Somerset, Jane's father calls down curses on the head of her lover, as Jane calls down curses on the Bishop in "Crazy Jane and the Bishop." The first line of the poem, "Bring me to the blasted oak," may have been suggested by a woodcut of Jane before a tree (Munch-Pedersen 68). Yeats's play *The Pot of Broth* (1904; first performance 1902) contains a song with a reference to Jack the Journeyman and a note pertaining to her name.

> The words and the air of "There's Broth in the Pot" were taken down from an old woman known as Cracked Mary, who wanders about the plain of Aidhne, and who sometimes sees unearthly riders on white horses coming through stony fields to her hovel door in the night time. (*Variorum Plays* 254)

Jack the Journeyman may have come from Lady Gregory's play *A Losing Game* in which she uses the common motif in Irish folklore of the jealous old husband and the young wife (Hoffman 72). Cracked Mary and Crazy Jane of the ballads, however, are heartbroken jilted lovers. Yeats transforms the character into a rebel against convention and a spokeswoman for sexual love: his Jane lives on, full of vigor, love, and hate.

Gaelic love songs reveal a delight in melancholy recklessness and wildness of speech. As Robert Welch argues in "Yeats's Crazy Jane Poems and Gaelic Love Song," their speakers' intensity of passion places them outside the pale of normalcy; their imaginations are distracted. Distracted feelings are not "normal," and we find the speaker saying that others advise him or her to have nothing to do with this craziness.[12] The theme of setting aside ordinary things is common in European love poetry, but in Gaelic songs it has immediacy, outrageousness, a mood of liberation, and frenzy (Welch 232). The lunatic, such as King Goll, can represent the spontaneity of the subjective animal world. Yeats, in the Crazy Jane poems, recovers a strong affinity with the Gaelic love songs, because these songs established a world of erotic anguish in which places and things are charged with immeasurable significance. In Yeats's version of "Love Song: From the Gaelic" the lovers express their faith that they will be safe in the woods:

> My love, we will go, we will go, I and you,
> And away in the woods we will scatter the dew;
> And the salmon behold, and the ousel too,
> My love, we will hear, I and you, we will hear,
> The calling afar of the doe and the deer.
> And the bird in the branches will cry for us clear,
> And the cuckoo unseen in his festival mood;
> And death, oh my fair one, will never come near
> In the bosom afar of the fragrant wood.
>
> (*Variorum Poems* 717)

Like Sweeney in *Buili Shuibhne* (*Mad Sweeney*), the peasant lovers become extremely sensitive to the details of the natural world around them.

Just as the speaker in "My Grief on the Sea" utters the pain of loss and unfulfilled desire, "Crazy Jane on the Day of Judgment" reveals erotic longing and the desire to be absorbed into the being of the other.

> 'Love is all
> Unsatisfied
> That cannot take the whole
> Body and soul';
> *And that is what Jane said.*

> (*Poems* 257)

The speakers in both poems lie in the grass and dream that their lovers come to them. Longing and secrecy lead to madness.

> 'Naked I lay
> The grass my bed;
> Naked and hidden away,
> That black day';
> *And that is what Jane said.*

In the Irish Gaelic poem, the lover hallucinates as she dreams that her beloved, who is on his way to America, returns to her:

> On a green bed of rushes
>   All last night I lay,
> And I flung it abroad
>   With the heat of the day.

> And my love came behind me—
>   He came from the South;
> His breast to my bosom,
>   His mouth to my mouth.

> (Hyde, *Love Songs* 31)

The two mysterious singers delight in irrationality and strangeness, in abandoning conventional mores, caution, and rationality. Jane becomes mad in order to find out what true love is, which cannot be shown until time is gone.

'What can be shown?
What true love be?
All could be known or shown
If Time were but gone.'
That's certainly the case, said he.

A tryst between a mad woman and the ghost of a dead lover, a common theme in Irish love poetry, frames the action of "Crazy Jane and the Bishop" (*Poems* 255–56), in which Jane's strength of feeling prevails over the religious strictures of the bishop. Crazy Jane cries out to be led to the "blasted" oak, like Lear upon the heath who cries out against betrayal. She wants to "call down curses" on the head of the bishop who banished her lover, Jack the Journeyman. He wasn't even a bishop when he accused them of living "like beast and beast," not even parish priest, yet he was fierce ("an old book in his fist"). His piousness and righteousness are powerful enough to prevent them from being together, but powerless to prevent the ugliness of old age—she states triumphantly that his skin is "Wrinkled like the foot of a goose"—nor can his habit conceal his physical deformity, "The heron's hunch upon his back."[13] Jack, who had been straight and tall ("But a birch-tree stood my Jack"), calls her to the oak tree, which is solid and stately (not the yew-tree of legend), to meet his ghost.

The second refrain in each stanza compares the two men. Jane has chosen the "solid man" who stands tall. The bishop is a "coxcomb" because he is ludicrous, waving his old book and ordering her about, and because he degrades love; furthermore, as a hunchback, belonging to Phase Twenty-Six, he is not an admirable character.[14]

The last line before the refrain echoes "The Lamentation of the Old Pensioner" (Poems 46) in which the speaker declares, "I spit into the face of Time / That has transfigured me." Jane declares that "should that other come, I spit." The "other" is the bishop, who apparently still tyrannizes her. The first refrain adds a level of difficulty to an otherwise straightforward poem. "Safety in the tomb" may derive from Synge's *Deirdre* play. The bishop is not likely to declare that "All find safety in the tomb," for he believes in sin and punishment. Clearly Jack has not found safety, for his ghost walks at night, although this refrain may be what he says to her. Jane will not be safe in the tomb,

for she is unrepentant. Nor is she, with her blasphemous and anticleri-
cal sentiments, the type to desire safety. Perhaps Jane as speaker of the
refrains wishes to live and to avoid "safety" that she thinks everyone
will eventually find in death.

In "Crazy Jane and Jack the Journeyman," Jane foretells the time
she will be in the tomb and will no longer be able to satisfy the lovers
who come to her at night. She does not care that they leave, physical
love being sufficient for her even though it is transient:

> I know, although when looks meet
> I tremble to the bone,
> The more I leave the door unlatched
> The sooner love is gone,
> For love is but a skein unwound
> Between the dark and dawn.
>
> (258)

The ghost which finally leaves the cycles of reincarnation and returns
to God is lonely, as were the saints and angels in the Irish poems who
were jealous of the living lovers. Jane does not desire union with God
but reunion with the other world from which she can enter into life
again:

> I—love's skein upon the ground,
> My body in the tomb—
> Shall leap into the light lost
> In my mother's womb.

She wants to continue to engage in free love. Had she remained faith-
ful to Jack, her life would have been unfulfilled, and her unhappy
spirit would walk the roads after her death, searching for what she
had missed:

> But were I left to lie alone
> In an empty bed,
> The skein so bound us ghost to ghost
> When he turned his head
> Passing on the road that night,
> Mine would walk being dead.

Having rejected both religion and fidelity, Crazy Jane expresses her faith in permanence, which to her is continuity, in "Crazy Jane on God" (258–59). *"All things remain in God"* she sings at the end of each stanza, equating all experience—personal (love), public (war), or cosmic (the cycles of history). Her unnamed lover leaves her after a night of love; armies meet "In the narrow pass" for battle; a house which represents generations burns to the ground; Jane herself who was "wild" Jack's lover becomes "like a road / That men pass over." She regrets nothing and asks for no pity. Her body (not her soul) rejoices ("sings on"), for although individuals and nations experience upheaval, she finds permanence in moments of great emotion—love or passion.

Declan Kiberd suggests that Crazy Jane may have been patterned on one of the most famous of all Old Irish poems, "The Hag of Beare," in which a licentious old woman, preparing for death in a monastery, unrepentently recalls her lifetime of sin.[15] The poem is a metaphorical account of a poet who served many lords before seeking refuge in religion. The old harlot of the poem turns unwillingly to religion after being rejected in old age by her lovers; similarly, Crazy Jane does not lament her sinful youth but nevertheless repeats words of devotion:

> Though like a road
> that men pass over
> My body makes no moan
> But sings on:
> *All things remain in God.*
>
> (259)

Crazy Jane reaches her greatest exuberance and irreligiousness in "Crazy Jane Talks with the Bishop" (259–60). She uses orthodox Christian symbols to refute the bishop's puritanical (and "sensible") argument. Jane personifies Love, as Christ was equated with Love. Her use of "mansion" echoes not only the Bishop's words ("Live in a heavenly mansion, / Not in some foul sty"), but Christ's: "In my Father's house are many mansions: if it were not so, I would have told you" (*John* 14: 2). Neither death nor love (grave nor bed) denies that the desirable (beauty) and undesirable (excrement)—fair and foul—are part of the same thing, just as Christ was simultaneously divine (fair) and human (foul). Fair and foul are "near of kin" and must exist together as love and death exist together with the "heart's pride." In the last stanza "Love" takes on a new meaning. When a woman is intent upon winning her love, she may be "proud and stiff." Love here is spiritual. But "Love," both spiritual and physical, "has pitched his mansion in / The place of excrement." The spiritual and physical are one now, inseparable. Mansions are seldom "pitched," as tents are, yet perhaps all things are possible for Love, or for a God who takes a human form, dies, and lives again.

Jane's depth of feeling prevails over the Bishop's stern advice, for she knows what he does not—that the spirit is not simple and pure, that it is part of the living body. She demonstrates the truth of her convictions not only through her argument but through her choice of words, not only "Love" and "mansion" (which she borrows from the Bishop) but "pitch," which means both "set up" and "throw"; "rent," another Biblical term ("And the sun was darkened, and the veil of the temple was rent in the midst" [*Luke* 23: 45]); and "sole" and "whole." She affirms that whatever is to be "sole" (one) or "whole" (unified) must be rent asunder, as the veil of the tabernacle was upon the death of Christ who would make the soul one with God; "sole" and "whole" pun on "soul"—that with which the Bishop is concerned—and "hole"—Jane's concern, although she too understands the importance of the spirit and love. To Jane, a "heavenly mansion" is lifeless and empty, as was the heaven in the Irish love poems, while an earthly mansion can be filled with love.

Gaelic poetry emphasizes the desire to escape from ordinary existence and live with passion and daring; love inspires the speakers in these poems to dream of an impossible life. Reality in the form of passing time or separation from the beloved threatens to annihilate this dream, and usually succeeds. The use of peasant speakers in love poetry and drama enables Yeats and Synge to be irreligious, outrageous, and earthy. Their speakers, like those in the Irish poems, do not inhabit a pastoral environment in which conflict is finally resolved in favor of the lovers; rather, civilization and necessity (old age, separation, poverty) keep the lovers apart. The only resolution is in the poetic expression of despair, loneliness, and depth of feeling which allows the lovers to share in the common bond of experience.

Chapter 5

"A man who does not exist": The Peasant as Wanderer, Outlaw, Beggar, Seer

In all of J. M. Synge's plays except *Riders to the Sea*, the heroes reject the "respectable" life offered them by society or community. The speakers of W. B. Yeats's peasant poems usually abandon conventional society. The peasant in these works is a wanderer or hermit, a seer or prophet who voices the unfulfilled desires of an individual or a nation. He protests against the oppression of his country by another country, the blindness of his own people, the necessity of old age and poverty, the restrictions of law and religion. The peasant can be eloquent or outrageous, for he has no need to live up to social expectations. Yeats and Synge both describe the peasants as resembling aristocrats more closely than members of the middle class, just as the wild horse more nearly resembles the thoroughbred than the hack or cart horse: the simile suggests that they viewed the vagrant or peasant as freer and nobler than those of the middle class. Physical deprivation gives him insight into the nature of life. Unencumbered by material possessions or desire for gain, the beggar or hermit is free to meditate on questions of ultimate truth or spiritual mystery. Although society frequently attempts to stifle the creativity of the wanderer, he remains—like Thoreau—spiritually free and superior to those who live within civilized society.

The literature of rogues, outlaws, and adventurers appealed to a literate peasant audience, according to Carleton's fictional accounts and many of Yeats's sources for *Fairy and Folk Tales of the Irish Peasantry* (Thuente 164). A good example of an Irish hero-rogue who is a projection of an angry population is that of Finn who is both noble, conquering hero and victor through cunning and guile.[1] In an article of 1891 Yeats celebrates the recklessness, turbulent spirit, and wild passion of the Irish rakes and duelists of the eighteenth century ("A Reckless Century. Irish Rakes and Duelists," *UP* 1: 198–202). These men—some of them Catholic gentlemen defeated at the Boyne, many of them shopkeepers, artisans, and the poor who had no longer any national leadership—were full of courage and cynical acceptance of death. National responsibility was not yet awakened in them.

> During all the early part of the eighteenth century the nation had little or no sense of national duty and public responsibility, the proper chiefs of the people were dead or exiled with foreign armies, the bards had passed away—the last bardic college came to an end in 1680—and the ballad-makers had only just begun to take their place. (201)

Although Yeats may be reaching far to create a tradition, what is more important is that he extols the tempestuous spirit of the people of these stories, which he interprets as the same "Celtic" intensity, fire, and daring that will give Ireland great poets and thinkers (201–2).

Synge adopted the view that the tramp represented the imaginative life because he had been liberated from the gnawing frustration of life on the island. In his essays on Wicklow and West Kerry, Synge suggests that the vitality and distinctive temperament of laborers beget tramps. Vagrants constituted the natural aristocracy of Wicklow: the laborer possessed a temperament of distinction, and the gifted progeny of peasants and laborers became tramps just as among the middle classes the gifted children were least likely to be economically successful.

> In the middle classes the gifted son of a family is always the poorest—usually a writer or artist with no sense for speculation—and in a family of peasants, where the average comfort is just over penury, the gifted son sinks also, and is soon a tramp on the roadside. ("The Vagrants of Wicklow," *CW* 2: 202)

The existence of tramps was not to be regretted, for their appearance in great numbers was evidence to Synge of this giftedness among the peasantry. In places where the laborers and peasants had preserved their vitality, a certain number of vagrants was to be expected. The tramp and Nora Burke of *The Shadow of the Glen*, Mary Byrne in *The*

Tinker's Wedding, and Martin Doul in *The Well of the Saints,* born into higher circles, could have been writers or artists. The wandering life nurtured individual vitality and imagination just as society stifled it.

> Man is naturally a nomad ... and all wanderers have finer intellectual and physical perceptions than men who are condemned to local habitations. The cycle, automobile and conducted tours are half-conscious efforts to replace the charm of the stage coach and of pilgrimages like Chaucer's. But the vagrant, I think, along with perhaps the sailor, has preserved the dignity of motion with its whole sensation of strange colours in the clouds and of strange passages with voices that whisper in the dark and still stranger inns and lodgings, affections and lonely songs that rest for a whole life time with the perfume of spring evenings or the first autumnal smoulder of the leaves. (Notebook entries, "[People and Places]," *CW* 2: 195–96)

The healthiness of the outdoor life allowed the tramps to live to great age, although many stories of longevity were exaggerated. The tramps' privilege was in being little troubled by laws or other restrictions. A few people inherited their status as wanderers, but often they were merely ordinary people who drifted from village life and did not differ from the classes from which they came (202).

Among the old vagrants Synge found wise people whose lives he believed resembled works of art. Their talk was humorous and their ideas distinctive; they lived more fully than most people whose lives were more conventional. Their revenge on strangers who did not accord them their due respect was to call down curses from heaven (195). The vagrants of Ireland bore no resemblance to the mendicants of Italy, for mobility was a condition of the existence of tramp life in Ireland, and the greater number he saw were vigorous women and men of fine physique. Unlike the poor of the Continent, they made no pretense of infirmity. When treated with tact they were courteous; when rudely answered they avenged themselves with a word of satire. They rarely committed crimes or were drunk or unseemly. The freshness of their wit, equally sure in the women and the men, never lost a point that could be turned to profit or revenge and further distinguished the Irish tramps from the beggars of Europe (196–97).

Synge's plays involve small communities and fugitives or wanderers of one sort or another. *The Tinker's Wedding* involves a camp and a church near a settlement at which there is a fair. The dichotomy is established between the camp and church—the profane and the sacred—and the camp and the community—the free and the restricted, the savage and the civilized, the poor and the (relatively) affluent. *The Well of the Saints* is set at a crossroads with a church near a settlement where the peasant tradespeople work. *The Shadow of the Glen* takes place in a farmhouse secluded on a hill with a village below. In *Riders to the Sea* the cottage and island are surrounded by the sea and the larger world of Donegal and Connemara. *The Playboy of the Western World* takes place entirely in a shebeen near a settlement on the shore of the west coast of County Mayo near Sligo, where "harvest hundreds" pass through for the boats that take them to England. For Christy, the shebeen represents a place of safety from the villagers and the people of the outside world, the peelers and Old Mahon, and from loneliness. Synge presents the tension between the community's mores, expectations, and customs, and the individual's imagination, desire for freedom, and creativity. In the wanderer's rebellion against social restrictions and conventional morality we see the artists' demand for freedom to create as well as Ireland's struggle for independence. At the same time, such marginalization as the tinkers experience represents the state of colonized Ireland and—more specifically to the artist's purposes—the voice of the writer who is forging a new "national" literature from a history of people forced onto the sidelines by a stronger power.

Irreverent and blasphemous, the tinkers in *The Tinker's Wedding* and Christy Mahon in *The Playboy* reject religious and parental authority and conformism. Sarah Casey need never look to the religion of the civilized world at all, for she is happier when restored to her unorthodox but natural life.[2] *The Tinker's Wedding* presents another aspect of the romantic picture presented in *The Shadow of the Glen*. Rather than leaving the civilized world to enter the natural world, as Nora Burke and the Tramp do, the tinkers Sarah Casey and Michael and Mary Byrne do not seek to enter the civilized world but rather request its sanction—in this case, the marriage rite. The tinkers loudly express their independence from the community: they steal from it and beg from it, but they feel no desire to be part of it. The tinkers prevail in the battle of wits. Mary Byrne's speech reveals her fine imagination as well as her stern grasp of reality. Her songs are full of heathen unbelief:

And when we asked him what way he'd die,
    And he hanging unrepented,
'Begob,' says Larry, 'that's all in my eye,
    By the clergy first invented.'

(CW 4: 17)

She appreciates beauty and independence. Although she terms her son a fool for wanting to marry Sarah Casey, she calls Sarah a "grand handsome woman, the glory of tinkers, the pride of Wicklow, the Beauty of Ballinacree," who should not be lying down lonesome to sleep at night "in a dark ditch when the spring is coming in the trees" (23). She wants to tell Sarah the finest story she would hear in the east of Ireland ("from Dundalk to Ballinacree"), a story of queens in fine silks making matches for themselves. She praises Sarah's strength as well as her looks: "I've a grand story of the great queens of Ireland with white necks on them the like of Sarah Casey, and fine arms would hit you a slap the way Sarah Casey would hit you" (25). Mary's talk, however, also reveals her longing and fear of loneliness.

What good am I this night, God help me? What good are the grand stories I have when it's few would listen to an old woman, few but a girl maybe would be in great fear the time her hour was come, or a little child wouldn't be sleeping with the hunger on a cold night? . . . Maybe the two of them have a good right to be walking out the little short while they'd be young; but if they have itself, they'll not keep Mary Byrne from her full pint when the night's fine, and there's a dry moon in the sky. (27)

She begs them not to leave her alone, but they walk off, ostensibly to steal hens from Tim Flaherty, but really to make love. Mary knows what they are about; she knows the happiness of youth, beauty that is temporal, and the loneliness of old age. She also knows how to deal with the priest, how to get him to talk for her own entertainment and how to take her revenge on him when he insults her. She matter-of-factly invites him to share a drink, remarking sardonically that the night is "cruel dry" and letting him know that she believes he is no better than the tinkers: "Aren't we all sinners, God help us!" (17). She commiserates with him not because she really feels sympathy but because she loves to talk: "It's destroyed you must be hearing the sins of the rural people on a fine spring" (19). She tells him it would break her heart to hear him talking and sighing, and she coaxes him into accepting a drink. When he refuses to hear her song, and rebukes her, saying she will soon die and that she should be on her knees praying (21), she gets her revenge by remarking casually that in all her travels the one thing she has never heard is "a real priest saying a prayer" (21); in other words, she has never felt the need for religion, nor does she fear death. She further scandalizes him by remarking that it would be "great game to hear a scholar," the like of him, "speaking Latin to the saints above" (21). When he says that he never met her like for hard abominations, she feigns innocence, asking "Is that the truth?" and accuses Sarah and him of making "whisper-talk" before "the face of the Almighty God" (21).

A conjurer almost as accomplished as Mary, Sarah encourages Michael to stir up the fire so the priest can see her face, since she knows he can be persuaded by beauty; she has seen him looking out his window and "blinking at the girls" (45). She tells the priest he is a "kind man with the poor" (13)—something he clearly is not—who would surely wed them for nothing. He refuses rudely, but she persuades him, by coaxing and flirting, to marry them for a crown and ten shillings, in addition to the gallon can that Michael is making (15). Before he leaves she extracts his promise, just as all three tinkers will extract his promise not to turn them over to the law for tying him up. Sarah reveals the hypocrisy behind established values when she tells Michael that he should look busy when the priest walks by, "for it's great love the like of him have to talk of work" (13). Michael knows that the priest himself does not work hard, that he indulges in the vices he says he abhors in others: "It's often his reverence does be in there playing cards, or drinking a sup, or singing songs until the dawn of day" (13), and Sarah remarks that they are more likely to make a bargain with the priest after he has been drinking. Mary pretends to disapprove of Sarah's hypocrisy when she flirts with the priest, "the fearfullest old fellow you'd see any place walking the world" (23), but the audience knows that she merely enjoys hearing herself talk.

The audience is on the tinkers' side, for they are right to poke fun at a man who is openly contemptuous of them and clearly hypocriti-cal. The play rejects the stereotype of the ignorant itinerant, for the tinkers' language shows that they are more imaginative and intelligent than the priest. He is greedy and lazy and desires an easy life.

> If it's starving you are itself, I'm thinking it's well for the like of you that do be drinking when there's a drouth on you, and lying down to sleep when your legs are stiff. [*He sighs gloomily.*] What would you do if it was the like of myself you were, saying Mass with your mouth dry, and running east and west for a sick call maybe, and hearing the rural people again and they saying their sins? . . . It's a hard life I'm telling you, a hard life, Mary Byrne; and there's the bishop coming in the morning, and he an old man, would have you destroyed if he seen a thing at all. (19)

Mary loves to sing and talk, to drink with her friends at a fair, and to sleep in the ditch when she is tired, but she does not, like the priest, pretend to be more virtuous than she is. He reveals his own lack of virtue and the selfishness inherent in the desire to be religious without being generous.

The tinkers' constant arguing and unkindness is not due to bad nature but rather liveliness, wit, and desire for entertainment. Mary calls Michael a fool for wanting to marry Sarah and implies that mar-riage will not stop a woman who has made up her mind to leave (35): the sanctity of the marriage rite is not as strong as the desire for freedom. Sarah teases him, saying she will go off with Jaunting Jim or the rich tinkers of Tibradden if he does not marry her (9). He insults Sarah by questioning her fidelity: " . . . it's new thoughts you'll be thinking at the dawn of day?" (7). He retorts that her nickname, the "Beauty of Ballinacree," is what they call horses in Arklow (11), and he groans at her words and his own confession to his mother that he plans to marry Sarah (35). Yet he loves her, for he looks at her in horror when she describes the thoughts of freedom that the springtime in-spires in her: "The like of that, Michael Byrne, when there is a bit of sun in it, and a kind air, and a great smell coming from the thorn trees is above your head" (9).

Even as they enjoy their freedom from the restrictions of religion and society, they are not free from necessity or passing time. Mary verbalizes what will come of Sarah's longing to be married:

It's as good a right you have surely, Sarah Casey, but what good will it do? Is it putting that ring on your finger will keep you from getting an aged woman and losing the fine face you have, or be easing your pains, when it's the grand ladies do be married in silk dresses, with rings of gold, that do pass any woman with their share of torment in the hour of birth, and do be paying the doctors in the city of Dublin a great price at that time, the like of what you'd pay for a good ass and a cart? (37)

Thus, for all their irreverence and satirical humor, the tinkers will face the same end as the priest and the great queens of their stories. They laugh at the rest of the world: " . . . it's little need we ever had of the like of you to get us our bit to eat, and our bit to drink, and our time of love when we were young men and women, and were fine to look at," Mary tells the priest (49). Still, they must run from him in the end, because he has the power to utter maledictions in Latin and to scare them into flight.

The story is drawn from a folktale Synge heard in Wicklow about a pair of tinkers who convinced a priest to marry them for half a sovereign and a tin can. They returned after three weeks to ask the priest again if he would wed them. When he asked for the can, they told him they had finished it but that the ass had kicked it and damaged it so that it wasn't fit for him. "Go on now," the priest retorted. "It's a pair of rogues and schemers you are, and I won't wed you at all" ("At a Wicklow Fair," *CW* 2: 228–29).

One of the most famous Irish indictments of clerical avarice is a song collected by Douglas Hyde for a volume called *Religious Songs of Connacht*, chapter two of the *Songs of Connacht*, from which Synge may have drawn part of the plot for *The Tinker's Wedding:*

Sure if you were dead to-morrow morning
And I were to bring you to a priest tied up in a bag,
He would not read a Mass for you without hand-money.
(quoted in Kiberd, *Synge* 143)[3]

Synge reverses Hyde here, where the priest himself is tied up in a sack as punishment for his selfishness. The occasion is not a death but a wedding, and the priest is tied up not before but after the refusal (144). Another story that may have served as a part of the plot of *The Tinker's*

Wedding was one which he heard on a mountain to the east of Augha-
vanna, in Wicklow. The informant told him that tinkers came from
every part of Ireland and were "gallous lads for walking round
through the world." One time he saw fifty of them on the road to
Rathdangan, matchmaking and marrying themselves for the year that
was to come.

> One man would take such a woman, and say he was going such
> roads and places, stopping at this fair and another fair, till he'd
> meet them again at such a place, when the spring was coming on.
> Another, maybe, would swap the woman he had with one from
> another man, with as much talk as if you'd be selling a cow. ("The
> Vagrants of Wicklow," CW 2: 204)

Synge reverses this story as well, for it is the woman Sarah Casey who
decides she will wed Michael and whose passions drive her in the
springtime of the year.

Synge wrote that peasants were precious possessions for any
country and blamed the middle class for supporting the status quo
that was so abhorrent in the Congested Districts. Even as he lamented
their poverty, however, he loathed the transformation of peasantry
into bourgeois proprietors. He felt that in Mayo the natural, wild,
intuitive life of the peasant had been demoralized and degraded by
religion and materialism; he distrusted religious dogma and detested
modern capitalism.[4] Still, in the tinkers of Wicklow he thought he
observed the kind of freedom that he wanted for all of them. An old
wanderer whom Synge met there had lived more fully than most other
people in the world.

> As he sleeps by Lough Bray and the nightjar burrs and snipe
> drum over his head and the grouse crow, and heather whispers
> round him, he hears in their voices the chant of singers in dark
> chambers of Japan and the clamour of tambourines and [the] fly-
> ing limbs of dancers he knew in Algeria, and the rustle of golden
> fabrics of the east. As the trout splash in the dark water at his feet
> he forgets the purple moorland that is round him and hears waves
> that lap round a boat in some southern sea. He is not to be pitied.
> His life has been a pageant not less grand than Loti's or George
> Borrow's and like all men of culture he has formed a strong con-

cept of the interest of his own personal aspect. He is no leech-gatherer such as Wordsworth met upon the moors but is still full of scorn and humour and impatience. . . . There is something grandiose in a man who has forced all kingdoms of the earth to yield the tribute of this bread and who, at a hundred, begs on the wayside with the pride of an emperor. The slave and beggar are wiser than the man who works for recompense, for all our moments are divine and above all price though their sacrifice is paid with a measure of fine gold. Every industrious worker has sold his birthright for a mess of pottage, perhaps served him in chalices of gold. . . . (CW "[People and Places]," 2: 196)

This is Synge at his most romantic: the wanderer is freer than the property owner because he can go where he likes, untroubled by laws, politics, or material possessions; the beggar can be proud because he makes his own decisions and is, moreover, able to force the kingdoms of the earth to provide for him; the provincial is more cultured than the city-dweller, for culture has nothing to do with education, company, or manners, but with vigorousness of mind and depth of emotion. Like Thoreau's walker, he leaves when he likes, not when he has saved enough for train fare. The countryman or wanderer is more likely to be able to contemplate spiritual matters because he is not materialistic or interested in achieving status. His "natural" life is superior to life in the crowded cities, because it allows him to get closer to God and Eden, the condition of innocent happiness.[5] This romantic view of the country life represented as well the aspirations of a nation long subjugated by another which was considered to be more sophisticated and was certainly more urbanized.

Far more romantic than Synge in his use of the wanderer as a poetic speaker, Yeats makes his beggars and hermits suffer physical privation in order to focus their thoughts on matters of the spirit or of art. In "The Municipal Gallery Re-visited" (Poems 319–21), Yeats wrote that "All that we did, all that we said or sang / Must come from contact with the soil." Heroic Ireland could put thought and art to "that sole test," the "Dream of the noble and the beggarman." Through this unlikely juxtaposition, Yeats tries to show that in order for a nation to be unified, all the people must share in its traditions.

The wanderer or beggar is of course deracinated, marginalized, spiritually homeless, and so is a fitting symbol of the Anglo-Irish predicament (neither truly Irish nor English, wherever he may live). Like the eighteenth-century bards who had an aristocratic self-image even as they wandered as *spalpeens* seeking labor, the Anglo-Irishman feels himself to be a leader but does not possess the loyalty of the people. In "The Curse of Cromwell" Yeats's speaker complains that he has traveled "far and wide" and finds "Nothing but Cromwell's house and Cromwell's murderous crew"; that is, the curse of the invader dooms his descendants to homelessness. An old wandering beggar comes from a line of good servants; the poet-speaker feels similarly exiled within his own nation. Those he would serve with his art are true aristocrats, who are all dead now. The poet aligns himself with aristocrat and peasant, both of whom are displaced by the modern desire for gain.

> All neighbourly content and easy talk are gone,
> But there's no good complaining, for money's rant is on,
> He that's mounting up must on his neighbour mount
> And we and all the Muses are things of no account.
>
> (*Poems* 305)

The poet dreams that he comes upon a great house where he is welcomed, but he wakes to find a ruin, and, like a beggar or peasant, he "must out and walk / Among the dogs and horses that understand my talk."

In this late poem Yeats seems to show that his heroic dream can never again be realized; his true masters are dead. Earlier Yeats wrote that images from the primitive imagination produced legends that informed great literature ("The Celtic Element in Literature," *Essays* 182). These images, expressed in the speech of the common people, could also be used by modern writers to bring the culture of Ireland to the world's attention. Yeats attempted to improve upon the tradition of the "popular" poets by imitating their speech but rejecting their sentimentality. Among his most successful ballad-like poems are those inspired by his contact with country people—"The Ballad of Father Gilligan," "The Ballad of Father O'Hart," "The Ballad of Moll Magee," "The Ballad of the Foxhunter," The Lamentation of the Old Pensioner," and "The Meditation of the Old Fisherman."[6]

Yeats's ballads achieved their lyric form in "Beggar to Beggar Cried" and "Running to Paradise" (Hoffman 41). By adopting the voice of the beggar he uses the simple and direct speech in order to make his feelings universal, something the words of aristocrats cannot do. The aristocratic speaker talks of the loneliness of leadership, and stands for everyone; the few who are heroes walk "proud, open-eyed, and laughing to the tomb." The common man, however, expresses pleasure in sunrise or sunset, an Easter wind from the south. In some of Yeats's later poems, the beggarman becomes one of his favorite poetic voices—one of his masks—because, free from the material world, the beggar, like the Shakespearean fool, can reveal ultimate truths and spiritual mysteries (43). The personalities of Crazy Jane, Tom the Lunatic, the Wild Old Wicked Man, and even the speaker in "The Statesman's Holiday" permit him the manipulation of emotion in dramatic speech, which ballad-like form enhances (48). Edwin Muir writes that Yeats's most consummate triumphs are his "simple riddling songs, filled with the realistic yet credulous imagination of the peasantry . . . that is the kind of song the peasantry might make if they still made songs, with its shrewd satirical evaluation of worldly good, and its belief in another world."[7] The songs of Crazy Jane and Tom the Lunatic, Muir writes, are written out of a peasant judgement of the world and with the images a peasant might use:

> 'Whatever stands in field or flood,
> Bird, beast, fish or man,
> Mare or stallion, cock or hen,
> Stands in God's unchanging eye
> In all the vigour of its blood;
> In that faith I live or die.'
>
> ("Tom the Lunatic," *Poems* 269)

"The peasant believes more strongly than any other class in another world, and is attached more closely by his vocation to this one," Muir writes (59). Irony of situation provides Yeats with the images for poems both spiritual and earthy.

The musing of the old crane of Gort, who concludes that nonchalance is the posture that will bring him his reward, frames the tale of "The Three Beggars" (*Poems* 111–13). Old King Guaire asks the beggars if they can answer a riddle: "Do men who least desire get most, / Or get the most who most desire?" He asks whether desire increases itself or whether indifference brings the greatest reward. The question precedes and anticipates the legendary one which the speaker of "The Tower" is to ask: "Does the imagination dwell the most / Upon a woman won or woman lost?" (*Poems* 197). One of the beggars answers that desire makes the individual strong ("And what could make their muscles taut /Unless desire had made them so?"), that he who possesses strength of will shall have the most. The king promises that the one who falls asleep first (that is, who can be indifferent to his desire) will have a thousand pounds and departs "merry as a bird / With his old thoughts." All the beggars accomplish is to lose three nights' sleep. The first beggar thinks of sexual desire: although he is old he will persuade a pretty girl to share his bed. The second values respectability and dignity: first he says he will learn a trade, then he says he will become a farmer. The third believes that status is important. He would imitate his betters ("the other gentlemen") by laying his thousand pounds on a horse, thereby making himself a gentleman. Their idleness had taught them to dream:

> One to another sighed and cried:
> The exorbitant dreams of beggary,
> That idleness had borne to pride,
> Sang through their teeth from noon to noon.

> (112)

None wins because none is able to put aside desire and adopt an attitude of indifference. The old crane (heron) concludes that he must be indifferent, although by the end of the poem he has not yet attained what he wanted, either.

"The Three Hermits" (113–14) live in a windy, stony place beside "a cold and desolate sea." Their lack of material possessions enables them to contemplate questions of reincarnation and blessedness. Although fearful of impending death and the possibility of returning to earth in "some most fearful shape," the first one cannot stay awake long enough to pray. The second one, though plagued with fleas, manages to keep his belief in just rewards, that men receive what they deserve in the afterlife, and that, should they be God-fearing yet weak of will, they shall have a finer life next time, as a poet, king, or "witty lovely lady." Unlike his counterparts, the third has achieved the gaiety and understanding of spiritual transcendence that will be described so vividly in "Lapis Lazuli." That he sings like a bird in spite of ragged clothes and fleas associates him with King Guaire of the previous poem, and with poets and visionaries, even saints. Unnoticed by those who are still concerned with the body (practicality) and the soul (religion), making no mark in the world, he sings because he is an artist.

A single speaker in "Beggar to Beggar Cried" (114–15) decides to change his life, to leave the world and find bodily and spiritual health, to "make" his "soul" (prepare for death) before he becomes bald. To do this he will live a middle-class life and acquire a wife and house so that he can have physical comfort ("To rid me of the devil in my shoes") and sexual satisfaction ("And the worse devil that is between my thighs"). His wife should not be either too wealthy or too beautiful, for wealth and beauty would prohibit his living comfortably: the rich are "driven" by their wealth as beggars are by the "itch" (and thus the wealthy and poor are equated), and as the comely are plagued by their beauty. Yet as he grows respected at his ease, he will lose the "humorous happy speech" which the poem itself celebrates. He still desires to wander, still is inspired by the "wind-blown clamour of the barnacle-geese." Although he declares that he will settle for the ordinary existence, his decision leaves him *"frenzy-struck."*

Beggars who value the wandering life, as well as those who sing even as they sit on their windy, stony places, are blessed; they are "running to paradise," as is the speaker in the following poem, which reinforces the theme that those who give themselves over to middle-class pursuits such as making money will become dull old men. The beggar here has a fine life, for as he runs toward Paradise, people along the way see to his needs. His brother, having decided to spend his life as a gentleman, has worn himself out in the pursuit of respectability: he beats his "big brawling lout," and keeps a gun, dog, and servants, but is bound down by his possessions. The rich and poor exchange places, the poor achieving wealth and the rich losing it, yet the process results in the loss of imagination, the "humorous happy speech" of the previous poem which is the hallmark of the "darling wit" in this one. He who was content to be bare-heeled at school abandoned the wandering life in order to stuff "an old sock full" of money and has consequently lost his wit and imagination. The speaker will make no such mistake. He cares nothing for material gain nor human company: the wind takes his fancy, for no one can "buy or bind" it. The discordant, unsingable refrain creates a dialectic between itself and the stanza. The king and beggar are the same in Paradise, yet the unitalicized *is* remains mysterious. Rather than implying that in Paradise all are equal in status, the speaker indicates that in consciousness they are one: the king, too, can be happy in Paradise.

Yeats unifies his beggarman poems with imagery of sight, sound, and touch. The series begins with three wrong-headed, silly beggars foolish enough to desire a different way of life and ends with one of Yeats's eloquent affirmations of life. The wind that no one can contain in "Running to Paradise" carries the clamor of the geese in "Beggar to Beggar Cried." The sea air which will bring health to the beggar chills the three hermits. All are ragged and live outdoors exposed to the elements in desolate, stony places. The hermits and beggars of the first two poems are plagued by lice and fleas. For all this, there is merriment, movement, noisy but vigorous cursing and argument ("brawling"), melodious singing. In spite of their poverty, these characters celebrate life.

All these images are brought together in the final poem of this series, "The Hour Before Dawn" (116–19), in which a beggar wanders in a "windy place." The beggar, "A bundle of rags upon a crutch," anticipates the aged man of "Sailing to Byzantium," who is merely a "tattered coat upon a stick." This beggar is at first a "cursing rogue," profane, not in pursuit of heaven or given to thinking about spiritual matters. He, like King Guaire, is "merry." At the magical hour before dawn, he finds himself on Cruachan (Roscommon), a magical mountain, for Maeve's nine Maines (the children of Ailill) were nursed there, and "an ancient history" declared that "Hell Mouth lay open near that place." Things look good at first, for he spies the possibility of a meal—he counts a pair of lapwings and a sheep with no house nearby—and of constructing a shelter out of stones. However, as he fumbles with the stones he uncovers a deep hollow in the mountain; he prepares to flee until his fears are dissipated by the sight of a "great lad with a beery face," who snores away, "no phantom by his look." He awakens the lad who mistakes him for one of Maeve's brawling sons who, sick of his grave, is walking.

In his first affirmation of life, the rogue angrily demands that he not be called a ghost. Nor will he be quiet, he says: he will talk as he helps himself to the beer. The sleeper, however, will not allow the beggar to drink his magical potion, the beer "from Goban's mountain-top" that enables him to sleep as long as he desires. The rogue would sleep away the winter, yet the lad remarks that he too began with such

a simple idea, but gradually lost interest in life until he desired only
to sleep to his death. His sleep is now nine centuries long. The rogue
cannot bear this insult to life. He cries out in a rage:

> 'It's plain that you are no right man
> To mock at everything I love
> As if it were not worth the doing.
> I'd have a merry life enough
> If a good Easter wind were blowing,
> And though the winter wind is bad
> I should not be too down in the mouth
> For anything you did or said
> If but this wind were in the south.'

(118–19)

The sleeper argues that "all life longs for the Last Day," that human
activity comes to nothing at all. Souls will be but "sighs," flesh and
bone will disappear, leaving behind nothing, not even a "smoking
wick." The sleeper, being blessed (he says), keeps to his cleft like a
rabbit and waits for God in a drunken sleep, for nothing matters but
heaven. The rogue cannot stand this idea. With "great pummelling"
he vents his rage on the sleeper—who is entirely impervious to physi-
cal abuse, unable to feel anything—then buries him in his mountain
hollow as if he were something evil, heaping up stone on stone and
then heaping up more stones, so eager is he to keep this denial of life
from being known in the world. The rogue embodies the contraries
of rage and merriment (anger and joy). The opposite of the sleeper,
he feels physical pain and the discomfort of living out of doors, and
he combines the sacred and the profane—he prays and curses to-
gether, for he loves life with all its privations. He affirms both life and
faith when he flees "From Maeve and all that juggling plain," then
gives thanks as the dawn breaks.

The peasant who abandons the life of the community and strikes
out on his own expresses his individuality as the artist does. Freedom
from social mores and restrictions leads to individuality rather than
to conformity. The tinkers of Synge's play create a life for themselves
which is far more vivid than that of the priest. Yeats's beggars and
hermits voice their desire to wander unfettered, to live essentially,
unmotivated by social aspirations. The hundred-year-old singing her-
mit and the "cursing rogue" are pure life; they celebrate *living* unen-

cumbered by useless things and repressive rules. They are poets who praise the world merely because they live in the world, because dawn follows night, and because, being poor, they have nothing to lose, and so do not have anything to fear. The desire to romanticize the wanderer because he is alone and free to go where he pleases, independent of obligation, springs from a deeply felt conviction that all human beings could be intellectually and spiritually free if they could only abandon materialism and fear of the unknown. Still, the insights of visionaries are not negotiable in a new society of peasant proprietors. Yeats's visionaries inveigh against the philosophy of calculation that was overtaking the rural population, and Synge's must always leave the stage before the curtain drops.

Chapter 6

"A man who is but a dream": The Peasant as Artist and Hero

Because poetry was regarded as a high form of discourse in Gaelic Ireland, poets and ballad singers held the status of those thought to be wise and to have magical powers (Ó hÓgain 44). For this reason, Yeats and Synge chose to exploit the stories of the old Irish wandering ballad singers in order to create a lasting Anglo-Irish literature. Synge was more interested in folktales and stories of the *seanchas*, or *seanchaí*, upon which he could base his plays, believing that art was rooted in peasant life. Yeats believed that all literature was but the perfection of an art that had once been practiced by everyone: Synge expressed this same idea when he wrote that the unlettered literature of lonely places was the real source of the art of words (Kiberd, *Synge* 159). He did not want to create a folk literature for a peasant audience, but he did want to incorporate the methods and themes of folklore into his poems and plays. Synge believed that Tolstoy was wrong when he wrote that art should be intelligible to the peasant but right in claiming a certain criterion for art: "... I think this is to be found in testing art by its compatibility with the outside world and the peasants or people who live near it. A book, I mean, that one feels ashamed to read in a cottage of Dingle Bay one may fairly call a book that is not healthy—or universal" (*CW* 2: 351).

Synge valued the folk stories, not the tales of fairies and heroes, as the best sources for modern literature. He wrote that poets should turn to ballads not for purposes of imitation but of finding new methods of expressing their own poetic ideas and believed that one of the greatest advantages enjoyed by the folk was their being indifferent to social mores and artistic conventions which inhibited their direct expression of emotion. Poets, he wrote, should not copy the peasant songs but adopt or use by instinct the peasant's inner mode of creating

(Kiberd, *Synge* 160). The universality of art was found in its relationship to ordinary life.

> In all the circumstances of this tramp life there is a certain wildness that gives it romance and a peculiar value for those who look at life in Ireland with an eye that is aware of the arts also. In all the healthy movements of art, variations from the ordinary types of manhood are made interesting for the ordinary man, and in this way only the higher arts are universal. ("The Vagrants of Wicklow," *CW* 2: 208)

Synge wrote in an unpublished essay, "On Literature and Popular Poetry" (1897–98), that folklore possessed artistic potential: with the growth of folk studies, people began to realize that the songs and stories of primitive people offered artistic suggestions, that the arts were losing their meaning in technical experimentation while peasant music and poetry were full of exquisitely delicate emotion. Ibsen and Zola, who attempted realism, were not beautiful but joyless and pallid. On the other hand, Synge found both beauty and realism in folk idiom (Kiberd, *Synge* 160).

Yeats reserved his highest praise for writers who were part of this tradition.

> Mr. Synge alone has written of the peasant as he is to all the ages; of the folk-imagination as it has been shaped by centuries of life among fields or on fishing-grounds. His people talk a highly coloured musical language, and one never hears from them a thought that is of to-day and not of yesterday. ("Samhain: 1905," *Explorations* 183)

Yeats envied the spontaneous inspiration of the anonymous songsters of Connacht, for the very difficulty in writing as a modern man made him acutely aware of the beauty of folk poetry ("Yeats as Critic-Reviewer," *UP* 1: 70). He considered a poem to be "an elaboration of the rhythms of common speech and their association with profound feeling" ("Modern Poetry," *Essays* 508). A poet should not be the "bundle of accident and incoherence that sits down to breakfast" but one who has been reborn "as an idea, something intended, complete" ("A General Introduction for My Work" 509). T. R. Henn writes that for Yeats, the peasant fisherman was but another mask he used to convey wisdom, simplicity, and loneliness, together with deliberate solitude and the skill of hand and eye which he found in Renaissance tradition.[1] He is the poet transformed—"A man who does not exist" (*Poems* 149), except in the imagination. Yeats and Synge were both interested in the theme of the artist's alienation from society because of the pursuit of the artistic vision.

Characters that move people speak to everyone of the universal emotions, Yeats wrote. The artist sorrowfully contemplates the great irremediable things, but remakes all that he experiences. The poet thus writes of everyone's desire, for if he is truly an artist he speaks for everyone ("Poetry and Tradition," *Essays* 255). Yeats found a "whimsical grace, a curious extravagance" in the western tales, told by people who live in wild and beautiful scenery, under a sky ever-changing with clouds. Those who told the tales were often poor but serious-minded fishing people who found in the doings of ghosts and spirits the fascination that gives vitality to their lives.

Yeats's most famous peasant poet was Red Hanrahan, whose character is based on stories of the Irish poet Owen O'Sullivan the Red.[2] Yeats intended to create a new myth from traditional elements. In his stories of the early 1890s, Yeats named his hero Owen O'Sullivan; in the stories of *The Secret Rose* (1897), patterned on the earlier work, the hero called Red Hanrahan is a peasant visionary and passionate poet (Thuente 195). Yeats then revised and simplified these stories with Lady Gregory's significant help in 1905 and published them as the *Stories of Red Hanrahan* (Finneran 347–49). In this version, Hanrahan is less a peasant hedge-schoolmaster (although he does continue this tradition, especially in "Red Hanrahan's Curse") and more a bardic poet (Thuente 210). O'Sullivan's quest for knowledge is replaced by Hanrahan's quest for love in *The Secret Rose* (Thuente 215). Although inadequate as a visionary, the Red Hanrahan of the 1905 versions of the stories is able to earn legendary knowledge and love. He appears in "The Tower" where the speaker calls up images from the surrounding countryside in order to ask his fundamental question, his need to learn from tradition whether the imagination dwells the most upon a woman won or a woman lost—whether it dwells on that which is desired or that which has been attained. He summons several local characters, including Mrs. French (from Sir Jonah Barrington's *Personal Sketches of his Own Time*, 1827) and Mary Hynes (made famous by Anthony Raftery), in order to enquire of them. Only Hanrahan, however, possesses the special knowledge he seeks—his "mighty memories," derived from the stories of Owen O'Sullivan and from Irish legend, to which Yeats was now turning for his sources of Irish material.

Yeats was aware of the ancient bardic schools which were followed in the eighteenth century by the "hedge-schools," so called because they had no permanent location. Qualifications for teachers included being able to read well, being able to write Irish, and having a strong memory.[3] The hedge schoolmasters were the heirs of the bards who could recite poetry about the ancient heroes at any gathering of the people; thus, the schoolmasters enabled the national literary tradition to become the heritage of the peasants (11). Although the hedge schools were clearly a peasant institution, there is much evidence that classical teaching was abundant, since writers of the eighteenth and nineteenth centuries from other countries remarked that many of the Irish peasants knew Latin well and were better educated than the Irish middle classes and certainly better than their counterparts on the Continent (50–53). The country schoolmasters were of the people themselves and performed the function of local historian, scribe, and organizer of secret political societies (108). Noteworthy country schoolmasters other than the famous Owen Roe O'Sullivan were Donnchadh Ruadh MacNamara and Brian Merriman, who wrote "The Midnight Court" (118–22). Yeats's Hanrahan fulfills the qualities of the classical scholar (*Mythologies* 239) and wandering poet, but while he can perform a peasant's duties (such as making a rope) he is clearly not one of the people. He is isolated and lonely, and, as his story goes through several revisions, he becomes increasingly sensual until by 1928 he is an "Old lecher with a love on every wind."

The stories of this wandering peasant poet and hedge schoolmaster involve the themes that dominated Yeats's poetry—alienation from community, acceptance of his own and Ireland's past, loss of love, old age. In the initial story, Hanrahan learns about his own alienation from Ireland's past. He refuses to question the meaning of the symbols he is confronted with—Pleasure, Power, Courage, and Knowledge, or the Cauldron of the Dagda, the Stone of Destiny, the Spear of Lug, the Sword of Nuada—Ireland's four great treasures. In the final story the treasures take the shape of the pot, knife, baking stone, and blackthorn stick—common articles of western cottages, which he finds in the cottage of Winny Byrne. Hanrahan, like the young Michael Gillane in *Cathleen Ni Houlihan*, learns that he must abandon worldly ambition and accept his fate and his role in Ireland's history, to identify his own with Ireland's destiny. He loses his loved one in the first story, to be reunited in the final one with his fairy bride. The stories reveal a pattern of sin, suffering, repentance, and redemption (352–54).

Yeats's Hanrahan stories fulfilled two of his artistic aspirations, to create myths and to project contrary aspects of the self.[4] Hanrahan is a ballad poet, a wanderer and visionary, yet he is alienated from the people. Yeats cherished the idea of the educated folk poet who knew Homer and Virgil, as Hanrahan does, as well as the Irish epics (Hoffman 6), just as Yeats himself desired both to be a member of an elite and also to write for the common people (32). The story of "Kidnappers" (*Mythologies* 70–76), which Yeats claimed he had collected from an old woman, can be identified with an early ballad, "The Host of the Air." This poem represents the first appearance of the supernatural card game found in "The Tower" and the story "Red Hanrahan." It is a mythic motif, a test of human beings by the creatures of the Other World in which a girl's life is at stake. By winning the card game, O'Driscoll could have won his wife from the dead, like Orpheus (Hoffman 71). The pack of hounds, like the flight of the barnacle-geese in "Beggar to Beggar Cried," represents a common motif of the card game, following a witch who has taken the shape of a hare (76). Thus Yeats adds to a traditional motif the figure of the wandering ballad poet. The stories are concerned with two of Yeats's important poetic themes—the rightful place of the poet in society and the terror of old age (Finneran 357).

In the first story, "Red Hanrahan," the poet wanders because he lacks the courage and strength to seek the truth. Tricked out of his true love and her inheritance by a magician with a supernatural pack of cards, Hanrahan encounters the four legendary women who demand of him the fundamental question. He cannot question them because he cannot find the right words to do so (*Mythologies* 221). Because of Hanrahan's weakness, Echtge, Daughter of the Silver Hand, will not be awakened from her eternal sleep.

The second story, "the Twisting of the Rope," also drawn from a folktale, begins with Red Hanrahan's meeting Oona, a daughter of a house, in Kinvara. She is attracted to Hanrahan because he sings a song he had heard or created during his lonely wanderings on Slieve Echtge, a song about the heroic, happy Other World:

> O Death's old bony finger
> Will never find us there
> In the high hollow townland
> Where love's to give and to spare;
> Where boughs have fruit and blossom
> At all times of the year;
> Where rivers are running over
> With red beer and brown beer.
> An old man plays the bagpipes
> In a golden and silver wood;
> Queens, their eyes blue like the ice,
> Are dancing in a crowd.
>
>   (229)

Oona's mother and father do not like Hanrahan because he has "no good name now among the priests, or with women that mind themselves" (225). Unable to refuse him entrance to their house nor force him to leave once he is there (for it is bad luck to expel a poet of the Gael and a singer from one's house), the girl's parents, like the old magician, trick Hanrahan: they get him to twist a rope with his own hands out of hay. As he does so the rope lengthens, so that he steps out of the door, which they immediately bolt shut. Hanrahan sits by the shore, his hands working as if he were twisting the rope, "but it seemed to him as he twisted that it had all the sorrows of the world in it" (232). The women of the Sidhe call to him, but he refuses them and writes a song called "The Twisting of the Rope." The Sidhe women mock him, saying he is weak and will never find comfort among the women of the earth.

"Hanrahan and Cathleen, the Daughter of Houlihan" associates the peasant poet with national sorrows, ideals, the soil itself. He thinks about Ireland's weight of grief and sings the song known as "Red Hanrahan's Song About Ireland." "Hanrahan's Vision," the fifth tale, relates him to all the great women of Irish love legend—Blanaid, Deirdre, Grania—but the only one who speaks to him is Dervorgilla, the unhappiest of all tragic women, for her sin brought Ireland into submission (251). In this story Hanrahan sings the entire song of "The Happy Townland" which came to him in one of his dreams; the song celebrates heroic life and laments its passing.

Hanrahan denies the proper attitude toward love in the fourth tale, "Red Hanrahan's Curse." Having coaxed the hearts from five girls whom he then abandoned (for he is a wanderer), he assists a young girl, Nora, in her desire to escape marriage to old Paddy Doe, a farmer with a hundred acres. Hanrahan puts her sorrow, along with his curse against old age, into a song which is sung in the village and succeeds in winning the enmity of the old men who drive him away again. Only before his death in the final story, "The Death of Hanrahan," does he learn to put his poetic skill to use in the service of love: he questions the old women about the Cauldron, the Stone, the Sword, and the Spear—the four talismans of the Tuatha De Danaan (*Variorum Poems* 188). Yeats's heroes never triumph. Only the soul triumphs, through transfiguration. Even Paradise is a dream of the soul. Hanrahan is reunited with a fairy bride, but he has never known perfection in earthly love.

In three of Yeats's plays in which peasants are heroes or antiheroes themselves—*Cathleen Ni Houlihan* (1902), *The Unicorn from the Stars* (1905), and *Purgatory* (1939)—we see a changed attitude toward the peasants and the kinds of ideals the peasants represent. In *Cathleen Ni Houlihan* and *The Unicorn from the Stars*, peasant characters are noble and fulfill roles worthy of the early Hanrahan. Just as *The Countess Cathleen* begins with Mary's question about what startled the hen in her coop, *Cathleen Ni Houlihan* begins with Peter Gillane's question about an unfamiliar noise that disturbs the people of the house, only this time the noise is the sound of cheering. Peter and Bridget Gillane, who are peasant farmers, talk of little at the beginning of the play but what they did not have when they were young and how poor they used to be, and what they will be able to buy with the dowry from their son Michael's wife. Their choices reflect peasants' values—they will buy stock and land—and they discuss their second son's chances of finding a suitable match. They are concerned only with getting on in life and their willingness to help the Old Woman who enters the house stems from a sense of duty, not generosity. Bridget tells Peter to give the Old Woman money, not because she feels empathy, but because if he does not, their luck will go from them (*Variorum Plays* 226).

Michael Gillane takes the greatest interest in the Old Woman, not in who she is or where she comes from as Peter and Bridget do, or how she lost her land, but in the meaning of her sad song and the identity of the brave men who died for love of her. Michael is a less complex character than Mary Bruin of *Land of Heart's Desire* and far less complex than Aleel of *The Countess Cathleen* or Martin Hearne of *The Unicorn from the Stars*, but he leaves the beautiful girl who is to be his wife and the prospect of a better life because like Mary Bruin and Martin Hearne he sees that the ordinary peasant's life is without inspiration. He possesses imagination and the desire to commit himself to something more than the mundane work and values of those around him. Even his love for Delia is too much a part of the ordinary world. He makes the sacrifice that Yeats believed all Irish people should make; he is a peasant because to Yeats the "people" of Ireland were the peasantry.

Martin Hearne is more rebellious than Michael Gillane or Mary Bruin and a greater visionary than Aleel, and his character is more fully developed than theirs. He is a tradesman—a coach builder—but he loves the land and knows the ancient traditions. He becomes a leader of the peasantry and fulfills the role of a bard by teaching his people about the world they will achieve. He is also a martyr, not for his people's freedom on earth, but for the salvation of their spirits. Only the peasants learn to value what he does.

Thomas Hearne, Martin's uncle and employer, wants Martin to be successful in the business of coach-building. Thomas embodies the values of a tradesman: he believes that only work is good, that the way to rid his brother Andrew and his nephew Martin of their "visions or trances" is to discipline them and force them to work. He achieves success with Andrew—a believer in ancient ways who was a dreamer like Martin before Thomas put him to work—but he fails entirely to convince Martin to give up his dream vision of the Celtic heaven. When Thomas accuses him of being drunk, Martin tells him,

I have been beyond the earth. In Paradise, in that happy townland, I have seen the shining people. They were all doing one thing or another, but not one of them was at work. All that they did was but the overflowing of their idleness, and their days were a dance bred of the secret frenzy of their hearts, or battle where the sword made a sound that was like laughter. (688)

Martin explains to dutiful Thomas that Paradise is really fullness of life, that a person's actions should lead to exultation and "the frenzy of contemplation" (688). "Events that are not begotten in joy are misbegotten and darken the world," Martin says, "and nothing is begotten in joy if the joy of a thousand years has not been crushed into a moment" (688). Martin expresses the exultation of engagement in timeless activity, like Yeats's fisherman, and the frenzy of thought and joy that the "cursing rogue" experiences. Yet Martin's convictions also symbolize the importance for Yeats of legend and ancient belief that must continue to live in every era.

Everyone in the play misunderstands Martin and everyone except Andrew tries to find a cure for his "illness." He seeks to lead the people—in this case, the local peasants—to spiritual freedom and belief in the exultant heart that would liberate them from bondage of mundane work and daily cares. Thomas believes first that Martin is ill, then drunk. Father John believes that he is cursed by a malaise of the spirit. The beggars, Johnny Bocach and Paudeen, as well as the other peasants, believe that Martin is a new leader who has come to drive out the landlords and the English and that their freedom will be freedom from poverty.

Martin does lead them to burn down two houses, because, as he later explains, he thought his mission was to destroy Church and Law. After the battle he sees another vision that makes plain the truth: like Christ's, his "business is not reformation but revelation" (704):

> ...The battle we have to fight is fought out in our own mind. There is a fiery moment, perhaps once in a lifetime, and in that moment we see the only thing that matters. It is in that moment the great battles are lost and won, for in that moment we are a part of the host of Heaven. (705)

Martin's followers still misunderstand him, Johnny accusing him of abandoning the men he inspired to fight, and Biddy Lally, also a beggar, saying that he has gone mad from awakening too suddenly from a trance. Biddy believes that his madness has given him great power "to get knowledge of the great cure for all things" (706).

Martin dies heroically for what he has done, and the beggars resolve to give him a funeral worthy of a great man, with his followers "coming on horses and bearing white rods in their hands" (710). The play ends on a darker note, however. Father John has no faith that he will ever learn the origin of Martin's vision. Thomas, who has no imagination, simply says that the world has gone very queer. Andrew's answer is the most ironic, for he rejects freedom of thought and embraces Thomas's utilitarian and safe philosophy—that to be "too headstrong and too open" is "the beginning of trouble"; people should keep themselves to what they know and desire a quiet life (711).

In an earlier play on the same theme of the search for spiritual redemption, *Where There is Nothing* (1902), a young man named Paul Ruttledge leaves his comfortable home and family because he cannot be content with the gentleman's life. He joins a group of tinkers because he too has wandering in his heart but finally seeks holy orders and meets his death because an angry mob believes he is spreading heresy. Like Martin Hearne, he speaks of breaking up all settled order, of bringing back "the old joyful, dangerous, individual life" (1157). In *The Unicorn from the Stars* Martin's vision has more to do with legendary Ireland, and clarifies what Yeats means by an inspired life and the dangers inherent in pursuing it.

Yeats speaks here as a poet of decolonization: he believes that an independent Ireland should become a society inspired by old legends and artistic vision, freed from the drudgery that a materialistic power has imposed. Thomas and Andrew represent the new group of middle-class Catholic proprietors, once peasants, who successfully turned Ireland into a society based solidly on bourgeois values.

The spirituality of the speakers in Yeats's beggarman poems is completely absent from the Old Man and his son, both peddlers, in *Purgatory* (1939). Yeats's noble Martin in *The Unicorn from the Stars* wants nothing to do with building ornate conveyances for the rich, but in *Purgatory* the great house and its way of life are the model for all the rest. Yeats's attitude here parallels that which he expresses in "Upon a House shaken by the Land Agitation," that the lower classes can never hope to acquire the gifts necessary for leadership. W. J. McCormack believes that Yeats's attitude toward the peasants changed around 1910 and that the change manifested itself in "Upon a House shaken" (373); Thuente says that the change took place far earlier, that Oona's materialistic parents in "The Rose of Shadow" represent Yeats's declining opinion of the peasantry (*W. B. Yeats and Irish Folklore* 219) and that his revisions of his plays in the 1890s indicate that the status of the peasants declined (for Yeats) as the ancient heroes became more important as subjects for art. Yeats's image of the peasants definitely deteriorated, Thuente writes, with *Land of Heart's Desire* in 1894.

In *Purgatory* Yeats explores the theme of destruction of venerated custom and traditional values. The dominant metaphor of the play may be the hereditary pollution that can never be erased, as McCormack writes (371), or it may be the Fall of Mankind from which no one escapes.

The Old Man, a tramp upon the roads, is the opposite of the lyrical "cursing rogue" who affirms life. This tramp, the lowest sort of antihero, destroys life in the pursuit of an ideal—the liberation of his mother from the cycle of guilt and repentance. However innocent his mother might have been, her decision to marry an inferior was based on love at first sight—lust—and for this mistake she bears the responsibility for the destruction of a house that produced great people (*Variorum Plays* 1043). On her wedding-night, the night the Old Man was begotten, his mother "is no better than her man" (1046) for "she is mad about him." Her lust and his depravity destroy the great tradition of the house. The son's cynicism and greed are the result of his upbringing; the mean life he has led as a peddler has made him careless and insensitive, not spiritual and free as Synge's wanderers and the beggars of Yeats's earlier poems. The Old Man chooses to live as a peddler because he thinks his way of life is fitting for one born of a father who brought tradition to ruin. There is no lovemaking in *Purgatory*: sexual intercourse is lust and pollution. The Old Man's son is "A bastard that a pedlar got /Upon a tinker's daughter in a ditch" (1044). The Old Man murdered his father and now he murders his son in order to end what he sees as the result of his mother's guilt—hereditary pollution—but he cannot release her soul from her dream—the nightmare of remorse.

The landscape of this play is composed not of a mountain and plains where the events of great legends took place but of a single backdrop—a burned facade of a house and a dead tree visible only by moonlight. The play suggests that the fate of Ireland, its traditions threatened by revolution—which had been created of both romance and violence [5]—had spawned only brutality. The spiritual treasure of the past had been destroyed, leaving a mean and ugly present. Yeats compared the destiny of artists with the destiny of the aristocracy; both, he said, needed tradition and permanence.

> Lady Gregory is planting trees; for a year they have taken up much of her time. Her grandson will be fifty years old before they can be cut. We artists, do not we also plant trees and it is only after some fifty years that we are of much value? Every day I notice some new analogy between [the] long-established life of the well-born and the artist's life. We come from the permanent things and create them, and instead of old blood we have old emotions and we carry in our head that form of society which aristocracies create now and again for some brief moment at Urbino or Versailles. We too despise the mob and suffer at its hands and when we are happiest we have some little post in the house of Duke Frederick where we watch the proud dreamless world with humility, knowing that our kingdom is invisible and that at the first breath of ambition our dreams vanish.[6]

In the rise of the lower classes, Yeats saw the destruction of the Ireland he valued, including the traditions of the peasantry.

McCormack writes that heroism is at the heart of Yeats's aesthetic, that in *Purgatory* Yeats confronts the cynicism of form upon which modernism depends (371). The past is a burden, like Joyce's nightmare of history. Yeats also confronts romanticism and idealism, at once mocking the old aesthetic of aristocrat, poet, and peasant, as well as reaffirming it. The Old Man fails to save his mother from her "dream" of guilt and remorse. The audience learns what he does not, that no act absolves another, that no one living or dead can escape the cycle of sin and guilt. The Old Man's act is as ghastly and destructive as his own father's, he suffers more deeply than his mother, and he lives a life of utter isolation and meaninglessness. His final cry to God voices the desperate hope that the cycle of torment will end, but nothing in the text indicates that it can. The Old Man is after all the heir of the Romantic tradition.

McCormack explains Yeats's interest in eugenics, apparent in *Purgatory*, as "one statement of the fascist longing to resolve all contradictions in a single conflagration" (398). This conflagration would engulf the heterogeneity of modern bourgeois society and restore to Ireland its traditional culture. Edward Said points out that Yeats's "aristocratic" values more closely resemble Italian or South American authoritarianism than European fascism (*Culture and Imperialism* 230). Yet McCormack also claims that the play itself reveals the noble past to be spurious because Yeats had created an "aristocratic" tradition out of a disunified, largely bourgeois history of Protestant Ascendancy (399). Tradition itself is thus evolutionary, with symbols borrowed selectively from experience.

Yeats's noble peasant fisherman led a life that approached the unity of art. For Synge the artistic peasant was not an image but a reality, and his way of life was to be celebrated. His peasant characters are not bucolic and rustic but vibrant, athletic, savage, and spirited and they embody the Irish character which he believed was imaginative and demonic. While Yeats sought to create a national literature, Synge wanted a hero for the modern world and he looked to country people to find one.

Christy Mahon achieves heroic stature because in his frustration with his father he strikes a blow he believes to have been fatal, and the people of Mayo praise him for it. Not his act or his illusion create his new identity but rather the adoration of people who desire a hero. By the time they turn against him, he has mastered his own life. Christy becomes a hero in that he transforms himself from a cowardly farm boy into a courageous athlete, lover, and leader of the people, in control of his own emotions and his will. He becomes an artist through his own inspired "poetry talk." Christy's discovery of his own will enables him first to strike at his father, then to defeat the Mayo athletes and his chief rival for Pegeen's hand, and finally to set himself completely free to "go romancing through a romping lifetime from this hour to the dawning of the judgement day" (CW 4: 173). The play is about the liberation of a victim of paternalistic tyranny, of provincialism, and of loneliness, but it also speaks of desire for national independence and individual freedom from social repression.

As we have seen, Synge collected the story that was to form the plot of The Playboy in the Aran Islands. A Connaught man killed his father with the blow of a spade when he was in a passion, and fled to the island where he threw himself at the mercy of the people. They hid him in a hole that Synge's informant, the oldest man on Inishmaan, showed him, and kept him safe for weeks. "This impulse to protect the criminal is universal in the west," Synge wrote (The Aran Islands, CW 2: 95), due partly to the association between legal justice and English law, but more directly to the people's conviction that a human being would not do wrong unless under the influence of a passion as "irresponsible as a storm on the sea." They did not believe that such passion *could* be controlled. A person who committed such a crime would be quiet for the rest of his life, they said, for no one would do such a thing if he could help it (95). Michael Flaherty echoes this sentiment in *The Playboy* when he remarks that Christy should have had good reason for doing what he did (*CW* 4: 73). A prototype for Christy may have been Hyde's description of Raftery, who was said to have been a "spare, thin Man" (Hyde, *Raftery* 25), the best in Ireland at wrestling and leaping bogholes (Hyde uses the term "lepping" as Synge does [25]). An adroit conversationalist, he captivated listeners. Synge may have adapted Christy's athletic feats from the horse races on the sands which he observed in Connaught ("In West Kerry," *CW* 2: 272) and the island riders who rode their Connemara ponies at full gallop with nothing to hold onto (*The Aran Islands* I, *CW* 2: 79).

The Playboy of the Western World is about awakening: personal awakening to freedom or national awakening to self-government. Christy begins to be aware of his own power when he realizes the men in the shebeen are interested in him (*CW* 4: 75). He boasts that he is the son of a "strong farmer . . . could have bought up the whole of your old house a while since from the butt of his tail-pocket and not have missed the weight of it gone" (69). Later he tells Pegeen, "We were great surely, with wide and windy acres of rich Munster land" (79), but he forgets this story entirely when he says that he committed his crime in a "cold, sloping, stony divil's patch of a field" (101). He becomes a hero because the people of Mayo are starved for someone to believe in. Possessing the ability, he needs the approval of the townspeople in order to learn to believe in himself. He wins Pegeen with his courage, daring, and fine talk, and he learns to be confident, gathering the courage to "slay" his father a second time, boasting that he will take some of the others before he goes (171). Finally he gives his triumphant speech, after defeating the athletes, his rival, the townspeople, and his father.

Stories about violence stimulate the people whose lives are so constricted. The Widow Quinn tells Christy he is a "fine, gamey, treacherous lad" (101). Pegeen also equates violence with courage, describing Christy as "a fine lad with the great savagery to destroy your da" (111), and says she will not marry a man the like of Shaneen who had "no savagery or fine words in him at all" (153). She declares, "I wouldn't give a thraneen for a lad hadn't a mighty spirit in him and a gamey heart" (113). The other characters delight in vivid personality and in violence for its own sake. Jimmy Farrell flatters Pegeen with her ability to "knock the head of any two men in the place" (63). Pegeen, chiding the reticent newcomer Christy, challenges him with "You did nothing at all. A soft lad the like of you wouldn't slit the windpipe of a screeching sow" (71). Susan remarks that Sara Tansey drove the ass cart ten miles to see "the man bit the yellow lady's nostril on the northern shore" (97). Sara answers, fitting on Christy's boots: "There's a pair do fit me well, and I'll be keeping them for walking to the priest, when you'd be ashamed this place, going up winter and summer with nothing worth while to confess at all" (97). Sins and crimes are to be lauded, while virtue equals boredom. The most cowardly of the men is the least respected, for good reason. The Widow Quinn remarks to Shawn, "It's true all girls are fond of courage and do hate the like of you" (117). When Shawn voices his opinion that Mayo is as good a place and now as good a time as any other, Pegeen makes clear the relationship between violence and romance:

> As good, is it? Where now will you meet the like of Daneen Sullivan knocked the eye from a peeler, or Marcus Quin, God rest him, got six months for maiming ewes, and he a great warrant to tell stories of holy Ireland till he'd have the old women shedding down tears about their feet. Where will you find the like of them, I'm saying? (59)

The heroes are both violent men and storytellers with vivid personalities.

Christy rebels against unbearable restraint, against Church and state: he is Messiah as well as hero. The girls' bringing him presents parodies the Epiphany. His triumphs in the sports parody the Palm Sunday adulation; Synge may also have had in mind triumphal exploits at Greek games. When Christy's pretensions are unmasked, he is vilified, ridiculed, tortured, and offered up for sacrifice. Yet the religious imagery is undermined by the blasphemous epithets and irreligious behavior of the characters. The allusions to mercenary marriage and Widow Quinn's mercenary matchmaking lead to sexual degradation. Pegeen is likened to a beast whom it were better to breed to a sturdy stud like Christy.[7] The villagers applaud Christy for his act of emancipation, for it is an embodiment of their own desires; when the tale becomes reality, however, they have no courage and no faith.

Christy's story is like Parnell's, a "gallous story" when told, but when publicly seen, it becomes a "dirty deed." The hypocritical townspeople act only out of vicarious pleasure and self-interest; Christy's actions, however, result from desire for liberty and anger at the appalling treatment he receives from his father.

Christy's artistic gifts—his storytelling and his poetic love-talk— like Raftery's spur those he meets into creating art, however dismal their stories seem when compared to his. Synge recorded this trait in the islanders: "The people have so few images for description that they seize on anything that is remarkable in their visitors and use it after- wards in their talk" (*The Aran Islands* III, *CW* 2: 129). Pegeen eagerly relates the story of the Widow, who reared a black ram at her own breast, so that the Lord Bishop of Connaught, eating the ram in a kidney stew, "felt the elements of a Christian," and who killed her husband by hitting him with a rusty pick, so that he died from blood poisoning.[8] "That was a sneaky kind of murder did win small glory with the boys itself," says Pegeen (*CW* 4: 89), who does not remark on the sneakiness in Christy's deed—he has hit his father on the back of the head. Jimmy Farrell tells of the skulls in the city of Dublin, "ranged out like blue jugs in a cabin of Connaught" (133). He declares the truth of it because a lad saw them as he returned in the Liverpool boat from harvesting: "'They have them there,' says he, 'making a show of the great people there was one time walking the world. White skulls and black skulls and yellow skulls, and some with full teeth and some haven't only but one'" (133–35). He also tells of a man who killed horses after he was kicked in the head, ate the insides of a clock and died afterwards (137). Philly also tells a story of death, of the graveyard beyond the house where he was a lad and the exposed skeleton of a man who had thighs "as long as your arm" (135). He imagines the people of the old days to have been larger than those of the present: "He was a horrid man, I'm telling you, and there was many a fine Sunday I'd put him together for fun, and he with shiny bones you wouldn't meet the like of these days in the cities of the world" (135). Michael Flaherty's story of Kate Cassidy's wake is derived from the stories of tremendous drunkenness at funerals that Synge heard on the islands (*The Aran Islands* I, *CW* 2: 76). The funeral served merely as an occasion for drunkenness, as Michael tells Christy: "... you'd never see the match of it for flows of drink, the way when we sunk her bones at noonday in her narrow grave, there were five men, aye, and six men, stretched out retching speechless on the holy stones" (*CW* 4: 151).

Old Mahon's storytelling is as vigorous, although not as artistic, as Christy's. He displays proudly his wounded head and declares triumphantly that his own son did it, that he walked hundreds of miles winning his bed and board for the telling of his tale (135). He too waxes gregarious when he believes he is being praised. When the Widow says that he must have vexed his son fearfully to make him strike such a blow (she assumes, like the islanders of Synge's acquaintance and like Michael Flaherty, that the fault lies with the victim and not with the criminal), Old Mahon echoes Christy's "Is it me?" (121). He delights in imagining brutality, telling the Widow, "There was one time I seen ten scarlet divils letting on they'd cork my spirit in a gallon can; and one time I seen rats as big as badgers sucking the life blood from the butt of my lug" (143), and he confirms Christy's description of his violent temper when he describes his having been locked in an asylum for battering peelers and assaulting men, and when he declares the welcome he shall have at the Union, for he is "a terrible and fearful case, the way that there I was one time screeching in a straitened waistcoat with seven doctors writing out my sayings in a printed book" (143–45).

Pegeen also becomes an artist in her changed tone when she makes love to Christy after he has won the sports. She, too, echoes Christy's incredulous, "Is it me?": "And to think it's me is talking sweetly, Christy Mahon, and I the fright of seven townlands for my biting tongue. Well the heart's a wonder, and I'm thinking there won't be our like in Mayo for gallant lovers from this hour to-day" (151).

Christy achieves the status of artist and hero because the people of Mayo encourage and flatter him. Pegeen declares that only his tiredness keeps him from talking the way Owen Roe O'Sullivan did or the poets of Dingle Bay: "... I've heard all times it's the poets are your like, fine fiery fellows with great rages when their temper's roused" (81). She tells him he must have had great people in his family and he should have lived like a king of Norway or the Eastern world (83). Christy finds his real courage, however, when the villagers turn against him and accuse him of being a fraud. He does not revert to his former, cowardly self but fearlessly orders them: "Shut your yelling, for if you're after making a mighty man of me this day by the power of a lie, you're setting me now to think if it's a poor thing to be lonesome, it's worse maybe go mixing with the fools of the earth" (165). He asserts his position in their society: "...I'm after hearing my voice this day saying words would raise the topknot on a poet in a merchant's town" (165). Finally, full of confidence in himself as athlete, hero, poet, and lover, he blesses them for what they have enabled him to find in himself: "Ten thousand blessings upon all that's here, for you've turned me a likely gaffer in the end of all, the way I'll go romancing through a romping lifetime from this hour to the dawning of the judgment day" (173).

The people of Mayo, however, cannot rise to the hero they have made. They desire security and peace over poetry and courage. Michael Flaherty declares what they all feel (except Pegeen), that "By the will of God, we'll have peace now for our drinks" (173). For the villagers, eloquence is not enough; they reject poetry for mundane life. Like Nora Burke, Pegeen is left without her vision of a happier life, but unlike Nora she can choose only between two unhappy conditions—spinsterhood or lonely marriage. Nora at least has the promise of some beauty in what is left of her life. The audience may feel that Pegeen deserves what she gets for turning against Christy, yet may also feel sympathy for her. This society has no room for Christy the artist, the wandering minstrel, for he is too brave and free-spirited. Christy will create a new society for himself, while Pegeen, who might have become his partner, has neither the imagination nor the will to leave the sterile way of life she knows.

Seamus Deane argues that Synge's drama both affirms and denies the "heroicizing impulse" of the Literary Revival (*Celtic Revivals* 58) because in his plays the community produces a hero who must leave it bereft of emotional vitality: "Self-realization involves social alienation. Those who walk away from society and those who remain within it represent two kinds of value which are not reconcilable" (58). In all Synge's plays except *Riders to the Sea*, the hero envisions revivified pastoral romance, such as that advocated by the writers of the Revival but rejected by the society in favor of the status quo, characterized by Michael Flaherty as "peace now for our drinks"; the masses desired bourgeois materialism reviled by Synge and Yeats.

Apart from *Riders to the Sea*, all of Synge's art praises the irresponsible spirit of the natural man, and he chooses the people of the west where he thought that this spirit had liberty to make itself felt. Synge wrote that the humor of the middle island (Inishmaan) was quaint and wild, but on the south island (Inishere) he met a humor that was close to ecstasy: "Perhaps a man must have a sense of intimate misery, not known there [Inishmaan], before he can set himself to jeer and mock at the world" (*The Aran Islands* III, *CW* 2: 140). The passionate spirit of all the islanders expressed itself in "magnificent words and gestures" (92). The temperament of the people of Connaught itself was "half savage" (122): "The man who feels most exquisitely the joy of contact with what is perfect in art and nature is the man who from the width and power of his thought hides the greatest number of Satanic or barbarous sympathies" ("Autobiography," *CW* 2: 6).

Christy Mahon fashions a new personality for himself, while the Douls in *The Well of the Saints* create a vision of a new world, an Eden that can be engendered only by a free imagination: the world is either beautiful or ugly according to the sensibilities of the perceiver. The Douls experience a world of sound and smell that sighted people ignore: "Isn't it finer sights ourselves had awhile since and we sitting dark smelling the sweet beautiful smells do be rising in the warm nights and hearing the swift flying things racing in the air, . . . till we'd be looking up in our own minds into a grand sky, and seeing lakes, and broadening rivers, and hills are waiting for the spade and plough" (*CW* 3: 141). Creatures of the senses, peculiarly aware of their state of being, they find the Saint's abstract religious truth to be defeating and deluding. Heaven and hell are within the physical world, the endurable and unendurable, the warm sun and stony path.

Synge described his visit to the old ruined church of the Ceathair Aluinn, "The Four Beautiful Persons," on Inishmaan, and a holy well near it that was famous for curing blindness and epilepsy. A woman of Sligo long ago had seen it in a dream and had taken her blind son to it where the water restored his sight (*The Aran Islands* I, *CW* 2: 56–57). The theme of the play—newly sighted people wishing to be blind again—comes from a folk tale about a blind man, who, having been cured, asks to be made blind again in order that he may not commit sin.[9] Yeats wrote that in primitive times blind men became poets, as in his own time they became fiddlers in the villages, and were content to praise life. Poets who suffered impediments plain to all sang of life with the ancient simplicity ("Discoveries," *Essays* 277–78).

The Douls' custom had been to sit by the wayside, inspiring sympathy in passersby—whom they despised—and indulging in vain dreaming and quarreling. The family altercations in *The Well of the Saints,* fought over simple things, provide drama for Martin and Mary, in order to break the tedium of familiarity; there is little real malice. They exchange their aloof and independent existence for one of drudgery: now they must work with their hands and are not only poor but also miserable, whereas earlier, when blind, they had been poor but free. Their outcry against injustice is the undoing of the countryside. Like Christy Mahon, they disturb the peace of the local people who want to punish them for it.

Theirs is a world of dreams. While newly sighted people would probably not wish to be blind again but would find each other, however wrinkled and old, to be beautiful, the Douls' wish tells us more about the world they live in. Their blindness is a metaphor: the sighted people in this play see very little and feel very little but desire for gain; the Douls imagine ("see") beautiful visions. Timmy the Smith is self-satisfied and abusive. Molly Byrne is foul-tempered, malicious, and vain. The Saint is a well-meaning but foolish reformer who is "blind" to Molly's nature and to the Douls' spiritual vision. The Douls prefer blindness and fantasy to drudgery and a "reality" that destroys their belief in themselves. Their descriptions of the world they cannot see are poetic; the world they can see, however, is devoid of beauty.

Mary and Martin Doul love nature. Martin knows the lay of the land as well as any sighted man: Mary calls him "a grand man the world knows at finding your way if there was deep snow itself lying on the earth" (*CW* 3: 133). Mary loves the outdoor life, as does the Tramp in *The Shadow of the Glen:* "Well, the sun's coming warm this day if it's late autumn itself" (71). However, like Adam and Eve, they wonder about the visible world, the knowledge that has been denied to them. Martin states his lack of faith: "I do be thinking odd times we don't know rightly what way you have your splendour..." (71). He is unsatisfied and says plaintively that if they could see themselves for one hour only they'd know for certain what they looked like and would never have to heed the lies of the rabble (73). He also laments that he is unable to see the young girls walking the road.

The play emphasizes the discrepancy between belief and reality, the poetic and the prosaic, the imaginative and the mundane. The Saint believes that young girls are "the cleanest holy people you'd see walking the world," and so he entrusts his holy water, cloak, and bell to Bride and Molly Byrne (83). Timmy the Smith and Mary Doul remark sarcastically on his naïveté. Molly Byrne fits the Saint's cloak on Martin and tells Mary that if she could see Martin she'd be as proud as Satan (85), and Martin believes that the cloak becomes him. Martin talks of Mary's "yellow hair, and her white skin, and her big eyes" (87) and declares that being a saint is not as good as being wedded "with the beautiful dark woman of Ballinatone" (87). Molly remarks scornfully to Martin, " . . . it's little you know of her at all" (87), while Timmy displays uncharacteristic charity when he says that they will see a "great wonder" this day and pities them, saying it was "bad work" that the people let on that Mary was fine looking, when in reality she was a "wizened hag" (91-93).

Molly's selfishness and materialism are inferior to the Douls' vision: "It'd be a fine thing if some one in this place could pray the like of him, for I'm thinking the water from our own blessed well would do rightly if a man knew the way to be saying prayers, and then there'd be no call to be bringing water from that wild place, where, I'm told, there are no decent houses, or fine-looking people at all" (91). Although she is about to be married, she has little faith in marital love: "If it's vexed he is itself, he'll have other things now to think on as well as his wife, and what does any man care for a wife, when it's two weeks, or three, he is looking on her face?" (93).

The play is unsatisfying in that newly-sighted people, blind from their seventh year, would presumably find everything in the world beautiful, even the bleeding feet of the Saint and the wrinkled face of an aged spouse. Martin's cruel comments to Mary reveal greater familiarity with the visible world than he could have had: "I'm telling you there isn't a wisp on any grey mare on the ridge of the world isn't finer than the dirty twist on your head. There isn't two eyes in any starving sow, isn't finer than the eyes you were calling blue like the sea" (97). It is difficult, furthermore, to believe that a newly-sighted person would wish to be blind again; yet the play's importance lies in Synge's use of the metaphor of blindness.

High incidence of blindness among Gaelic poets was due to the fact that many of the blind, unable to do manual labor, turned to poetry. Daniel Corkery in *The Hidden Ireland* describes the peasants' cabins and lists some of the names of famous Irish poets who were blind:

Chimney there was none, but a hole in the roof allowed portion of the smoke (sic) to emerge when the interior had become filled with it. The smoke was often seen to rise up like a cloud from almost every inch of the roof, percolating through as the thatch grew old and thin. The soot that in time came to encrust the walls and thatch within was occasionally scraped off and used as manure.

Between the absence of windows and the ever-present clouds of smoke, the people dwelt in darkness: it did not make for health, nor for quick convalescence when sickness broke out; quite commonly it led to blindness; though one must not forget to add the many prevalent fevers and plagues if one would understand why in any list of the poets of these days one comes so frequently on the word "Dall" (blind)—Tadhg Dall Ua h-Uigín, Liam Dall Ua h-Ifearnáin, Seumas Dall Ua Cuarta, Donnachadh Dall Ua Laoghaire; Carolan might also have been called "Dall," while Donnchadh Ruadh Mac Conmara (MacNamara) became blind in his old age. Blind poets, blind fiddlers, blind beggars of all kinds were to be seen tapping their way on every road in the country, from fair to fair, from house to house. (13–14)

Paul de Man, in *Blindness and Insight*, writes that the metaphor of blindness provides penetrating but problematic insight into the nature of literary language.

The insight exists only for a reader in the privileged position of being able to observe the blindness as a phenomenon in its own right—the questions of his own blindness being one which he is by definition incompetent to ask—and so being able to distinguish between statement and meaning. He has to undo the explicit results of a vision that is able to move toward the light only because, being already blind, it does not have to fear the power of this light. But the vision is unable to report correctly what it has perceived in the course of its journey.[10]

In Synge's play, the Douls come to understand more than the sighted people because functional blindness heightens their insight in other areas. Martin possesses an extreme auditory imagination, and he is, as Mary says, adept at finding his way (*CW* 3: 133). He states that only those who have been blind truly "see" anything (117). The Douls, having created their own beautiful world, find the visible one dissatisfying. Unlike the Douls, the materialistic people of the village mistake drudgery for virtue. When the community tries to force these wandering dreamers to conform to their customs and values, the Douls rebel against the constraints. In the process they force the people to examine their own way of life. Timmy the Smith complains that Martin and Mary have made everyone uneasy: "But it's a queer thing the way yourself and Mary Doul are after setting every person in this place, and up beyond to Rathvanna, talking of nothing, and thinking of nothing, but the way they do be looking in the face" (111). Deprived of their dream, the Douls force everyone else to question their own complacencies.

Martin's poetic language captivates Molly Byrne against her will. She tells him he sounds like a man who is losing his mind, but she is nevertheless intrigued by his words (117). He insists that he can see her as no one has ever been able to see her because he has been blind, and that together they can find a more beautiful world: "Let you come on now, I'm saying, to the lands of Iveragh and the Reeks of Cork, where you won't set down the width of your two feet and not be crushing fine flowers, and making sweet smells in the air . . . " (117). His most poetic speech reveals his despair at his disillusion:

Grand day, is it? . . . Or a bad black day when I was roused up and found I was the like of the little children do be listening to the stories of an old woman, and do be dreaming after in the dark night that it's in grand houses of gold they are, with speckled horses to ride, and do be waking again, in a short while, and they destroyed with the cold, and the thatch dripping maybe, and the starved ass braying in the yard? (113)

After they again lose their sight, the Douls return to each other to find new dreams and create a new world for themselves. Mary persuades herself that she is becoming a beautiful old woman with white hair, and Martin creates a new image of himself as an old man with a long, silken beard. They return to their lost Eden through their senses: Mary hears the sound of birds that herald the springtime and says that there will be fine warmth in the sun and sweetness in the air, that they will sit in the quiet and smell the new flowers growing. Martin hears the lambs of Grianan and the full river rushing in the glen. After they have refused the Saint's offer to cure them again, Martin describes the new world they have found and the world they are leaving:

> We're going surely, for if it's a right some of you have to be working and sweating the like of Timmy the smith, and a right some of you have to be fasting and praying and talking holy talk the like of yourself, I'm thinking it's a good right ourselves have to be sitting blind, hearing a soft wind turning round the little leaves of the spring and feeling the sun, and we not tormenting our souls with the sight of the grey days, and the holy men, and the dirty feet is trampling the world. (149)

After the Douls have gone, Timmy the Smith remarks that in the south, where they are going, lie many rivers in which they may be drowned (151). They have regained their paradise, but reality proves to be stronger than their dream in the end. Still, the Douls triumph over their tormentors and embrace a destiny of their own choosing. Synge speaks here for the underrepresented: the Douls are marginalized people living outside a small, regional community, itself outside the main current of Irish life, which was struggling to find its own cultural identity as a colonized nation. His answer parallels Yeats's in *Where There Is Nothing*: turn away from materialism to find freedom and beauty.

Heroic or artistic achievement means isolation and exile. Nora Burke and the Tramp, Christy Mahon, and Mary and Martin Doul, are all forced to leave their communities or homes. Red Hanrahan too is outcast, although his story ends with the hope that he has entered the Other World. Martin Hearne and Michael Gillane must leave their homes in order to fulfill their destinies. The fate that Yeats and Synge see in store for the artist or hero is that he will lose his people (or at least be misunderstood by them) but will yet possess his imaginative vision.

Conclusion

Because they desired to create a new sense of nationality (as opposed to nationalism) in Ireland, Yeats and Synge romanticized and idealized the way of life of Irish peasants. The primitivism of Yeats and Synge stemmed from nineteenth-century romanticism and the belief that modernity—industrialism and technology—meant loss of beauty. Unable to accept the values of the urban middle class, they looked to the countryside and the peasants for artistic inspiration. They may be seen as imaginatively repossessing the landscape at the very moment when their class was losing it. Those who own the land never truly "see" it, and those who "see" it never actually own it. Ownership, then, is the stumbling block, and the poet's task is to teach the Irish to see their own landscape and understand its irreplaceable importance for Irish tradition. Yeats created new myths for Ireland from old ones and new images from tradition. Synge expressed the language he heard in the rural places of Ireland, in order to portray the vitality he believed the peasants possessed and to help preserve their way of life. Both found in nature a mysterious power, and in folklore they found subjects for art.

Yeats records in his *Autobiography* that, when he first began to write, he had hoped to find his audience in Sligo (10). He never abandoned his belief in the traditional hierarchy of aristocracy and peasantry, for he believed that an independent Ireland should be founded on old values. The aristocrat, who was worldly and sophisticated, must represent higher values; the significance of his actions was political and influential in nature. The peasant, on the other hand, could voice the cry of the heart against necessity—old age, loss of love, dispossession. The peasant could be more vital and less cautious; his language could be extravagantly outrageous. His actions—farming and fishing—preserved a timeless way of life. Synge, however, could have dispensed with the aristocrat altogether, for in the peasants and wanderers of Wicklow and the west he thought he saw a greater nobility. Jack B. Yeats wrote in a letter that while Synge was well traveled, the Irish countryside and its people were what he loved.

> Synge must have read a great deal at one time, but he was not a man you would see often with a book in his hand; he would sooner talk—or rather listen to talk—almost anyone's talk...I think the Irish peasant had all his heart. He loved them in the east as well as he loved them in the west, but the western men on the Aran Islands and in the Blaskets fitted in with his humour more than any—the wild things they did and said were a joy to him. (*CW* 2: 402)

Yeats and Synge looked to folklore to find a tradition, almost a religion, upon which to build a new literary movement. Seán Ó'Faoláin wrote that imagination alone cannot formulate a religion, nor even aspire to it (*The Irish* 32), and Yeats himself acknowledged the impossibility of any conscious invention taking the place of tradition ("The Message of the Folk-lorist," *UP* 1: 288). Yeats and Synge failed to create a peasant literature in the tradition of William Carleton, for neither had grown up in peasant culture and therefore could never fully understand it.

Still, Yeats and Synge succeeded in creating a peculiarly Irish and modern form of the pastoral. Their characters stand out against a harsh and beautiful—as well as unmistakably Irish—landscape, which itself becomes symbolic of human emotion, and, in Yeats's case, aspects of the poet's memory. If Yeats and Synge ignored localized social norms and exaggerated the peasants' artistic sensibilities, they nevertheless also presented the very dark side of their lives. The world of Synge's plays is not the rediscovered Eden that we find in some of his journal entries, nor, for all his writing about the artistic traditions of the Irish peasants, is Yeats able to find his ideal audience. If the urban world suffered from the degradation of modern times, so too did the countryside: bitterness, anger, jealousy, avarice, lust, uncertainty, and cruelty plague the rural life as Yeats and Synge present it. Dreams of beauty, love, and an impossibly noble life remain dreams, which are usually denied to the people.

Even though they were the key figures in the Irish Literary Revival, Yeats and Synge were outsiders, being Protestant, middle-class, and essentially urban in outlook. Their writing about the peasants was derived not from personal background but from artistic necessity, and each one, according to his own personal bent, found confirmation of his ideas about them. While not indulging in sentimental pastoral, both transformed the peasants into ideal figures, whether they were tragic or comic, heroic or ignoble. What was important about the peasants to Yeats and Synge was not what would interest an anthropologist, historian, or sociologist; they were interested in whatever gave them images for art: thus, the peasant became a wanderer, a mystic, a man of nature. Such artistic recreation characterizes the Irish Literary Revival as a whole, in which Irish culture and history were idealized in order to create a tradition. This idealization was necessary for writers who created a literary tradition outside their personal experience and who tried to forge a national culture from ideals and from art.

Appendix

The Irish Peasants

So striking was the distinctiveness in nineteenth-century Ireland of the large landowning class in race and religion, and so enormous was its political power and influence, that it is tempting to see Irish history in the prefamine rural areas in terms of two social classes, the landowners and the tenants; and yet the social fracture between owners and cultivators was no larger than the fractures that divided the cultivating class itself. There were differences regarding sizes of holdings, which varied greatly, between large farms of fifty, a hundred, or several hundred acres and small holdings of one, five, or ten acres; indeed, half the holdings in 1844 were under eleven acres. By 1926, this figure had not substantially improved, as half the holdings were then under fifteen acres.[1] There were, in addition, differences between small landholders and those who had no land: in the early 1840s, twenty-five percent of the adult male population may have held no land at all. Differences in holdings resulted from the practice of subletting. In the eighteenth century, it was common for landowners to let land to middlemen; however, during the nineteenth century many proprietors tried to eliminate tenancies. There were fewer "gentry-middlemen" than in the eighteenth century and fewer land agents, lawyers, Protestant clergy, and owners' sons who leased and then let portions of estates.

The essential distinctions between farmers and laborers were that farmers were occupiers whose produce was sufficient, in normal times, to feed their families, pay their rents, and enable them to purchase some goods that were not produced at home. Farmers who were independent landholders (as differentiated from landowners) spent the better part of their working days in self-employment. "Peasants" were small tenant farmers, while "laborers," who were worse off, often worked on large farms given over to grazing (*The Irish Peasant* 110). Laborers had no land or insufficient land to support themselves without also working for someone else. Not only did they not own land, they could not be said to "hold" land either, even as tenants. Yet there was often more in common between small farmers and laborers than between small and large farmers. Besides small farmers and subtenants who employed no labor, laborers were also interested in preserving tillage because they sometimes depended for their livelihoods on obtaining land in conacre; that is, they might rent enough land to grow subsistence produce. Grazing also did not require sufficient labor to employ the available work force. Those who were truly landless, such as farm servants, often came from families of small landholders. The question of whether to increase grazing or tillage was to haunt the Irish agricultural community through the nineteenth century and well into the twentieth, when large farmers and graziers who supported Cosgrave and the Free State struggled for power with de Valéra and the Republicans in the 1920s and early 1930s.

The greatest division within the rural community in Ireland in the eighteenth and nineteenth centuries, however, was between large landowners and the rest, and a major source of this division was religion.[2] The principal means by which the Protestant Ascendancy had been established was confiscation of land owned by Catholics and the enactment of a series of repressive penal laws. Small farmers, laborer-landholders, and landless laborers were the rural poor, to which three-fourths of the adult male agricultural force belonged. Although the Penal Laws were repealed in 1829, the Protestant Ascendancy remained entrenched, a source of resentment for Catholics who suffered social disadvantages because of religion. Consequently, they had a strong sense of shared opposition to the Protestant landowners. Three major political movements in the prefamine period were the Emancipation Campaign of 1829, which won Catholics the right to hold high judicial and political posts; the Repeal movement which was aimed at getting rid of the Act of Union passed in 1800 (which had united Ireland to Great Britain with one Parliament in London); and the Tithe War of the 1830s which was aimed at repealing tithes to the established church. There was an unmistakable class bias in the Emancipation movement; the most active support came from towns and large farmers (Clark 18–20).

The postfamine years saw changes in land ownership, with many evictions, clearances, and attention to "business principles." Closely related to the decrease in population was the increase in size of landholdings and the overwhelmingly pastoral nature of Irish agriculture following the famine (Clark 107–8). The years between 1851 and 1876 saw large increases in the number of acres achieved from conversion of unused land to rough pasture. Reports from the *Poor Law Inspectors on the Wages of Agricultural Labourers in Ireland in* 1870 revealed:

> Previous to the famine the labourer enjoyed his cabin, attached to some farm, with rood, or half acre, or acre of land, and facilities for obtaining conacre land to sow a crop of potatoes. He was able to rear his pig and keep fowl . . . the social changes and custom of the last twenty years render it most difficult for a labourer to get an allotment of land. Landlords' views are generally opposed to it; and let it be viewed as it may, the fact remains, that you cannot convince an Irishman that he is better off as a daily labourer, even with fair wages, than he would be with the possession of a bit of land. (Reprinted in Clark 115.)

Before the famine, the agricultural community could be divided into three groups—landowners, large farmers, and small farmers and laborers—of which the largest class was the last and the smallest the first. After the famine, the classes could be divided into landowners, tenant farmers, and laborers, of which the middle class was the largest (121–22). Although there were differences in size of holdings, the distinctions between large, rent-receiving farmers and small, rent-paying farmers had clearly diminished and, although there were more tenant farmers in the postfamine days, the laborers were worse off than earlier.

This increasing polarization of rural society into commodity producers and wage laborers did *not* mean the disappearance of small farmers. In spite of increased agricultural commercialization, "middle peasants" survived in Ireland during the last half of the nineteenth century and into the twentieth. The persistence of this class of peasant, more striking in Ireland than elsewhere, was, however, not unique. Large capitalist farms failed to replace small family farms during the late nineteenth century in western Europe, and consequently rural society was not separated into a simple dichotomy between a stratum of large commercialized farmers on one hand and one of landless laborers on the other. Between the large-scale commodity producers and the wage laborers there was a class of small-scale producers, usually poor and relying on subsistence tillage (150-51). The poor western peasant may be seen as a connecting link between the "small holder" and the laborer.

One of the biggest weaknesses of the system was that landlords and tenants were divided by culture and religion. Alexander M. Sullivan wrote, in *New Ireland: Political Sketches and Personal Reminiscences of Thirty Years of Irish Public Life*, that the land had been "given over to be owned by men of one nation and creed, and tilled by men of another race and faith," and "lord and peasant represented conqueror and conquered."[3] This overstates the religious homogeneity of both landowning class and tenant population and underestimates the complexity of the land system. Before the famine, the majority of landlords were Catholic, if we include landlords who did not own land but leased it and then sublet it. Religious fidelity, nevertheless, united and divided Irish society. There was an increase in the number of Catholic owners after the famine, although Catholic-owned estates were generally smaller than those owned by Protestants.

Both Protestant and Catholic proprietors were actually removed from the rural population by virtue of the higher rank they held and the social circles in which they interacted, although Protestant separation was much greater, due to their almost exclusive marriage within their own group. Many landowners were absentee; however, it was not true that most of the land in Ireland was owned by persons living outside the country. In 1870, 13.3 percent of owners, whose estates totaled 23.5 percent of the land at 22.3 percent of total value, lived outside of Ireland. By contrast, 45.8 percent of owners lived on or near their property, which represented 49.2 percent of value (Clark 158). Had statutory reform of the tithe and land system been carried out in 1762 when proposals were made to permit Catholics to take mortgages on land, it might have considerably altered the course of Irish agrarian history. Instead, in 1765, an act was passed (called the first "coercion" act) which served to defeat all efforts by Catholics, and by the government, to alter the system of land ownership devised in the seventeenth century. Coercion was an admission that Ireland existed in a state of "smothered war" and encouraged the masses of the rural population to refuse to cooperate with the authorities and to distrust legal methods and institutions as a means of redressing their wrongs. Prefamine Ireland, far from being a peaceful peasant society, was a country of remarkable violence, often committed by secret societies and oathbound groups such as Ribbonmen and Whiteboys (66). "Whiteboy-ism" was an eighteenth-century class phenomenon, a vast trades union for protection of Irish peasantry, not to regulate wages or hours, but to keep the actual occupants in possession of their land and to regulate the relations of landlord and tenant for the benefit of the latter.[4] In spite of clerical admonition, denunciation, and even excommunication, these oathbound societies continued to exist, particularly in times of distress, and to draw people's loyalty.

For generations, rural people in Ireland had used violence to defend what they saw as customary rights. During the social and economic crises before the famine, the tradition of popular violence became a desperate struggle to preserve the very means of the peasants' existence. Chief Secretary for Ireland Henry Hardinge (not a man who was noted for taking the side of the people) wrote to Prime Minister Peel in 1822 that "ranks of tenants" had been evicted in "want and despair" upon the country, and that violent groups recruited them. A Protestant landowner, Sir Robert Hudson, ejected four hundred Catholics from his Cavan estate. Lord William Beresford evicted five hundred Catholics to be replaced with Protestant tenants, even though the previous tenants had occupied the land for generations and paid their rent faithfully. It was reasonable, Hardinge concluded, for popular discontent to turn to vengeance and outrage (Clark 69).

Four significant political rivals vied for the people's loyalty in postfamine Ireland: the Catholic clergy, the conservative nationalists ("Home Rule" advocates), the extreme nationalists (Fenians and members of the Irish Republican Brotherhood, who spanned all social classes), and the agrarian labor movements. Charles Stewart Parnell, a nationalist, saw potential political power behind the land question and joined forces with the Fenians. His "New Departure" policy advocated peasant proprietorship, abolition of arbitrary evictions, and agitation over the land question (20). Parnell's movement tried to restore to the Catholic peasants their land. In the process, the Irish Catholic peasantry had been molded into nationalists in pursuit of Grattan's ideal, which was an independent parliament in Ireland, in control of its own affairs, linked with Great Britain only through the Crown.

Alliance between landed gentry and urban middle class would have prevented the agrarian direction of Irish nationalism (277). Parnell himself was both a Protestant landowner and a nationalist who had become interested in land agitation even before Michael Davitt realized its potential. Davitt's contribution was to help organize early meetings in Connaught in 1879; Parnell's was to take a leading part in uniting these clubs with Leinster and Munster. Fenian nationalists provided leadership; farmers' societies began the land agitation.[5]

An agrarian economic crisis resulting from falling prices, crop failure, and exceptionally wet weather threatened many farmers in the winter of 1878–79 with bankruptcy, starvation, and eviction. The Irish National Land League was founded in 1879 in order to prevent dispossession of the rural population. The League combined in one great agrarian movement nationalists of all kinds, from moderate home-rule supporters to more radical republicans, Fenians, the Clan na Gael, and the parish clergy. While the League provided relief, its major task was to organize resistance to landowners in order to prevent eviction and to bring about reductions in rent and finally to transform tenants into owners.

In the greatest mass movement in modern Irish history, the "Land War" of 1879–82, the tenant farmers as a class faced the landowners. Because the Land League was a lawful organization, the government could not prevent its success. The League perfected resistance by non-violent means: although violence did erupt, there were also more peaceful demonstrations at process-serving evictions, embargoes on farms from which tenants had been evicted, social ostracism, and the boycott. The League provided defense funds and family relief for those prosecuted.[6] By 1913, the Irish rural population was relatively satisfied with its lot (Fitzpatrick 282), and after 1918 their main demands had been met (Goldring 20).

Notes

Introduction

1. Mary Helen Thuente, *W. B. Yeats and Irish Folklore* (Dublin: Gill and Macmillan, 1980), 27. Hereafter referred to in the text as "Thuente."

2. Birgit Bramsbäck, *Folklore and W. B. Yeats: The Function of Folklore Elements in Three Early Plays. Studia Anglistica Upsaliensia* 51 (Uppsala, Sweden: Acta Universitatis Upsaliensis, 1984). Hereafter referred to in the text as "Bramsbäck."

3. Declan Kiberd, *Synge and the Irish Language* (Totowa, N.J.: Rowman and Littlefield, 1979). Hereafter referred to in the text as "Kiberd."

Chapter 1

1. W. B. Yeats, *The Poems. A New Edition*, ed. Richard J. Finneran (New York: Macmillan, 1983), 148. Hereafter referred to in the text as "*Poems.*"

2. John Unterecker, *A Reader's Guide to William Butler Yeats* (New York: Octagon Books, 1971), 140, 147.

3. W. B. Yeats, "The Stirring of the Bones," in *The Autobiography of William Butler Yeats* (New York: Collier Books, 1971), 240.

4. Edward Hirsch, "The Imaginary Irish Peasant," *PMLA* 106.5 (October 1991): 1116–33.

5. Seamus Heaney, "Yeats as an Example?" in *Preoccupations: Selected Prose 1968–1978* (London: Faber and Faber, 1980), 108–9.

6. Edward W. Said, *Culture and Imperialism* (New York: Alfred A. Knopf, 1993), 233. Hereafter referred to in the text as "Said, *Culture.*"

7. Quoted in Maurice Goldring, *Faith of Our Fathers: The Formation of Irish Nationalist Ideology, 1890–1920* (Dublin: Repsol, Ltd., 1982), 105. Hereafter referred to in the text as "Goldring."

8. Seamus Deane, "Introduction," in Terry Eagleton et al., *Nationalism, Colonialism, and Literature* (Minneapolis: University of Minnesota Press, 1990), 3. Hereafter referred to in the text as "Deane, 'Introduction.'"

9. W. B. Yeats, "Four Years: 1887–1891," *Autobiography*, 131.

10. W. B. Yeats, *The Letters of W. B. Yeats*, ed. Allan Wade (London: Rupert Hart-Davis, 1954), 440. Hereafter referred to in the text as "Wade, *Letters.*"

11. J. M. Synge. *Collected Works* 2, general ed. Robin Skelton (Washington, D.C.: Catholic University of America Press, 1982), 142. Hereafter referred to in the text as *"CW."*

12. Declan Kiberd, in letter to the author, 1993.

13. W. B. Yeats, *The Collected Letters of W. B. Yeats* 1 (1865–95), ed. John Kelly (Oxford: Clarendon Press, 1986), 232. Hereafter referred to in the text as "Yeats, *Collected Letters."*

14. W. B. Yeats, *The Variorum Edition of the Poems of W. B. Yeats,* ed. Peter Allt and Russell K. Alspach (New York: Macmillan, 1973), 799. Hereafter referred to in the text as *"Variorum Poems."*

15. See, for example, notes to "The Ballad of Father Gilligan" (*Variorum Poems* 800), "The Ballad of Father O'Hart" (797), "Down by the Salley Gardens" (797), "The Stolen Child" (797), "The Madness of King Goll" (796), "The Meditation of the Old Fisherman" (797), "The Ballad of the Foxhunter" (798), "The Lamentation of the Old Pensioner" (799), and "The Host of the Air" (803).

16. Mary Helen Thuente, "Foreword," in W. B. Yeats, *Representative Irish Tales* (Atlantic Highlands, N.J.: Humanities Press, 1979), 7. Hereafter referred to in the text as "Thuente, 'Foreword'."

17. *Letters to the New Island* (Cambridge: Harvard University Press, 1934), 103–4, 107, 174. Hereafter referred to in the text as *"New Island."*

18. *Essays and Introductions* (New York: Collier Books, 1972), 511, 510. Hereafter referred to in the text as *"Essays."*

19. W. B. Yeats, "Ireland Bewitched," in *Uncollected Prose by W. B. Yeats* 2 (1897–1939), ed. John P. Frayne and Colton Johnson (New York: Columbia University Press, 1976), 169. Hereafter referred to in the text as *"UP 2."*

20. Nicholas Grene, *Synge: A Critical Study of the Plays* (London: Macmillan, 1975), 13–16. Hereafter referred to in the text as "Grene."

21. *States of Ireland* (London: Hutchinson and Company, 1972), 71–72.

22. (London: Croom Helm, 1979), 26. Hereafter referred to in the text as "Watson."

23. (London: Macmillan, 1967), 154.

24. Liam O'Dowd, "Town and Country in Irish Ideology," *The Canadian Journal of Irish Studies* 13.2 (December 1987), 44.

25. Quoted in "Preface" to *Views of the Irish Peasantry 1800–1916,* ed. Daniel J. Casey and Robert E. Rhodes (Hamden, Conn.: Archon Books, 1977), 10.

26. Quoted in Daniel Corkery, *Synge and Anglo-Irish Literature: A Study* (Cork: Cork University Press, 1931), vi. Hereafter referred to in the text as "Corkery, *Synge."*

27. *The Best of Myles* (Harmondsworth, England: Penguin Books, 1983), 234–35.

28. *The Hidden Ireland: A Study of Gaelic Munster in the Eighteenth Century,* 2d ed. (Dublin: Gill and Son, 1925), 11. "The cabins of the eighteenth century were sometimes built of stone, mortared or unmortared, but far more frequently of sods and mud. They were thatched with bracken, furze, fern or heath; and must have been often indistinguishable from the bogland, perhaps with advantage. Usually there was but one room, sometimes divided by a rough

partition; and often a sort of unlighted loft lay beneath the roof" (13). Hereafter referred to in the text as "Corkery, *Hidden Ireland.*"

29. L. M. Cullen, "The Hidden Ireland: Re-assessment of a Concept," *Studia Hibernica* 9 (1969): 24.

30. A. A. Roback, *A Dictionary of International Slurs* (Cambridge, Mass.: Sci-Art Publishers, 1944), 41–43, 57, 182.

31. Edward W. Said, *Orientalism* (New York: Vintage Books, 1979), 32. Hereafter referred to in the text as "Said, *Orientalism.*"

32. Michel Foucault, *The Archaeology of Knowledge,* trans. A. M. Sheridan Smith (New York: Random House, 1972), 183.

33. (London: Downey and Company, 1889), 7.

34. Quoted in "Tours in Ireland," *Quarterly Review* 85.170 (September 1849), 518.

35. *Critical and Miscellaneous Essays* 4 (Boston: Dana Estes and Company, 1869), 54–55.

36. L. P. Curtis, Jr., *Anglo-Saxons and Celts: A Study of Anti-Irish Prejudice in Victorian England* (Bridgeport, Conn.: The Conference on British Studies at the University of Bridgeport, 1968), 5.

37. William Graham Sumner, *Folkways* (Boston: Ginn and Company, 1906), 13.

38. In *Views of the Irish Peasantry,* 59.

39. "The Incompatibles," in *English Literature and Irish Politics* (Ann Arbor: University of Michigan Press, 1973), 265.

40. "On the Study of Celtic Genius," in *Lectures and Essays in Criticism* (Ann Arbor: University of Michigan Press, 1962), 344–48.

41. *A Short History of the English People,* 1 (New York: Harper and Brothers, 1893), 308.

42. For an understanding of the turbulent reception of Synge's plays, especially *The Playboy of the Western World,* see the following sources: Hilary Berrow, "Eight Nights at the Abbey," in *J. M. Synge Centenary Papers 1971,* ed. Maurice Harmon (Dublin: Dolmen Press, 1972), 75–87; David H. Greene, "The Playboy and Irish Nationalism," in *The Journal of English and Germanic Philology* 46 (1947): 199–204; Lady Augusta Gregory, *Our Irish Theatre* (New York: G. P. Putnam's Sons, 1913); Richard M. Kain, "A Scrapbook of the 'Playboy Riots,'" *Emory University Quarterly* 22.1 (Spring 1966): 5–17; James Kilroy, *The 'Playboy' Riots* (Dublin: Dolmen Press, 1971); Daniel J. Murphy, "The Reception of Synge's *Playboy* in Ireland and America: 1907–1912," *Bulletin of the New York Public Library* 64.10 (October 1960): 515–33; Alan Price, *Synge and Anglo-Irish Drama* (London: Methuen, 1961).

43. (London: H. G. Bohn, 1854).

44. (London: Bradbury, Agnew, and Company, 1887).

45. (Edinburgh: Foules, 1910), 24.

46. Roy F. Foster, *Paddy and Mr. Punch: Connections in Irish and English History* (London: Penguin, 1993), p. 174.

47. In *Views of the Irish Peasantry,* 25.

48. Patrick Pearse, "O'Donovan Rossa: A Character Study," in *Collected Works of Padraic H. Pearse: Political Writings and Speeches* (Dublin: Phoenix Publications, 1924), 128.

49. Quoted in Paul Bew, "The Land League Ideal: Achievements and Contradictions," in *Irish Studies* 2, 87. Hereafter referred to in the text as "Bew."

50. Quoted in Richard Ellmann, *Yeats: the Man and the Masks* (New York: Macmillan, 1948), 113.

51. (Harmondsworth, England: Penguin Books, 1969), 39. Hereafter referred to in the text as "Ó'Faoláin."

52. In fact, Yeats's literary pastoralism may have had a serious impact on present-day Irish agriculture in that it can be seen as partly responsible for the rather barren emphasis from the Land War to the present on land *ownership* rather than land *use*. The bulk of vegetables consumed in Ireland are now imported from French, Polish, Spanish, and Israeli farms because Irish farmers prefer husbandry to cultivation.

53. George Dalton, "Peasants in Anthropology and History," *Current Anthropology* 13 (1972): 386–87.

54. George M. Foster, "What Is a Peasant?" in Jack M. Potter, May N. Diaz, and George M. Foster, *Peasant Society: A Reader* (Boston: Little, Brown and Company, 1967), 11.

55. *The Races of Britain* (London: Trubner and Company, 1885), 267.

56. *The Irish Peasant: A Sociological Study* (New York: Charles Scribner's Sons, 1892), 29. Hereafter referred to in the text as "*The Irish Peasant.*"

57. Samuel Clark, *Social Origins of the Irish Land War* (Princeton: Princeton University Press, 1979), 27. Hereafter referred to in the text as "Clark."

58. On agrarian violence in Ireland in the twentieth century, see Maurice Manning, *The Blueshirts* (Dublin: Gill and Macmillan, 1970), 126–32.

59. See the appendix for a discussion of the history of agriculture and agrarian sociology in Ireland in the nineteenth and twentieth centuries.

60. Paul Bew writes in his essay "The Land League Ideal: Achievements and Contradictions" that Michael Davitt was to compromise his support for the United Irish League in 1898 by consorting with Catholic graziers in a way he never would have done with Protestant landlords (Bew 85).

61. David Fitzpatrick, *Politics and Irish Life 1913–1921: Provincial Experience of War and Revolution* (Dublin: Gill and Macmillan, 1977), 239.

62. Synge's plays offended nationalist opinion, writes Conor Cruise O'Brien in *States of Ireland* (New York: Vintage Books, 1973), because they showed the Catholic country people "in what their urbanized children considered to be an unfavorable light" (71). When Synge's plays were staged in Connemara, many in the audience walked out, complaining that, "we can see the like of that any day of the week among ourselves," thereby proving Synge's accuracy and the falseness of the original allegation that *The Playboy* travestied the west. What the audience expected was kings and queens. More recently, John C. Messenger, in *Inish Beag: Isle of Ireland* (New York: Holt, Rinehart, and Winston, 1969, hereafter referred to in the text as "Messenger, *Inish Beag*"), describes the "delirious response" of the islanders to the plot of Synge's play:

"The act which so horrified viewers of nativistic persuasion in Dublin and Boston half a century ago arouses the opposite effect among the folk" (77). What really galled audiences was Synge's remorseless realism.

63. Declan Kiberd, "Irish Literature and Irish History," in *The Oxford History of Ireland*, ed. Roy F. Foster (Oxford: Oxford University Press, 1992), 268. Hereafter referred to in the text as "Kiberd, 'Irish Literature.'"

64. (New York: Brentano's, 1943), 58.

65. Synge wrote in some unpublished notes (1889) that in many ways the people of the islands had the best joys of life—simplicity, contentment, and affection—and yet they also had hard work and a good deal of the savage in their lives (Synge Manuscript Collection, Trinity College Dublin, Ms. 4382.31v, 4382.34v. Hereafter referred to in the text as "TCD."). That Synge became a fluent reader and speaker in Irish is clear from his correspondence and notes. In February, 1899, his friend from Aran, Martin McDonagh, indicates in a letter that Synge knew some Irish but was not fluent. By February of 1902 Martin writes to Synge entirely in Irish (TCD 4424 and 4384). Synge writes that in August of 1905 in Ballyferriter (West Kerry) a group of young men made him tell them of his travels and insisted that he talk in Irish the whole time (TCD 4403.2v).

66. W. B. Yeats, *Uncollected Prose* 1, ed. John P. Frayne (London: Macmillan, 1970), 293. Hereafter referred to in the text as "*UP* 1."

67. In *The Empire Writes Back: Theory and Practice in Post-Colonial Literature*, Ashcroft et al. use the term *postcolonial* to cover all cultures affected by imperial process from the moment of colonization to the present (2). They list all colonies of Britain, France, Portugal, and Spain, including African, Carribbean, Southeast Asian, and South Pacific nations, India, Pakistan, New Zealand, Australia, Canada, and even the United States. They make no mention of Ireland (New York: Routledge, 1989).

68. Lloyd, *Anomalous States: Irish Writing and the Postcolonial Moment* (Durham, NC: Duke University Press, 1993), 69.

69. Seamus Deane, *Celtic Revivals: Essays in Modern Irish Literature 1880–1980* (London: Faber and Faber, 1985), 38. Hereafter referred to in the text as "Deane, *Celtic*."

Chapter 2

1. Ralph Linton, "Nativistic Movements," *American Anthropologist* 45 (1943): 230.

2. In "Man of Aran Revisited: An Anthropological Critique," a revision and expansion of a paper read before the American Committee for Irish Studies in 1964: 12.

3. John C. Messenger, *Inish Beag*, 4–5.

4. Arthur O. Lovejoy and George Boas, *Primitivism and Related Ideas in Antiquity*, vol. 1 of *A Documentary History of Primitivism and Related Ideas* (Baltimore: The Johns Hopkins Press, 1935), 1.

5. Raymond Williams, *The Country and the City* (New York: Oxford University Press, 1973), 139.

6. Nicholas Grene, "The Landscape of Ireland," in *Synge: A Critical Study of the Plays* (London: Macmillan, 1975), 16.

7. James Turner, *The Politics of Landscape* (Cambridge: Harvard University Press, 1979), 163, 165.

8. Turner names this ironic construct "green Thought" (4) as distinguished from present-day environmentalist philosophy which demands that parts of the "natural" world be left alone and which equally implies a separation from the "human" consciousness.

9. Quoted in G. J. Watson, *Irish Identity and the Literary Revival: Synge, Yeats, Joyce, and O'Casey* (London: Croom Helm, 1979), 24.

10. Quoted in Arthur Power, *Conversations with James Joyce*, ed. Clive Hart (London: Millington, 1975), 33.

11. Alf MacLochlainn, "Gael and Peasant—A Case of Mistaken Identity?" in *Views of the Irish Peasantry*, 24.

12. Conrad M. Arensberg, *The Irish Countryman: An Anthropological Study* (New York: Macmillan, 1937), 96–99. Arensberg describes in these pages the way in which the ownership of land became a central value in the lives of country people in the early years of the twentieth century.

13. W. J. McCormack, in *Ascendancy and Tradition in Anglo-Irish Literary History from 1789 to 1939* (Oxford: Clarendon, 1985) writes that the tensions of Modernism are made manifest in the primitive—"that paradoxical discovery of high European civilization in its violent imposition upon the globe." Artistic obsession with primitive culture, McCormack writes, is ambiguously related to gunboat diplomacy; "That ambiguity, in turn, contributes to the truly central place of Yeats in Anglophone Modernism, for Yeats's Ireland provided access to an allegedly primitive society which was still European" (293–94). Hereafter referred to in the text as "McCormack."

14. Hoxie Neal Fairchild, *The Noble Savage: A Study in Romantic Naturalism* (New York: Columbia University Press, 1928), 2.

15. Walter W. Grey, *Pastoral Poetry and Pastoral Drama* (London: A. H. Bullen, 1906), 4.

16. Sir Philip Sidney, *The Countess of Pembroke's Arcadia*, in *Prose of the English Renaissance*, ed. J. William Hebel et al. (New York: Appleton-Century Crofts, Inc., 1952), 316–17.

17. From *The Complete Works of Tacitus*, trans. by Alfred John Church and William Jackson Brodribb, ed. Moses Hadas (New York: Random House, 1942), 718–19.

18. Miguel de Montaigne, *The Essays of Michael, Seigneur de Montaigne*, trans. by Charles Cotton (London: Ward, Lock, and Co., n.d.), 721.

19. Percy Bysshe Shelley, *Shelley's Prose*, ed. David Lee Clarke (Albuquerque: University of New Mexico Press, 1954), 277–78.

20. W. B. Yeats, "By the Roadside," in *Mythologies* (London: Macmillan, 1962), 139. Hereafter referred to in the text as "*Mythologies*."

21. "Cuchulain of Muirthemne," in *Explorations* (New York: Collier Books, 1962), 10. Hereafter referred to in the text as *"Explorations."*

22. Manuscripts of Trinity College, Dublin, ms. #4349.

23. James Olney, *The Rhizome and the Flower: The Perennial Philosophy—Yeats and Jung* (Berkeley: University of California Press, 1990).

24. Carl Gustav Jung, *Two Essays on Analytical Psychology*, trans. by R. F. C. Hull, Bollingen Series 20, vol. 7 (New York: The Bollingen Foundation, 1953), 64. Hereafter referred to in the text as "Jung, *Two Essays.*"

25. Carl Gustav Jung, *The Archetypes of the Collective Unconscious*, trans. by R. F. C. Hull, Bollingen Series 20, vol. 9, part 1 (New York: The Bollingen Foundation, 1959), 22.

26. In "Sex and the Dead: *Daimones* of Yeats and Jung" (1981), James Olney describes the relationship between Yeats's and Jung's Great Memory and the *daimones*, forces of nature (or "residue of experience"), which seize on the individual and manifest themselves in visions and dreams:

When an archetype takes hold of us (nor can we avoid possession by them since we are human and possessed of all the instincts specific to humans), then—as Yeats and Jung jointly maintain—events of the day do not (as in Freud) determine the images of our dreams nor does experience in the world determine our vision; rather our vision breaks the world and reforms it according to an image that comes from deep within and from far in the past. An instinct insistently forces its own self-portrait on us, and it is not—nor will it ever be—the portrait of anyone in the world; so that all our Freudian incestuous desires—Yeats and Jung agree—are deeper and other than the son's desire for his mother or the brother's for his sister. They are nothing less than the serpent's closing on his own tail, Antaeus returning to the earth, the self wedding the anti-self in a *hieros gamos*, Narcissus joined to his daimonic image, Leda's Egg turning inside out and outside in without ever breaking the shell. The figures of such visions and dreams, Yeats one place declares, are 'shadows of the impulses that have made them, messages . . . out of the ancestral being of the questioner'(*Essays* 36). Another way—less poetic but more psychological—of saying this is that such visionary and dream figures are self-portraits of specifically human instincts which are themselves the inherited product of the accumulated experience of the race. In yet other words, they are archetypal images from the collective unconscious, symbolic figures from *Anima Mundi*, *daimones* reflecting the cumulative experience and psychic possibilities of humankind and, at the same time, shaping that experience and those possibilities. (*Critical Essays on W. B. Yeats*, ed. Richard J. Finneran [Boston: G. K. Hall and Co., 1986], 222)

27. Seán Ó Súilleabháin, "Irish Oral Tradition," in *A View of the Irish Language*, ed. Brian Ó Cuív (Dublin: Stationery Office, 1969), 55–56.

28. Daniel A. Harris, *Coole Park and Ballylee* (Baltimore: Johns Hopkins University Press, 1974), 58–59.

29. Kiberd, Declan. "Irish Literature and Irish History," in Roy F. Foster, ed., *The Oxford History of Ireland* (Oxford University Press, 1992), 241.

Chapter 3

1. Alwyn and Brinley Rees, *Celtic Heritage: Ancient Tradition in Ireland and Wales* (London: Thames and Hudson, 1961; repr. 1975), 89–92. Hereafter referred to in the text as "Rees."

2. E. Estyn Evans, "Peasant Beliefs in Nineteenth Century Ireland," in *Views of the Irish Peasantry*, 44–45.

3. Anthony G. Bradley, "Pastoral in Modern Irish Poetry," *Concerning Poetry* 14.2 (Fall 1981): 84. Hereafter referred to in the text as "Bradley."

4. Synge described his theory about the origin of superstition and the interrelationship between the natural and supernatural in writings that were published after his death under the title "Autobiography":

One evening when I was collecting on the brow of a long valley in County Wicklow wreaths of white mist began to rise from the narrow bogs beside the river. Before it was quite dark I looked round the edge of the field and saw two immense luminous eyes looking at me from the base of the valley. I dropped my net and caught hold of a gate in front of me. Behind the eyes there rose a black sinister forehead. I was fascinated. For a moment the eyes seemed to consume my personality, then the whole valley became filled with a pageant of movement and colour, and the opposite hillside covered itself with ancient doorways and spires and high turrets. I did not know where or when I was existing. At last someone spoke in the lane behind me—it was a man going home—and I came back to myself. The night had become quite dark and the eyes were no longer visible, yet I recognized in a moment what had caused the apparition—two clearings in a wood lined with white mist divided again by a few trees which formed the eye-balls. For many days afterwards I could not look on these fields even in daylight without terror. It would not be easy to find a better instance of the origin of local superstitions, which have their origin not in some trivial accident of colour but in the fearful and genuine hypnotic influence such things possess upon the prepared personality. (*CW* 2: 10)

5. Anonymous, "Winter Cold" (eleventh century), in *A Celtic Miscellany: Translations from the Celtic Literatures*, ed. Kenneth Hurlstone Jackson (London: Penguin, 1971), 65. Hereafter referred to in the text as "Jackson."

6. Frank Kinahan, *Yeats, Folklore, and Occultism: Contexts of the Early Work and Thought* (Boston: Unwin Hyman, 1988), 17. Hereafter referred to in the text as "Kinahan."

7. Peter Alderson Smith, *W. B. Yeats and the Tribes of Danu: Three Views of Ireland's Fairies* (Gerrards Cross, Buckshire: Colin Smythe, 1987), 155. Hereafter referred to in the text as "Smith."

8. This story is first related by Yeats in "Irish Fairies, Ghosts, Witches, Etc.," 1889 (*UP* 1: 134).

9. Dáithí Ó hÓgain, in "The Visionary Voice: A Survey of Popular Attitudes to Poetry in Irish Tradition," writes that the ancient Irish concept of the poet as having visionary powers and of his poetry as a verbal manifestation of occult knowledge survived in peasant traditions. In *Image and Illusion: An-*

glo-Irish Literature and its Contexts. A Festschrift for Roger McHugh, ed. Maurice Harmon (Dublin: Wolfhound Press, 1979), 49. Hereafter referred to in the text as "Ó hÓgain."

10. In "Ireland Bewitched" (1899), Yeats retells the story he collected from an old woman from the borders of Sligo and Mayo about a "wild old man" who knew how to move the cards until a hare leaped out of them followed by a hound (*UP* 2: 169).

11. Linda L. Revie, "The Little Red Fox, Emblem of the Irish Peasant in Poems by Yeats, Tynan, and Ní Dhomhnaill," in *Learning the Trade: Essays on W. B. Yeats and Contemporary Poetry,* ed. Deborah Fleming (West Cornwall, Conn.: Locust Hill Press, 1993), 113–34.

12. The story in *Mythologies* differs from the Lear theme of Gerald Griffin's story "The Knight of the Sheep" that Yeats included in *Representative Irish Tales.* In Griffin's story the father, who is turned out of his home by ungrateful sons to whom he has prematurely given their birthright, is saved by people whom his one good son has helped. At the end, the father gains comic revenge and the bad sons realize their mistake. Yeats's story is a character tale about a man who will not accede to anyone's authority.

13. W. B. Yeats, *The Variorum Edition of the Plays of W. B. Yeats,* ed. Russell K. Alspach and Catharine C. Alspach (New York: Macmillan, 1973), 169. Hereafter referred to in the text as *"Variorum Plays."*

14. W. B. Yeats, *Collected Plays* (New York: Macmillan, 1973), 45.

15. Paul F. Botheroyd, "J. M. Synge's *The Aran Islands, Riders to the Sea,* and Territoriality: The Beginnings of a Cultural Analysis," in Dapo Adelugba, *Studies on Synge* (Ibadan, Nigeria: Ibadan University Press, 1977), 82. Hereafter referred to in the text as "Botheroyd."

16. Robin Skelton, *The Writings of J. M. Synge* (London: Thames and Hudson, 1971), 44. Hereafter referred to in the text as "Skelton, *Writings.*"

17. Seán Ó Súilleabháin, *Irish Folk Custom and Belief* (Cork: Mercier Press, 1977; first ed. 1967), 19–20. Hereafter referred to in the text as "Ó Súilleabháin, *Irish Folk Custom.*"

18. Reidar Th. Christiansen, "The Dead and the Living," *Studia Norvegica* 2 (Oslo, 1946): 15.

19. Augusta Gregory, *Visions and Beliefs in the West of Ireland* (New York: G. P. Putnam's Sons, 1920), 24.

20. Declan Kiberd, "J. M. Synge: 'A Faker of Peasant Speech'?" in *Review of English Studies* N.S. 30 (1979) 117: 60. Hereafter referred to in the text as "Kiberd, 'J. M. Synge'."

21. Jeanne A. Flood, "Thematic Variation in Synge's Early Peasant Plays," *Éire-Ireland* 7.3 (1972): 74.

22. In a passage omitted from an article published on May 9, 1907, in the *Manchester Guardian,* Synge praises the peasant shepherds' virtues which he says increase the beauty of the landscape itself:

The herds who spend half their time walking through the mountains in dense clouds or mist are one of the most remarkable classes left in Ireland. To know these people in their own glens, to talk with them when it is raining and in the cold dawns and the twilights is a pleasure and privilege like few others. [There are] men who have a simplicity and sincerity that would cure any cynicism, and a fineness of form—in at least some of the men and women—with an expression of curious whimsical humour or despondency that never loses its interest. Beautiful as these Wicklow [glens] are in all seasons, when one has learned to know the people one does not love them as Wordsworth did for the sake of their home, but one feels a new glory given to the sunsets by the ragged figures they give light to. (*CW* 2: 228 fn.)

23. This detail comes from a folk belief Synge collected on Inishmaan. Pat Dirane advised Synge to keep a sharp needle under the collar of his coat in order to ward off the fairies. Synge attributes this belief to the sanctity of the instrument of toil, a folk belief common in Brittany, and to the fact that iron was a common talisman among primitive people (*The Aran Islands* I, *CW* 2: 80).

24. Seán Ó Súilleabháin, *Irish Wake Amusements* (Cork: Mercier, 1967), 85–87.

Chapter 4

1. Douglas Hyde (1860–1949) was the most important of Ireland's folklorists and the first to render Irish folklore materials into the Anglo-Saxon idiom (Thuente 65–66, 68).

2. Douglas Hyde, *The Love Songs of Connacht: The Fourth Chapter of the 'Songs of Connacht'* (Shannon, Ireland: Irish University Press, 1969), 61. Hereafter referred to in the text as "Hyde, *Love Songs.*"

3. Douglas Hyde, *Songs Ascribed to Raftery: The Fifth Chapter of the 'Songs of Connacht'* (New York: Barnes and Noble, 1973), 107. Hereafter referred to in the text as "Hyde, *Raftery.*"

4. Yeats would not again praise Hyde so exuberantly until 1929. Yeats believed that the scholar in Hyde would overcome the poet and he did not like Hyde's being drawn into politics by the Gaelic League. Lady Gregory replaced him as Yeats's most important guide in his study of Irish folklore (*UP* 1: 292). Later, however, in "Coole Park, 1929," Yeats praised Hyde as a member of the company of artists who had created the Irish Literary Renaissance:

There Hyde before he had beaten into prose
That noble blade the Muses buckled on,
. . . .
Found pride established in humility,
A scene well set and excellent company.

(*Poems* 243)

5. That is: "'Tis a pity that I am not married."
6. "B'yore" means "beer."
7. The fourth and fifth stanzas of this poem are as follows:
My grief, and my trouble!
  Would he and I were

In the province of Leinster,
    Or county of Clare.

Were I and my darling—
    Oh, heart-bitter wound:—
On board of the ship
    For America bound.

The literal translation follows:

> My grief on the sea. It is it that is big. It is it that is going between me And my thousand treasures. I was left at home Making grief, Without any hope of (going) over sea with me, For ever or aye. My grief that I am not, And my white moorneen, In the province of Leinster Or County of Clare. My sorrow I am not, And my thousand loves On board of a ship Voyaging to America. A bed of rushes Was under me last night And I threw it out With the heat of the day. My love came To my side, Shoulder to shoulder And mouth on mouth. (Hyde, *Love Songs* 29)

8. One of Mary Hynes's more mysterious utterances is her telling Raftery, "The cellar is strong in Ballylee." This "cellar" alludes to a deep pool in the river, near a house. Yeats knew the legend, for he describes the pool in the river in "Coole and Ballylee, 1931": "Then darkening through 'dark' Raftery's 'cellar' drop" (*Poems* 243).

9. Donal O'Sullivan, *Songs of the Irish: An Anthology of Irish Folk Music and Poetry with English Verse Translations* (Dublin: Mercier Press, 1981), 73–74.

10. Daniel Hoffman, *Barbarous Knowledge: Myth in the Poetry of Yeats, Graves, Muir* (New York: Oxford University Press, 1967), 71. Hereafter referred to in the text as "Hoffman."

11. Robert Welch, "Yeats's Crazy Jane Poems and Gaelic Love Songs," in Heinz Kosok, ed., *Studies in Anglo-Irish Literature* (Bonn: Bouvier Verlag Herbert Grundmann, 1982), 230.

12. Ole Munch-Pedersen, "Crazy Jane: A Cycle of Popular Literature," *Éire-Ireland: A Journal of Irish Studies* 14.1 (Spring 1979): 67.

13. In *A Vision*, Yeats writes that such a man desires emotion but becomes completely solitary because all normal communication has passed. Lacking personality, "he is forced to create its artificial semblance. . . . The deformity may be of any kind, great or little, for it is but symbolised in the hump that thwarts what seems the ambition of a Caesar or of an Achilles. He commits crimes, not because he wants to, or like Phase 23 out of phase because he can, but because he wants to feel certain that he can; and he is full of malice because, finding no impulse but in his own ambition, he is made jealous by the impulse of others. He is all emphasis, and the greater that emphasis the more does he show himself incapable of emotion, the more does he display his sterility. If he live amid a theologically minded people, his greatest temptation may be to defy God, to become a Judas, who betrays, not for thirty pieces of silver, but that he may call himself creator" (New York: Collier Books, 1966), 176–78.

14. In *Studies in Anglo-Irish Literature,* ed. Heinz Kosok (Bonn: Bouvier Verlag Herbert Grundmann, 1982), 230–32.

15. *Men and Feminism in Modern Literature* (New York: St. Martin's Press, 1985), 131.

Chapter 5

1. James MacKillop, "Finn MacCool: The Hero and the Anti-Hero in Irish Folk Tradition," in *Views of the Irish Peasantry,* 104.

2. D. E. S. Maxwell, *A Critical History of Modern Irish Drama 1891–1980* (Cambridge University Press, 1984), 51.

3. Yeats uses this anticlerical sentiment in *The Unicorn from the Stars* (1908). One of the beggars, Biddy Lally, says, "Is it the priest you are bringing in among us? Where is the sense in that? Aren't we robbed enough up to this with the expense of the candles and the like?" Nanny, another beggar, answers her, "I tell you, if you brought him tied in a bag he would not say an Our Father for you, without you having a half-crown at the top of your fingers" (*Variorum Plays,* 698).

4. Robin Skelton, "The Politics of J. M. Synge," *Massachusetts Review* 18 (1977): 18–19.

5. Oscar Wilde writes in "The Soul of Man Under Socialism" that the possession of private property by a class of owners not only oppresses the poor who have nothing but also demoralizes the owners themselves. With the abolition of private property would come a healthy society and beautiful individualism wherein people would be free to choose their own work (*Plays, Prose Writings, and Poems* [London: Everyman's Library, 1975], 259, 263).

6. Ernest A. Boyd, *Ireland's Literary Renaissance* (New York: John Lane, 1916), 133.

7. *The Estate of Poetry* (Cambridge: Harvard University Press, 1962), 58.

Chapter 6

1. *The Lonely Tower: Studies in the Poetry of William Butler Yeats* (London: Methuen, 1950), 75.

2. Richard J. Finneran, "'Old lecher with a love on every wind': A Study of Yeats's *Stories of Red Hanrahan,*" *Texas Studies in Language and Literature* 14.1 (Spring 1972): 350. Hereafter referred to in the text as "Finneran."

3. Patrick John Dowling, *The Hedge Schools of Ireland* (London: Longmans, Green, and Company, 1935), 1–3.

4. Lester I. Connor, "A Matter of Character: Red Hanranhan and Crazy Jane," in *Yeats, Sligo, and Ireland: Essays to Mark the Twenty-First Yeats International Summer School,* ed. A. Norman Jeffares. *Irish Literary Studies* 6 (Gerrards Cross, England: Colin Smythe, 1980), 1.

5. John Rees Moore, *Masks of Love and Death: Yeats as Dramatist* (Ithaca and London: Cornell University Press, 1971), 326.

6. *Memoirs,* ed. Denis Donoghue (New York: Macmillan, 1972), 155–56.

7. Robin Skelton, "The Politics of J. M. Synge," 20–21.

8. Synge records the folktale in 1905 of a woman who suckled a lamb at her breast. Later, a doctor, eating the lamb, detected the elements of a Christian (TCD 4400, 5v, 7).

9. Seán Ó Súilleabháin, "Synge's Use of Irish Folklore," in *Centenary Papers,* 21.

10. *Blindness and Insight: Essays in the Rhetoric of Contemporary Criticism* (New York: Oxford University Press, 1971), 106.

Appendix

1. Padraic Colum, *The Road Round Ireland* (New York: Macmillan, 1926), 23.

2. Samuel Clark, "The Importance of Agrarian Classes: Agrarian Class Structure and Collective Action in Nineteenth-Century Ireland," in *Irish Studies 2. Ireland: Land, Politics, and People,* ed. P. J. Drudy (Cambridge University Press, 1982), 57.

3. (London: Cameron and Ferguson, 1882), 146.

4. David Fitzpatrick, "Class, Family, and Rural Unrest in Nineteenth-Century Ireland," in *Irish Studies 2,* 37.

5. Most Irish nationalists advocated reduction of the "pure grazing system" and its replacement by a "mixed system" of farming which demanded more labor. This ideal of tillage and grazing (which could support both population and profit) haunted Irish nationalist organizations, permeating social statements of the Irish Republican Brotherhood, which had been founded in 1858 (Bew 85), and even playing its part in bringing Fianna Fáil to power in 1932. A flaw in the Land League's project was that some of its leaders consorted with large cattle graziers to the exclusion of some smaller farmers. The result was the Land League Crisis in 1879–82, the formation of the United Irish League in 1898, and the Ranch War of 1906–10.

6. T. W. Moody, "Fenianism, Home-Rule and the Land War (1850–91)," in *The Course of Irish History,* ed. T. W. Moody and F. X. Martin (Cork: Mercier Press, 1967), 286–87.

Bibliography

Adelugba, Dapo, ed. *Studies on Synge*. Ibadan, Nigeria: Ibadan University Press, 1977.

Archibald, Douglas. *Yeats*. Syracuse University Press, 1983.

Arensberg, Conrad. *The Irish Countryman: An Anthropological Study*. New York: Macmillan, 1937.

Arensberg, Conrad, and Solon T. Kimball. *Family and Community in Ireland*. Cambridge: Harvard University Press, 1948.

Arnold, Matthew. "The Incompatibles." In *English Literature and Irish Politics*. Ann Arbor, Mich.: University of Michigan Press, 1973.

———. "On the Study of Celtic Genius." *Lectures and Essays in Criticism*. Ann Arbor, Mich.: University of Michigan Press, 1962.

Ashcroft, Bill, Gareth Griffiths, and Helen Tiffin. *The Empire Writes Back: Theory and Practice in Post-Colonial Literature*. New York: Routledge, 1989.

Bakhtin, M. M. *The Dialogic Imagination. Four Essays*. Ed. Michael Holquist. Trans. Caryl Emerson and Michael Holquist. Austin: University of Texas Press, 1981.

Barnett, Pat. "The Nature of Synge's Dialogue." *English Literature in Transition* 10, no. 3 (1967): 119–29.

Barnwell, William C. "Utopias and the 'New Ill-Breeding': Yeats and the Politics of Perfection." *Éire-Ireland* 10, no. 1 (1975): 54–68.

Bauman, Richard. "John Millington Synge and Irish folklore." *Southern Folklore Quarterly* 27, no. 4 (1963): 267–79.

Beckett, J. C. *The Anglo-Irish Tradition*. London: Faber and Faber, 1976.

Beddoe, John. *The Races of Britain*. London: Trubner and Company, 1885.

Berrow, Hilary. "Eight Nights at the Abbey." In *J. M. Synge Centenary Papers, 1971*, ed. Maurice Harmon. Dublin: Dolmen Press, 1972.

Bew, Paul. *Conflict and Conciliation in Ireland, 1890–1910: Parnellites and Agrarian Radicals*. Oxford: Clarendon Press, 1987.

———. "The Land League Ideal: Achievements and Contradictions." In *Irish Studies 2. Ireland: Land, Politics, and People*, ed. P. J. Drudy. Cambridge University Press, 1982. 77–92.

Botheroyd, Paul F. "J. M. Synge's *The Aran Islands, Riders to the Sea* and Territoriality: The Beginnings of a Cultural Analysis." In *Studies on Synge*, ed. Dapo Adelugba. Ibadan, Nigeria: Ibadan University Press, 1977. 75–86.

Boyd, Ernest A. *Ireland's Literary Renaissance*. New York: John Lane, 1916.

Bradley, Anthony G. "Pastoral in Modern Irish Poetry." *Concerning Poetry*. 14.2 (Fall 1981): 79–96.

Bramsbäck, Birgit. *Folklore and W. B. Yeats: The Function of Folklore Elements in Three Early Plays*. *Studia Anglistica Upsaliensia* 51. Uppsala: Acta Universitatis Upsaliensis. 1984.

———. "William Butler Yeats and Folklore Material." *Beáloideas: The Journal of the Folklore of Ireland Society*. 39–41 (1971–73): 56–68.

Brown, Malcolm. *The Politics of Irish Literature from Thomas Davis to W. B. Yeats*. Seattle: The University of Washington Press, 1972.

Buchanan, R. H. "Rural Change in an Irish Townland, 1890–1955." *The Advancement of Science* 14, no. 56 (March 1958): 291–300.

Carlyle, Thomas. *Critical and Miscellaneous Essays* 4. Boston: Dana Estes and Company, 1869.

Casey, Daniel J. and Robert E. Rhodes, eds. *Views of the Irish Peasantry, 1800–1916*. Hamden, Conn.: Archon Books, 1977.

Christiansen, Reidar Th. "The Dead and the Living." *Studia Norvegica* 2 (Oslo, 1946): 15.

———. "Some Notes on the Fairies and the Fairy Faith." *Beáloideas: The Journal of the Folklore of Ireland Society* 39–41 (1971–73): 95–111.

Clark, David R. "Vision and Revision: Yeats's *The Countess Cathleen*." In *The World of W. B. Yeats*, ed. Robin Skelton and Ann Saddlemyer. Revised ed. Seattle: University of Washington Press, 1965. 158–76.

Clark, Samuel. "The Importance of Agrarian Classes: Agrarian Class Structure and Collective Action in Nineteenth-Century Ireland." In *Irish Studies* 2. *Ireland: Land, Politics, and People*, ed. P. J. Drudy. Cambridge University Press, 1982. 11–36.

———. *Social Origins of the Irish Land War*. Princeton University Press, Princeton, N. J., 1979.

Clarke, Austin. *The Celtic Twilight and the Nineties*. *The Tower Series of Anglo-Irish Studies I*. Dublin: Dufour Editions, 1970.

Colum, Padraic. *The Road Round Ireland*. New York: Macmillan, 1926.

Connor, Lester I. "A Matter of Character: Red Hanrahan and Crazy Jane." In *Yeats, Sligo, and Ireland: Essays to Mark the Twenty-First Yeats International Summer School*. *Irish Literary Studies* 6, ed. A. Norman Jeffares. Gerrard's Cross, England: Colin Smythe, 1980. 1–16.

Corkery, Daniel. *The Hidden Ireland: A Study of Gaelic Munster in the Eighteenth Century*. 2d ed. Dublin: Gill and Son, 1925.

———. *Synge and Anglo-Irish Literature: A Study*. Cork University Press, 1931.

Cullen, L. M. "The Hidden Ireland: Re-assessment of a Concept." *Studia Hibernica*, no. 9 (1969): 7–47.

Curtis, L. P., Jr. *Anglo-Saxons and Celts: A Study of Anti-Irish Prejudice in Victorian England*. Bridgeport, Conn.: The Conference on British Studies at the University of Bridgeport, 1968.

Dalton, George. "Peasants in Anthropology and History." *Current Anthropology* 13 (1972): 386–87.

Dawe, Gerald, and Edna Longley, eds. *Across a Roaring Hill: The Protestant Imagination in Modern Ireland. Essays in Honour of John Hewitt.* Belfast and Dover, N.H.: The Blackstaff Press, 1985.

Deane, Seamus. *Celtic Revivals: Essays in Modern Irish Literature 1880–1980.* London: Faber and Faber, 1985.

———. "Introduction." In *Nationalism, Colonialism, and Literature,* Terry Eagleton et al. Minneapolis: University of Minnesota Press, 1990. 3–20.

de Man, Paul. *Blindness and Insight: Essays in the Rhetoric of Contemporary Criticism.* New York: Oxford University Press, 1971.

Donnelly, James S., Jr. "The Land Question in Nationalist Politics." In *Perspectives on Irish Nationalism,* ed. Thomas E. Hachey and Lawrence J. McCaffrey. Lexington: University Press of Kentucky, 1989. 79–98.

Dowling, Patrick John. *The Hedge Schools of Ireland.* London: Longmans, Green and Company, 1935.

Drudy, P. J., ed. *Irish Studies 2. Ireland: Land, Politics, and People.* Cambridge University Press, 1982.

Dumbleton, William A. *Ireland: Life and Land in Literature.* Albany: State University of New York Press. 1984.

Edwards, R. Dudley. *A New History of Ireland.* University of Toronto Press, 1972.

Ellman, Richard. *Yeats: The Man and the Masks.* New York: Macmillan, 1948.

Evans, E. Estyn. "Peasant Beliefs in Nineteenth-Century Ireland." In *Views of the Irish Peasantry, 1800–1916,* ed. Daniel J. Casey and Robert E. Rhodes. Hamden, Conn.: Archon Books, 1977. 37–56.

Fairchild, Hoxie Neale. *The Noble Savage: A Study in Romantic Naturalism.* New York: Columbia University Press, 1928.

Fallis, Richard. *The Irish Renaissance.* Syracuse University Press, 1977.

Farag, Fahmy F. "The Ireland that Sings: Yeats and the Heresy of Universal Education." In *Studies in Anglo-Irish Literature,* ed. Heinz Kosok. Bonn: Bouvier Verlag Herbert Grundmann, 1982.

Ferris, William R., Jr. "Folklore and Folklife in the Works of John M. Synge." *The New York Folklore Quarterly* 27, no. 4 (1971): 339–56.

Field Day Theatre Company. *Ireland's Field Day.* Notre Dame, Ind.: University of Notre Dame Press, 1986.

Finneran, Richard J. "'Old lecher with a love on every wind': A Study of Yeats's Stories of Red Hanrahan." *Texas Studies in Language and Literature* 14, no. 1 (Spring 1972): 347–58.

———, ed. *Critical Essays on W. B. Yeats.* Boston: G. K. Hall and Company, 1986.

Fitzpatrick, David. "Class, Family, and Rural Unrest in Nineteenth-Century Ireland." In *Irish Studies 2. Ireland: Land, Politics, and People,* ed. P. J. Drudy. Cambridge University Press, 1982. 37–76.

———. *Politics and Irish Life, 1913–1921: Provincial Experience of War and Revolution.* Dublin: Gill and Macmillan, 1977.

Flood, Jeanne A. "Thematic Variation in Synge's Early Peasant Plays." *Éire-Ireland* 7, no. 3 (1972): 72–81.

Foster, George M. "What Is a Peasant?" In *Peasant Society: A Reader*, ed. Jack M. Potter, May N. Diaz, and George M. Foster. Boston: Little, Brown and Company, 1967. 2–14.

Foster, John Wilson. *Colonial Consequences: Essays in Irish Literature and Culture.* Dublin: Lilliput Press, 1991.

———. "The Revival of Saga and Heroic Romance During the Irish Renaissance: The Ideology of Cultural Nationalism." In *Studies in Anglo-Irish Literature*, ed. Heinz Kosok. Bonn: Bouvier Verlag Herbert Grundmann, 1982. 126–35.

Foster, Roy F., ed. *The Oxford History of Ireland.* Oxford University Press, 1992.

———. *Paddy and Mr. Punch: Connections in Irish and English History.* London: Penguin, 1993.

Foucault, Michel. *The Archaeology of Knowledge.* Trans. A. M. Sheridan Smith. New York: Random House, 1972.

Gaskell, Ronald. "The Realism of J. M. Synge." *Critical Quarterly* 5 (1963): 242–48.

Goldring, Maurice. *Faith of our Fathers: The Formation of Irish Nationalist Ideology.* Dublin: Repsol Ltd., 1982.

Green, John Richard. *A Short History of the English People.* Vol. 1. New York: Harper and Brothers, 1893.

Greene, David H. "The *Playboy* and Irish Nationalism." *The Journal of English and Germanic Philology* 46 (1947): 199–204.

———, and Edward M. Stephens. *J. M. Synge, 1871–1909.* New York: Macmillan, 1959.

Greg, Walter W. *Pastoral Poetry and Pastoral Drama.* London: A. H. Bullen, 1906.

Gregory, Lady Augusta. *Our Irish Theatre.* New York: G. P. Putnam's Sons, 1913.

———. *Visions and Beliefs in the West of Ireland.* New York: G. P. Putnam's Sons, 1920.

Grene, Nicholas. *Synge: A Critical Study of the Plays.* London: Macmillan, 1975.

Grossman, Alan R. *Poetic Knowledge in the Early Yeats: A Study of "The Wind Among the Reeds."* Charlottesville: University Press of Virginia, 1969.

Hall, Anna Maria. *Tales of Irish Life and Character.* Edinburgh: Foules, 1910.

Hall, Keith N. "Nature's Storms and Stormy Natures in Synge's Aran Islands." *Éire-Ireland* 7, no. 3 (1972): 63–71.

Hardy, Barbara. "The Wildness of Crazy Jane." In *Yeats, Sligo, and Ireland: Essays to Mark the Twenty-Fifth Yeats International Summer School. Irish Literary Studies* 6, ed. A. Norman Jeffares. Gerrard's Cross, England: Colin Smyth, 1980. 31–53.

Harmon, Maurice. "Cobwebs Before the Wind: Aspects of the Peasantry in Irish Literature from 1800–1916." In *Views of the Irish Peasantry, 1800–1916*, ed. Daniel J. Casey and Robert E. Rhodes. Hamden, Conn.: Archon Books, 1977. 129–59.

———, ed. *Fenians and Fenianism.* Seattle: University of Washington Press, 1970.

————, ed. *Image and Illusion: Anglo-Irish Literature and its Contexts. A Festschrift for Roger McHugh*. Dublin: Wolfhound Press, 1979.

————, ed. *J. M. Synge Centenary Papers, 1971*. Dublin: Dolmen Press, 1972.

Harris, Daniel A. *Yeats: Coole Park and Ballylee*. Baltimore: Johns Hopkins University Press, 1974.

Heaney, Seamus. "Yeats as an Example?" In *Preoccupations: Selected Prose 1968–1978*. London: Faber and Faber, 1980. 98–114.

Henn, T. R. *The Lonely Tower: Studies in the Poetry of W. B. Yeats*. London: Methuen and Company, 1950.

Hirsch, Edward. "The Imaginary Irish Peasant." *PMLA* 106, no. 5 (October 1991): 1116–33.

Hoffman, Daniel. *Barbarous Knowledge: Myth in the Poetry of Yeats, Graves, Muir*. New York: Oxford University Press, 1967.

Hyde, Douglas. *Love Songs of Connacht: the Fourth Chapter of the 'Songs of Connacht.'* Shannon, Ireland: Irish University Press, 1969. First Dublin edition, 1893.

————. *Songs Ascribed to Raftery: the Fifth Chapter of the 'Songs of Connacht.'* New York: Barnes and Noble, 1973. First Dublin edition, 1903.

The Irish Peasant: A Sociological Study. New York: Charles Scribner's Sons, 1892.

Jackson, Kenneth Hurlstone, ed. *A Celtic Miscellany: Translations from the Celtic Literatures*. London: Penguin, 1971.

Jeffares, A. Norman, ed. *Yeats, Sligo, and Ireland. Essays to Mark the Twenty-fifth Yeats International Summer School. Irish Literary Studies* 6. Gerrards Cross: Colin Smythe, 1980.

Jochum, K. P. S. *W. B. Yeats: A Classified Bibliography of Criticism*. Urbana: University of Illinois Press, 1978.

Jung, Carl Gustav. *The Archetypes and the Collective Unconscious*. Trans. R. C. Hull. Bollingen Series 20. Vol. 9, pt. 1. New York: The Bollingen Foundation, 1959.

————. *Two Essays on Analytical Psychology*. Trans. R. F. C. Hull. Bollingen Series 20. Vol. 7. New York: The Bollingen Foundation, 1953.

Kain, Richard M. "A Scrapbook of the 'Playboy Riots'." *Emory University Quarterly* 22, no. 1 (spring 1966): 5–17.

Kelly, John. "Choosing and Inventing: Yeats and Ireland." In *Across a Roaring Hill: The Protestant Imagination in Modern Ireland. Essays in Honour of John Hewitt*, ed. Gerald Dawe and Edna Longley. Belfast and Dover, N.H.: The Blackstaff Press, 1985.

Kenner, Hugh. "Notes Toward an Anatomy of 'Modernism'." In *A Star-Chamber Quiry*, ed. E. L. Epstein. New York: Methuen, 1982. 3–42.

————. "The Sacred Book of the Arts." In *Critical Essays on W. B. Yeats*, ed. Richard J. Finneran. Boston: G. K. Hall and Company, 1986.

Kiberd, Declan. "Irish Literature and Irish History." In *The Oxford History of Ireland*, ed. Roy F. Foster. Oxford: Oxford University Press, 1992. 230–81.

————. "J. M. Synge: 'A Faker of Peasant Speech'?" *Review of English Studies*. N.s. 30 (1979) 117: 59–63.

———. *Men and Feminism in Modern Literature.* New York: St. Martin's Press, 1985.

———. *Synge and the Irish Language.* Totowa, N.J.: Rowman and Littlefield, 1979.

Kilroy, James. *The 'Playboy' Riots.* Dublin: Dolmen Press, 1971.

Kinahan, Frank. *Yeats, Folklore, and Occultism: Contexts of the Early Work and Thought.* Boston: Unwin Hyman, 1988.

Kinsella, Thomas. *Davis, Mangan, Ferguson? Tradition and the Irish Writer.* Dublin: Dolmen Press, 1970.

Kopper, Edward A., Jr. *A J. M. Synge Literary Companion.* New York: Greenwood Press, 1988.

Kosok, Heinz, ed. *Studies in Anglo-Irish Literature.* Bonn: Bouvier Verlag Herbert Grundmann, 1982.

Lebow, Ned. "British Images of Poverty in Pre-Famine Ireland." In *Views of the Irish Peasantry, 1800–1916,* ed. Daniel J. Casey and Robert E. Rhodes. Hamden, Conn.: Archon Books, 1977. 57–85.

Lever, Charles. *Lord Kilgobbin.* London: Downey and Company, 1899.

Linton, Ralph. "Nativistic Movements." *American Anthropologist* 45 (1943): 230–40.

Lloyd, David. *Anomalous States: Irish Writing and the Post-Colonial Moment.* Durham, N.C.: Duke University Press, 1993.

Loftus, Richard J. *Nationalism in Modern Anglo-Irish Poetry.* Madison and Milwaukee: The University of Wisconsin Press, 1964.

Lovejoy, Arthur O., and George Boas. *Primitivism and Related Ideas in Antiquity.* Vol. 1 of *A Documentary History of Primitivism and Related Ideas.* Baltimore: The Johns Hopkins Press, 1935.

McCartney, Donal. "The Quest for Political Identity: The Image and the Illusion." In *Image and Illusion: Anglo-Irish Literature and its Contexts, A Festschrift for Roger McHugh,* ed. Maurice Harmon. Dublin: Wolfhound Press, 1979. 13–22.

McCormack, W. J. *Ascendancy and Tradition in Anglo-Irish Literary History from 1789 to 1939.* Oxford: Clarendon Press, 1985.

MacDonagh, Thomas. *Literature in Ireland: Studies in Irish and Anglo-Irish.* New York: Frederick A. Stokes Co., 1916.

McHugh, Roger. "Yeats and Irish Politics." *Texas Quarterly* 5, no. 3 (1962): 90–100.

MacKillop, James. "Finn MacCool: The Hero and the Anti-Hero in Irish Folk Tradition." In *Views of the Irish Peasantry, 1800–1916,* ed. Daniel J. Casey and Robert E. Rhodes. Hamden, Conn.: Archon Books, 1977. 86–106.

MacLochlainn, Alf. "Gael and Peasant—A Case of Mistaken Identity?" In *Views of the Irish Peasantry, 1800–1916,* ed. Daniel J. Casey and Robert E. Rhodes. Hamden, Conn.: Archon Books, 1977. 17–36.

MacNeice, Louis. *The Poetry of W. B. Yeats.* New York: Oxford University Press, 1941.

Manning, Maurice. *The Blueshirts.* Dublin: Gill and Macmillan, 1970.

Marcus, Phillip L. *Yeats and the Beginning of the Irish Renaissance*. Ithaca and London: Cornell University Press, 1970.

Maxwell, D. E. S. *A Critical History of Modern Irish Drama 1891–1980*. Cambridge University Press, 1984.

———. "J. M. Synge and Samuel Beckett." In *Across a Roaring Hill: The Protestant Imagination in Modern Ireland. Essays in Honour of John Hewitt*, ed. Gerald Dawe and Edna Longley. Belfast and Dover, N.H.: The Blackstaff Press, 1985. 25–38.

Maxwell, W. H. *A Critical History of the Irish Rebellion in 1798*. London: H. G. Bohm,1854.

Meir, Colin. *The Ballads and Songs of W. B. Yeats: The Anglo-Irish Heritage in Subject and Style*. London: Macmillan, 1974.

Messenger, John C. "Bibliography." In *Views of the Irish Peasantry, 1800–1916*, ed. Daniel J. Casey and Robert E. Rhodes. Hamden, Conn.: Archon Books, 1977. 203–18.

———. *Inis Beag: Isle of Ireland*. New York: Holt, Rinehart and Winston, 1969.

———. "*Man of Aran* Revisited: An Anthropological Critique." A revision and expansion of a paper read before the American Committee for Irish Studies in 1964.

Michaelson, Evalyn Jacobson, and Walter Goldschmidt. "Female Roles and Male Dominance among Peasants." *Southern Journal of Anthropology* 27, no. 4 (Winter 1971): 330–52.

Montaigne, Miguel de. *The Essays of Michael, Seigneur de Montaigne*. Trans. Charles Cotton. London: Ward, Lock, and Company. N.d.

Moody, T. W. "Fenianism, Home Rule and the Land War (1850–91)." In *The Course of Irish History*, ed. Moody and F. X. Martin. Cork: Mercier Press, 1967.

———, and F. X. Martin, eds. *The Course of Irish History*. Cork: Mercier Press, 1967.

Moore, John Rees. *Masks of Love and Death: Yeats as Dramatist*. Ithaca and London: Cornell University Press, 1971.

Mr. Punch's Victorian Era. London: Bradbury, Agnew, and Company, 1887.

Muir, Edwin. *The Estate of Poetry*. Cambridge: Harvard University Press, 1967.

Munch-Pedersen, Ole. "Crazy Jane: A Cycle of Popular Literature." *Éire-Ireland* 14, no. 1 (spring 1979): 56–73.

Murphy, Daniel J. "The Reception of Synge's *Playboy* in Ireland and America: 1907–1912." *Bulletin of the New York Public Library* 64, no. 10 (October 1960): 515–33.

naGopaleen, Myles. *The Best of Myles*. Ed. Kevin O'Nolan. Harmondsworth, England: Penguin Books, 1968.

O'Brien, Conor Cruise. *States of Ireland*. London: Hutchinson and Company, 1972.

O'Connor, Frank. *A Short History of Irish Literature: The Backward Look*. London: Macmillan, 1967.

Ó Danachair, Caoímhim. "Oral Tradition and the Printed Word." In *Image and*

Illusion: Anglo-Irish Literature and its Contexts. A Festschrift for Roger McHugh, ed. Maurice Harmon. Dublin: Wolfhound Press, 1979. 31–41.

O'Dowd, Liam. "Town and Country in Irish Ideology." *The Canadian Journal of Irish Studies* 13, no. 2 (December 1987): 43–54.

Ó'Faoláin, Seán. *The Irish: A Character Study.* Harmonsworth, England: Penguin Books, 1969.

Ó hÓgain, Dáithí. "The Visionary Voice: A Survey of Popular Attitudes to Poetry in Irish Tradition." In *Image and Illusion: Anglo-Irish Literature and its Contexts. A Festschrift for Roger McHugh,* ed. Maurice Harmon. Dublin: Wolfhound Press, 1979. 44–61.

Olney, James. "The Esoteric Flower: Yeats and Jung." In *Yeats and the Occult,* ed. George Mills Harper. Canada: Macmillan, 1975. 27–54.

———. *The Rhizome and the Flower: The Perennial Philosophy—Yeats and Jung.* Berkeley: University of California Press, 1980.

———. "Sex and the Dead: Daimones of Yeats and Jung." In *Critical Essays on W. B. Yeats,* ed. Richard J. Finneran. Boston: G. K. Hall and Company, 1986. 207–23.

Ó Súilleabháin, Seán. *Irish Folk Custom and Belief.* Cork: Mercier Press, 1977. First ed. 1967.

———. "Irish Oral Tradition." In *A View of the Irish Language,* ed. Brian Ó Cuív. Dublin: Stationery Office, 1969. 47–56.

———. *Irish Wake Amusements.* Cork: Mercier Press, 1967.

———. "Synge's Use of Irish Folklore." In *J. M. Synge Centenary Papers, 1971,* ed. Maurice Harmon. Dublin: Dolmen Press, 1972.

O'Sullivan, Donal. *Songs of the Irish: An Anthology of Irish Folk Music and Poetry with English Verse Translations.* Dublin: Mercier Press, 1981.

O' Sullivan, Sheila. "Yeats's Use of Irish Oral and Literary Tradition." *Beáloideas* 39–41 (1971–73): 266–79.

O'Sullivan, T. F. "Synge and the Ireland of his Day." In *Studies on Synge,* ed. Dapo Adelugba. Ibadan, Nigeria: Ibadan University Press, 1977. 1–9.

Ó Tuama, Seán. "Synge and the Idea of a National Literature." In *J. M. Synge Centenary Papers, 1971,* ed. Maurice Harmon. Dublin: Dolmen Press, 1972. 1–17.

Partridge, A. C. *Language and Study in Anglo-Irish Literature.* Dublin: Gill and Macmillan. 1984.

Pearse, Patrick. *Collected Works of Padraic Pearse: Political Writings and Speeches.* Dublin: Phoenix Publications, 1924.

Power, Arthur. *Conversations with James Joyce,* ed. Clive Hart. London: Millington, 1975.

Price, Alan. *Synge and Anglo-Irish Drama.* London: Methuen, 1961.

Quinn, Peter A. "Yeats and Revolutionary Nationalism: The Centenary of '98." *Éire-Ireland* 15, no. 3 (1980): 47–64.

Rees, Alwyn, and Brinley Rees. *Celtic Heritage: Ancient Tradition in Ireland and Wales.* London: Thames and Hudson, 1961; reprinted 1975.

Revie, Linda K. "The Little Red Fox, Emblem of the Irish Peasant in Poems by Yeats, Tynan, and Ní Dhomhnaill." In *Learning the Trade: Essays on W. B.*

Yeats and Contemporary Poetry, ed. Deborah Fleming. West Cornwall, Conn.: Locust Hill Press, 1993. 113–34.

Roback, A. A. *A Dictionary of International Slang*. Cambridge, Mass.: Sci-Art Publishers, 1944.

Robinson, Paul N. "Synge's Aran Island Journals." In *Studies in Anglo-Irish Literature*, ed. Heinz Kosok. Bonn: Bouvier Verlag Herbert Grundmann, 1982. 161–66.

Rose, Marilyn Gaddis. "Jack B. Yeats's Picture of the Peasant." In *Views of the Irish Peasantry, 1800–1916*, ed. Daniel J. Casey and Robert E. Rhodes. Hamden, Conn.: Archon Books, 1977. 192–202.

Saddlemyer, Ann. "'All Art is a Collaboration'? George Moore and Edward Martin." In *The World of W. B. Yeats*, ed. Robin Skelton and Ann Saddlemyer. Revised ed. Seattle: University of Washington Press, 1965. 203–22.

———. "The Cult of the Celt: Pan-Celticism in the Nineties." In *The World of W. B. Yeats*, ed. Robin Skelton and Ann Saddlemyer. Revised ed. Seattle: University of Washington Press, 1965. 19–21.

———. "Image-Maker for Ireland: Augusta, Lady Gregory." In *The World of W. B. Yeats*, ed. Robin Skelton and Ann Saddlemyer. Revised ed. Seattle: University of Washington Press, 1965. 195–202.

———. "'The noble and the beggar-man': Yeats and Literary Nationalism." In *The World of W. B. Yeats*, ed. Robin Skelton and Ann Saddlemyer. Revised ed. Seattle: University of Washington Press, 1965. 22–39.

———. "'A Share in the Dignity of the World': J. M. Synge's Aesthetic Theory." In *The World of W. B. Yeats*, ed. Robin Skelton and Ann Saddlemyer. Revised ed. Seattle: University of Washington Press, 1965. 241–53.

Said, Edward W. *Culture and Imperialism*. New York: Alfred A. Knopf, 1993.

———. *Orientalism*. New York: Vintage, 1979.

Seiden, Morton Irving. *William Butler Yeats: The Poet as a Mythmaker, 1865–1939*. East Lansing: Michigan State University Press, 1962.

Shaw, G. B. *John Bull's Other Island*. London: Constable and Co., Ltd. 1907.

Shelley, Percy Bysshe. *Shelley's Prose*. Ed. David Lee Clark. Albuquerque: University of New Mexico Press, 1954.

Sidney, Sir Philip. *The Countess of Pembroke's Arcadia*. In *Prose of the English Renaissance*, ed. J. William Hebel et al. New York: Appleton-Century-Crofts, Inc., 1952.

Skelton, Robin. *J. M. Synge and His World*. New York: Viking, 1971.

———. "The Politics of J. M. Synge." *Massachusetts Review* 18 (1977): 7–22.

———. *The Writings of J. M. Synge*. London: Thames and Hudson, 1971.

———, and Ann Saddlemyer, eds. *The World of W. B. Yeats*. Revised ed. Seattle: University of Washington Press, 1965.

Smith, Peter Alderson. *W. B. Yeats and the Tribes of Danu: Three Views of Ireland's Fairies*. Gerrard's Cross, England: Colin Smythe, 1987.

Stallworthy, Jon. "The Poetry of Synge and Yeats." In *J. M. Synge Centenary Papers, 1971*, ed. Maurice Harmon. Dublin: Dolmen Press, 1972.

Sullivan, Alexander M. *New Ireland: Political Sketches and Personal Reminiscences of Thirty Years of Irish Public Life*. London: Cameron and Ferguson, 1882.

Sumner, William Graham. *Folkways*. Boston: Ginn and Company, 1906.

Synge, John Millington. *The Collected Letters of John Millington Synge* 1 (1871–1907). Ed. Ann Saddlemyer. Oxford: Clarendon Press, 1983.

———. *J. M. Synge. The Collected Works*. Gen. ed. Robin Skelton. New York: Catholic University of America Press, 1982. Four volumes.

———. Synge Manuscript Collection, Trinity College Dublin.

———. *The Synge Manuscripts in the Library of Trinity College, Dublin: A Catalogue Prepared on the Occasion of the Synge Centenary Exhibition*. Dublin: Dolmen Press, 1971.

Tacitus. *The Complete Works of Tacitus*. Trans. Alfred John Church and William Jackson Brodribb. Ed. Moses Hadas. New York: Random House, 1942.

Thackery, William M. Quoted in "Tours in Ireland." *Quarterly Review* 85, no. 170 (September 1849): 491–562.

Thuente, Mary Helen. "The Folklore of Irish Nationalism." In *Perspectives on Irish Nationalism*, ed. Thomas E. Hachey and Lawrence J. McCaffrey. Lexington: University Press of Kentucky, 1989. 42–60.

———. "Foreward" to *Representative Irish Tales*. Ed. W. B. Yeats. Atlantic Highlands. N.J.: Humanities Press, 1979.

———. *W. B. Yeats and Irish Folklore*. Dublin: Gill and Macmillan, 1980.

Turner, James. *The Politics of Landscape*. Cambridge: Harvard University Press, 1979.

Unterecker, John. "Countryman, Peasant, and Servant in the Poetry of W. B. Yeats." In *Views of the Irish Peasantry, 1800–1916*, ed. Daniel J. Casey and Robert E. Rhodes. Hamden, Conn.: Archon Books, 1977. 178–91.

———. *A Reader's Guide to William Butler Yeats*. New York: Octagon Books, 1971.

Warner, Alan. *A Guide to Anglo-Irish Literature*. New York: Gill and Macmillan, 1981.

Waters, Martin J. "Peasants and Emigrants: Considerations of the Gaelic League as a Social Movement." In *Views of the Irish Peasantry, 1800–1916*, ed. Daniel J. Casey and Robert E. Rhodes. Hamden, Conn.: Archon Books, 1977. 160–77.

Watson, G. J. *Irish Identity and the Literary Revival: Synge, Yeats, Joyce, and O'Casey*. London: Croom Helm, 1979.

Welch, Robert. "Yeats's Crazy Jane Poems and Gaelic Love Songs." In *Studies in Anglo-Irish Literature*, ed. Heinz Kosok. Bonn: Bouvier Verlag Herbert Grundmann, 1982. 227–35.

White, Terence De Vere. *The Anglo-Irish*. London: Victor Gollancz Ltd., 1972.

Wilde, Oscar. *The Importance of Being Earnest: A Trivial Comedy for Serious People*. New York: G. P. Putnam's Sons, 1895.

———. "The Soul of Man Under Socialism." In *Plays, Prose Writings, and Poems*. London: Everyman's Library, 1975. 255–88.

Wilgus, D. K. "Irish Traditional Narrative Songs in English: 1800–1916." In *Views of the Irish Peasantry, 1800–1916*, ed. Daniel J. Casey and Robert E. Rhodes. Hamden, Conn.: Archon Books, 1977. 107–28.

Williams, Raymond. *The Country and the City*. New York: Oxford University Press, 1973.

Yeats, William Butler. *The Autobiography of William Butler Yeats*. New York: Collier Books, 1971.

———. *The Collected Letters of W. B. Yeats*. Ed. John Kelly and Eric Domville. Vol. 1 (1865–1895). Oxford: Clarendon Press, 1986.

———. *The Collected Plays of W. B. Yeats*. New York: Macmillan, 1973.

———. *Essays and Introductions*. New York: Collier Books, 1968.

———. *Explorations*. London: Macmillan, 1962.

———. *Letters to the New Island*. Cambridge: Harvard University Press, 1934.

———. *The Letters of W. B. Yeats*. Ed. Allan Wade. London: Rupert Hart-Davis, 1954.

———. *Memoirs*. Ed. Denis Donoghue. New York: Macmillan, 1972.

———. *Mythologies*. London: Macmillan, 1962.

———. *The Poems of W. B. Yeats: A New Edition*. Ed. Richard J. Finneran. New York: Macmillan, 1983.

———. *Purgatory: Manuscript Materials Including the Author's Final Text*. Ed. Sandra F. Siegel. Ithaca and London: Cornell University Press, 1986.

———. *Representative Irish Tales*. Atlantic Highlands, N.J.: Humanities Press, 1979. First published 1891. Foreword 7–23. Introduction 25–32.

———. *The Secret Rose, Stories by W. B. Yeats: A Variorum Edition*. Ed. Phillip L. Marcus, Warwick Gould, and Michael J. Sidnell. Ithaca and London: Cornell University Press, 1981.

———. *The Speckled Bird*. With variant versions. Annot. and ed. by William H. O'Donnell. Toronto: McClelland and Stewart, 1976.

———. *Uncollected Prose by W. B. Yeats*. Vol. 1 (1886–96). Ed. John P. Frayne. New York: Columbia University Press, 1970.

———. *Uncollected Prose by W. B. Yeats*. Vol. 2 (1897–1939). Ed. John P. Frayne and Colton Johnson. New York: Columbia University Press, 1976.

———. *The Variorum Edition of the Plays of W. B. Yeats*. Ed. Russell K. Alspach and Catharine C. Alspach. New York: Macmillan, 1966.

———. *The Variorum Edition of the Poems of W. B. Yeats*. Ed. Peter Allt and Russell K. Alspach. New York: Macmillan, 1973.

———. *Views of the Irish Peasantry*. New York: Collier Books, 1965.

———. *A Vision*. New York: Collier, 1965.

———, ed. *Fairy and Folk Tales of Ireland*. New York: Macmillan, 1973. Contains *Fairy and Folk Tales of the Irish Peasantry*, first published 1888, and *Irish Fairy Tales*, first published 1892.

Index

Ibsen, Henrik, 158
"If I Were to Go West," 121–22
"In a Real Wicklow Glen," 113
Inishere, 175
Inishmaan, 10, 38, 53, 101, 109, 113,
    169, 175, 200n.23
Inishmore, 68
Ireland, 6, 8, 10, 13–15, 17–18, 21, 25,
    27, 29–31, 33, 36, 41–42, 45–46,
    49, 50, 52, 58, 63, 68, 73–74, 77–
    78, 90, 122, 130, 140–43, 147–
    48, 160, 162, 164, 166–68, 170,
    181, 185–88, 194nn.52, 58, 59,
    195n.67, 196n.13
Irish Free State, 186
Irish Literary Theatre, 18, 50
Irish Literary Renaissance, 2, 200n.4
Irish National Land League, 190
Irish Peasant, The, 185
Irish Republican Brotherhood, 24,
    189, 203n.5
Irish Literary Revival, 46, 73, 182–83
    (*see also* Literary Revival)
Irish Revival, 1, 8–9, 38, 43, 46

Jacobite War (1690–91), 34
James I, 34
James II, 35
Joyce, James, 17, 52, 168
Jung, Carl Gustav, 2, 9, 66–67, 197n.26
    "Collective Unconscious," 2, 9, 66–
    67
    Two Essays on Analytical Psychology,
    67

Kain, Richard M., 193n.42
    "A Scrapbook of the 'Playboy Ri-
    ots,'" 193n.42
Kavanagh, Patrick, 9, 17
Keating, Geoffrey, 62
Keats, John, 63, 84
Kerry, County, 1, 60
Kiberd, Declan, 2, 8, 41, 74, 111–13,
    118, 127–28, 146, 157–58
    "Irish Literature and Irish His-
    tory," 74

"J. M. Synge: 'A Faker of Peasant
    Speech'?" 111
Synge and the Irish Language, 2, 112–
    13, 118, 128, 146, 157–58
Kinahan, Frank, 81–82, 89, 90
Kingsley, Charles, 26

Land Act of 1909, 73
Land Acts, 37
Land Bill, 25
Land League, 24, 45–47, 49, 51, 203n.5
Land League Crisis, 1879–82, 203n.5
Land Question, The, 34, 36
"Land War, The," 1879–82, 190,
    194n.52
Lawrence, D. H., 58
Lebow, Ned, 24
    "British Images of Poverty in Pre-
    Famine Ireland," 24
Leitrim, County, 90
Lever, Charles, 21
Lewis, Matthew Gregory, 132
Literary Revival, 15, 17, 33, 45, 49, 53,
    174 (*see also* Irish Literary Re-
    vival)
Lloyd, David, 41
London, 10, 50, 132
"Long Am I Going," 123
Lover, Samuel, 39

Macaulay, Lord, 26
MacLochlainn, Alf, 27
MacNamara (MacConmara),
    Donnchadh Ruadh, 160, 178
Madden, John, 125
Magee, Moll, 39
"An Maidrín Rua," 92
Manchester Guardian, 199n.22
Mangan, James Clarence, 121
Martin, Henri, 25
Martyn, Edward, 18
Maxwell, W. H., 27
    History of the Irish Rebellion, 27
Mayo, County, 142, 147, 169, 170–71,
    173–74
McCormack, W. J., 73, 166–68